Autism & Asperger's Syndrome in Layman's Terms

Revised E

CW01572709

DISCLAIMER AND/OR LEGAL NOTICES

The information presented herein represents the views of the author as of the date of publication. Because of the rate with which conditions change, the author reserves the right to significantly alter and amend his opinions based on the new conditions. This book is for educational and informational purposes only and the author does not accept any responsibility for any liabilities resulting from the use of this information. The content is not intended to be a substitute for professional medical advice, diagnosis, or treatment. Always seek the advice of your physician or other qualified health provider with any questions you may have regarding a medical condition. Never disregard professional medical advice or delay in seeking it because of something you have read.
aa
While every attempt has been made to verify the information provided, the author and his affiliates cannot assume any responsibility for errors, inaccuracies or oversights, applicability, fitness, or completeness of the content. Therefore, if you wish to apply ideas contained in this book, you are taking full responsibility for your actions.

The author and publisher shall in no event be held liable to any party for any direct, indirect, punitive, special, incidental or other consequential damages arising directly or indirectly from any use of this material, which is provided "as is," and without warranties.

As always, the advice of a competent legal, tax, accounting, medical or other professional should be sought. The author and publisher do not warrant the performance, effectiveness or applicability of any sites listed or linked to in this book.

Any similarities with people or organizations are unintentional.

Cranendonck Coaching
2012

Autism & Asperger's Syndrome in Layman's Terms

Revised Edition

Your Guide to Understanding Autism, Asperger's Syndrome, PDD-NOS, and Other Autism Spectrum Disorders (ASDs)

Autism, Causes, Symptoms, Signs, Diagnosis, and Treatments – Everything You Need to Know About Autism & its Effects on Life

Raymond Le Blanc

Table Of Contents

Introduction

This book was written for people who want to know more about Autism Spectrum Disorders.

This book can help you and your loved ones come to terms with and understand how autism is diagnosed and how to successfully manage this condition.

You will gain a better understanding of autism and how to deal effectively with its impact on your family.

We are convinced that having in-depth knowledge of autism and understanding the potential impacts of this condition on you and your family is vital.

This book on Autism Spectrum Disorders will give you the information you need to allow your family to lead as normal a life as possible, while giving your loved one with autism the best start possible.

This guide was initially developed to support parents and other caregivers.

Reading tip
You do not necessarily have to read the book from front to back at once. You can pick out the pieces that appear most relevant to you now. Either way is fine.

Note
Where ASD (Autism Spectrum Disorders) is mentioned you may also read PDD (Pervasive Development Disorder).

About the author
Raymond Le Blanc holds a master's degree in economics from the Erasmus University Rotterdam and a master's degree in clinical psychology from the Open University in Heerlen. He is also an NLP master practitioner. Raymond is the author of several books including "Singapore. The Socio-Economic Development of a City State," "Achieving Objectives Made Easy!" "Understanding and Overcoming Anxiety and Panic Attacks," and "Depressief?"

Raymond lives with his wife Karin and their two children Brigitte and Vincent in a small village, Maarheeze, the Netherlands.

You can read more about the author at http://raymondleblanc.com.

AUTISM DEFINED

Chapter 1 Living with an autism spectrum disorder

What does living with autism mean? This seems to be a simple question but it's difficult to answer. We will begin by giving a few short sketches as an introduction to autism. They are from different perspectives but they all have something to do with 'living with an Autism Spectrum Disorder.' We hope that the image will become clear and that this significant question will more or less be answered during the larger part of this book.

Boy with 'classic' autism
Jamie, a baby boy, is born into an average family, in a small town. This town could be anywhere. As he enters the world, he is overwhelmed by sounds, smells, feelings, tastes and sensations, so he shuts his eyes and goes to sleep. During his babyhood, he either sleeps a lot or screams hysterically when his senses become overloaded by information that he cannot deal with.

He understands the world in a different way and he struggles to survive. Jamie becomes attached to his mommy and begins to learn meaning from her sounds and her movements. He feels secure when she is nearby; the scent, feel and sound of her body are comforting. He does not feel safe when he is separated from her or held by other members of his family, so he yells and screams until his mommy can calm him.

As he grows, he starts to understand more about his world and trusts more adults. They make allowances for his condition and they try to help. Children are a different matter. Jamie wants to join in but he cannot cope with the strange movements and the way they use sounds – the rules of their games are impossible for him to understand, so he plays by himself or with children who are older or younger than he is. When he does join games he often changes the rules or disrupts the play.

When Jamie first goes away from home to the playgroup or nursery, he screams at the separation from his mommy and takes hours to quiet down when she comes to collect him. He gradually learns to make some sounds and move his face and body in an attempt to make himself understood, but some children and adults make fun of him. To deal with this confusing and frightening world he develops rituals and habits that help him feel safe – he likes things to stay the same and not change.

The same occurs when he eventually goes to school. The routine of the day is soothing and he often practices "school" at home, organizing the day into timed sections, expecting his food at precisely the same time every day, checking the clock and thinking about what he might be doing each day. He likes to dress in the same way each day and put clothes on in the same order. Jamie develops obsessive interests that the children cannot follow. They like to play baseball; Jamie is interested in a strange game called football – he is so weird! When he occasionally manages to be interested in the same things as the other children, he continues his obsession long after the others have moved on to something else.

Jamie has safe people and places at school. During lessons, he can cope to some extent, although he lives in a permanent state of high anxiety from the effort of trying to understand not only the content of the lesson, but also the body language and speech of the teachers and other students. His heart rate is extremely rapid as he lives in his own world of worry and fear. He takes teachers' comments literally and struggles to understand irony, sarcasm and jokes – if he is asked to "wait a minute," he times 60 seconds on his watch and then goes back to the teacher again.

Panic really hits Jamie at breaks and lunch times. Then, the rules and routines are often adapted by students and he cannot understand why the other children get angry when he reminds them that they should not drop litter, be late for lessons, or run in the corridors.

The levels of anxiety that Jamie lives with all of the time are just about manageable on most days. Sometimes, however, people like to change things around him without any warning. They love breaks from routine called parties, when all rules are different. Also, some of Jamie's most trusted friends like to change and develop things, so that new ideas can be carried out.

All of this sometimes makes him lose his temper and "explode." Usually, he can stop himself from doing this at school and so he waits until he gets home and then erupts over his parents. He knows that they love him and will tolerate his outbursts. However, they are exhausted from living with a growing adolescent human boy who causes huge tension in the family. Jamie is particularly difficult during the run-up to a party and can ruin the whole holiday for the rest of his family.

Jamie is loved passionately by his mommy and daddy and tolerated, for the most part, by his sister. His teachers are pleased by his progress, although they struggle to understand him. Jamie did not ask to be born autistic and sometimes he wishes that he could be normal too!

Mother of an autistic child
"I clearly remember when my oldest daughter, Ivy, was first diagnosed with autism, over 6 years ago, at the age of 2. The only positive thing I can say about it... maybe... is that, at last, we knew what the problem was. Then again, even this was nothing positive because, now, there definitely was a BIGGER problem, a problem too big for me to handle, I was sure of that! I'm sure you understand.

"Now, there were so many new things to worry about because of her diagnosis: 'How can we help her; can we assist her; what should we do next; who can we trust to help her; how can we protect her from situations she doesn't (and maybe never will) understand; why did this happen; why us; will our other children suffer this same fate; will my husband and I survive this; will our families welcome us or be full of excuses; etc.?' Again, I'm certain you understand. The list went on and on."

Adult with Asperger's syndrome
"I am a highly functioning autistic. I hold down a responsible job and live independently. My social life does not exist. I rarely interact with anyone outside of work. I basically hate people. I have been so misunderstood and as a result suffered so much abuse that I hate people and want nothing to do with them. My family hates me because of my autism, so I have nothing to do with any of them because they are so abusive. This is what happens when an autistic child is not properly diagnosed and treated."

Adult with Asperger's syndrome
"I have some Asperger's syndrome traits. You can barely recognize it in me. But often I have difficulties. Maybe these problems are small compared to yours, but let's consider them. The most frequent problem is people never let me talk. I took speech and discussion lessons – nothing, nothing worked. I could not understand that my facial expression is different, that my sight is different, and that people have a different expression in their eyes before they start to talk. I still do not have big success in jumping in to talk but I came to understand that people do not neglect me – they do not understand me; I do not give them a signal that I am ready to talk."

Sister of an autistic girl
"When I was seven I often wondered why my sister did not mingle with other kids. My mom couldn't get her to do anything, like playing tag with other kids or her homework; neither could my dad. For some reason my sister trusted me; if I said it was time to eat she would come with me to the dinner table. It wasn't until later I found out my sister had autism."

Adult with 'classic' autism
"Reality to an autistic person is a confusing mass of events, people, places, sounds and sights. There seem to be no clear boundaries, order or meaning to anything. A large part of my life is spent just trying to work out the pattern behind everything."

Boy with childhood disintegrative disorder
"John's early history was within normal limits. By age 2 he was speaking in sentences and his development appeared to be proceeding appropriately. At age 30 months he was noted to abruptly exhibit a period of marked behavioral regression shortly after the birth of a sibling. He lost previously acquired skills in communication and was no longer toilet trained. He became uninterested in social interaction, and various unusual self-stimulatory behaviors became evident. Comprehensive medical examination failed to reveal any conditions that might account for this developmental regression. Behaviorally, he exhibited features of autism. At follow-up at the age of 12 he still was not speaking, apart from an occasional single word, and had been placed in a school for the severely disabled."

Looking At The World Through A Different Set Of Lenses

People have long established the norms of society. Long ago they founded the textbook that would dictate what is acceptably "normal" to civilization at large. They have branded what they encountered but could not understand as "abnormal." People who sought their own answers, rather than accepting those that society fed them, were branded heretics and blasphemers.

Now these people are said to have "special needs," a subtle way of noting that they do not conform to the standards of "normal" society. They are regarded as abnormal because in their own world everything is peaceful and beautiful. The "real world" where "normal people" live, meanwhile, is a world of chaos, greed, lack, and suffering.

Our society is plagued by several kinds of developmental disabilities. Most of them are caused by the family's genetic codes or hereditary flaws in the gene structure. Some result from near miscarriages or trauma while others result from birth defects due to substance abuse. One of the most common forms of developmental disability is autism.

Opening up to autism

Autism is a complex developmental disability that causes troubles with societal relations and contact. Indications typically start by age three and can cause interruptions or problems in many diverse skills that build up from childhood to maturity. Autism hinders a child's ability to communicate with other people because of differences between the developmental paces of a person with autism and a normally developing baby.

A person with autism may be a few years behind when it comes to maturity. Because of this people with autism usually develop inter- and intra-personal skills very late in their lives, and in some cases never. People with autism can also experience difficulties talking to people and expressing their thoughts.

In older times, people with autism were said to be manifestations of the sins of the family. That meant deformities affiliated with autism were a very powerful stigma. Thus, families traditionally hid people with autism to avoid public dishonor and shame.

But in modern times, people have begun to realize the importance of understanding things that baffle and elude us. People who were called heretics and blasphemers for their quests for answers are now the same people we look up to for guidance and knowledge. Studies and researches have been undertaken in the past few decades that may shed light on people with autism. Breakthroughs have included separating fact from fiction when it comes to autism.

Here are a couple of myths that are helpful in understanding people with autism
- Myth number 1: Autistic people are the same in all aspects and ways.
- Fact: The only thing that people with autism have in common is their difficulty in communication. Everything else is a myth. Autistic people develop different personalities, emotions, and gestures that make them different from one another.

- Myth number 2: Autistic people are emotionless rocks.
- Fact: Contrary to popular belief, people with autism are actually some of the most emotion-filled people you will ever encounter. They can express love and are surprisingly sweet and very empathic.

- Myth number 3: People with autism are different so they should be treated differently.
- Fact: People with autism are not so different from you and me. They can also build relationships, marry, have children, achieve great things, and do everything that a normal person can do. The only difference is that they see the world as their beautiful playground and they see life through a different set of lenses.

Summary
Living with an Autism Spectrum Disorder offers challenges to the patient and his or her surroundings that can differ widely from person to person, from very difficult to cope with to mildly difficult.

In most cases 'normal' development is more or less hindered in all aspects of life and living. Autism is a lifelong developmental disability that affects social and communication skills.

People with an ASD may find it difficult to understand how the world and people around them operate and also find it hard to interact.

People with an ASD may particularly have trouble learning, understanding, and interpreting the unwritten rules of social interaction and relationships that most people without an ASD take for granted.

Chapter 2 What are autism spectrum disorders?

Not until the middle of the twentieth century was there a name for a disorder that now appears to affect an estimated 1 out of every 500 children, a disorder that causes disruption in families and unfulfilled lives for many children.

We will start this chapter with a brief historical overview of Autism Spectrum Disorders. After that, we will give a short definition of these disorders, before moving on to the definition of 'Pervasive.'

Myths surrounding Autism Spectrum Disorders will also be mentioned in this chapter.

Though there is some debate concerning the proper use of the terms "autism," "autistic," and "ASD," in this book, the terms will be used interchangeably.

2.1 History of Autism Spectrum Disorders

The word "autism" was first used by Swiss psychiatrist *Eugene Bleuler* in a 1912 issue of the American Journal of Insanity. It comes from the Greek word for "self" (autos). Bleuler used it to describe the schizophrenic's apparent difficulty in connecting with other people. Though the term was used to describe individuals displaying the autistic tendency to isolate themselves from personal interaction, the condition itself was not specifically defined until the 1940s.

Leo Kanner was the first physician in the United States to be identified as a child psychiatrist. His first textbook, Child Psychiatry (1935), was the first English language textbook to focus on the psychiatric problems of children. His seminal 1943 paper Autistic Disturbances of Affective Contact, together with the work of Hans Asperger, forms the basis of the modern study of autism.

In 1943 Dr. Leo Kanner of the Johns Hopkins Hospital meticulously studied a group of 11 children and introduced the label 'early infantile autism' into the English language. He suggested the term "autism" to describe the fact that the children seemed to lack interest in other people. Kanner's first paper on the subject was published in a now defunct journal, The Nervous Child, and almost every characteristic he originally described is still regarded as typical of Autism Spectrum Disorders.

At the same time a German scientist, Dr. *Hans Asperger*, made similar observations, describing a milder form of the developmental disorder that became known as 'Asperger's syndrome.' Interestingly, as a child, Hans Asperger appears to have exhibited features of the very condition named after him. He was described as a remote and lonely child, who had difficulty making friends. He was talented in language; he was particularly interested in the Austrian poet, Franz Grillparzer whose poetry he would frequently quote to his uninterested classmates. Asperger died before his identification of this pattern of behavior became widely recognized because his work was mostly in German and little-translated.

The first person to use the term "Asperger's syndrome" in a paper was British researcher *Lorna Wing*. As a result of having an autistic daughter, she became involved in researching developmental disorders, particularly Autism Spectrum Disorders.

Her paper, Asperger Syndrome: A Clinical Account, was published in 1981 and challenged the previously accepted model of autism presented by Leo Kanner in 1943. The paper popularized the research of Hans Asperger and introduced the term 'Asperger's syndrome.' Unlike Kanner, his findings were ignored and disregarded in the English-speaking world in his lifetime. Finally from the early 1990s, his findings began to gain notice, and nowadays Asperger's syndrome is a recognized worldwide condition.[i]

Although the papers of Kanner and Asperger represented the first explanation of ASDs, not much progress toward understanding the disorder was made until the 1960s.

In fact, in the 1950s and early 1960s, the widespread belief was that autism was not a biological disorder, but a psychological one, caused by a cold and detached style of mothering. Therefore, mothers of children with autism were, at the time, seen as the cause of their children's difficulties.

This erroneous notion was based on the findings and ideas of Dr. *Bruno Bettelheim*, who specialized in child development and was among the first to concentrate on autism. In retrospect, it seems incredible – and quite disturbing – that the medical establishment should have based its understanding of autism on a sweeping comparison made by one man. His explanation for its origin was breathtakingly wrong.

Bettelheim, who had spent time in a Nazi concentration camp, believed he saw parallels between the behavior of some camp prisoners and autistic children. This led him to posit that autism was a psychological disturbance arising from detached and "frigid" mothering – something akin to how prisoners reacted to the cold authority of camp guards.

The shock is not so much that Bettelheim could be so wrong as that it took decades before anyone in the medical community listened to the few lone voices, such as Dr. *Bernard Rimland*, Dr. *Eric Schopler*, and the mothers themselves, who had been challenging the unfounded theory of mother-blame since the early 1960s.[ii]

Dr. Rimland went on to present an authoritative review of existing evidence that proved autism to be a biological condition rather than a psychological one.

A groundbreaking study of autistic twins (1977) co-authored by Dr. *Susan Folstein*, professor of psychiatry at Tufts University, replaced the bad parenting theory with evidence that autism has complex genetic roots.

The study, published in the Journal of Child Psychology and Psychiatry, implicated regions of chromosomes 7 and 13 as possibly being involved in autism.

In the 1990s, researchers focusing on the genetic component of autism began to find connections between the disorder and people with irregularities on chromosome 15.

In 1992, Dr. *Stanley Greenspan*'s book, Infancy and Early Childhood: The Practice of Clinical Assessment, brought Floortime to the fore, though Greenspan and co-creator Dr. *Serena Wieder* began using it on children with autism spectrum disorders in the mid-1980s. Floortime, or play therapy as some refer to it, is a competing method to behaviorism and now the fastest growing intervention in the field, though ABA [See Chapter 21.1] still dominates.

In 1998 Dr. *Andrew Wakefield* came to public attention when Lancet medical journal published his study that suggested a possible link between rising rates of autism and the measles, mumps and rubella vaccine.

A report by the National Academy of Sciences' Institute of Medicine concluded in 2004 that the evidence did not support the vaccine-autism theory.

By 2001, researchers had discovered several genomic regions possibly related to autism.[iii]

Time Lime[iv]:

1911:   Dr. Eugen Bleuler, an influential Swiss psychiatrist, first introduces the term autism when he applies it to adult schizophrenia.

1943:   Child psychiatrist Leo Kanner publishes a paper that establishes autism as a childhood psychiatric disorder. He coins the condition "early infantile autism."

1944:   Unaware of Kanner's work, Dr. Hans Asperger publishes an account of the disorder, calling it 'autistic psychopathy.' But the term "Asperger's Syndrome" wasn't used in a research paper until 1981.

1950s: Autism is believed to be a psychological disorder caused by distant mothering.

1962:   British psychiatrist Lorna Wing founds the National Autistic Society (NAS) in the United Kingdom.

1964:   Infantile Autism: The Syndrome and Its Implication for a Neural Theory of Behavior is credited with changing the view of autism from an emotional illness to a neurodevelopmental disorder. Dr. Bernard Rimland wrote the book after the diagnosis of his son, Mark.

1965:   Dr. O. Ivar Lovaas and his team of researchers at the University of California in Los Angeles develop a treatment that alternates between shocking roughness and persistent and loving attention (Applied Behavior Analysis treatment). It is based on the idea of rewarding good behavior when children are good and punishing them when they're bad. The method becomes known as applied behavior analysis. Bernard Rimland founds the Autism Society of America (ASA).

1969:   Parents found the Autism Society of America.

1977:   First study of autism among twins is published, showing evidence of a genetic link. American psychiatrist Susan Folstein and British psychiatrist Michael Rutter publish a study of autistic twins in which they prove that autism has a genetic basis.

1980:   Autism is officially added to the DSM, the Diagnostic and Statistical Manual of Mental Disorders.

1980-   ABA reigns as a treatment for autism. ABA is a teaching strategy that changes behavior by manipulating a child's environment. Discrete trial training, or DTT, is often used interchangeably with ABA, but DTT is one of several methods that employ the strategy. How? DTT breaks down learning into simple steps with one-on-one tutoring.

1981:   Dr. Lorna Wing, a British researcher and mother of a child with autism, is the first person to use the term "Asperger's syndrome" in a paper, Asperger's Syndrome: A Clinical Account. This paper challenges the previously accepted model of autism that Leo Kanner presented in 1943.

1988:   The movie Rain Man is released, starring Tom Cruise as Charlie Babbitt and Dustin Hoffman as his autistic brother Raymond.

1990s: Link between autism and chromosome 15 is found.

1992:   Floortime emphasizes a child's emotional, social and imaginative abilities – autism's core deficits – and is developed from brain research showing that human development hinges on interactions and the relationships that develop from them.

1994:   Asperger's syndrome is officially added to the DSM-IV as a progressive developmental disorder. Two nonprofit groups, the National Alliance for Autism Research and Cure Autism Now, are founded to stimulate autism research and raise awareness about the disorder[v].

1998:   British-born Canadian surgeon Andrew Wakefield and others publish a controversial study in the Lancet about bowel symptoms of MMR-vaccinated children diagnosed with autism spectrum disorders.

2000:   In response to broad government concerns, vaccine makers remove thimerosal, a mercury-based preservative, from all routinely given childhood vaccines. Public fears grow that exposure to the preservative may be tied to autism[vi].

2001:   Several genomic regions are identified as possibly related to autism.[vii]

2003:   The Centers for Disease Control and Prevention (CDC) states there is no direct link between thimerosal and autism.

2004:   The Institute of Medicine, which advises the government on scientific matters, finds no credible evidence of a link between thimerosal and autism... or between the measles-mumps-rubella vaccine and autism.

2007:   Scientists find genetic bases of autism spectrum disorders.

2010:   Creators of the upcoming DSM-V propose to merge Asperger's under autism. Instead of keeping Asperger's syndrome as a separate disorder, creators of the upcoming DSM-V have proposed to eliminate it and merge it entirely under the Autistic Spectrum Disorder classification, ranking those with it from mild to severe. Many groups and Asperger's specialists including Tony Attwood have voiced opposition to the change.

Both Asperger's syndrome and autism are today listed in the Diagnostic and Statistical Manual of Mental Disorders DSM-IV-TR (fourth edition, text revision) as two of the five Pervasive Developmental Disorders (PDD), more often referred to today as Autism Spectrum Disorders (ASD). These disorders are all characterized by varying degrees of impairment in communication skills, social interactions, and restricted, repetitive and stereotyped patterns of behavior.

The Pervasive Developmental Disorders, or Autism Spectrum Disorders, range from a severe form, called autistic disorder, to a milder form, Asperger's syndrome.

If a child has symptoms of either of these disorders, but does not meet the specific criteria for either, the diagnosis is called pervasive developmental disorder not otherwise specified (PDD-NOS). The intent of the DSM-IV is that the diagnostic criteria should not be used as a checklist but, rather, as guidelines for the diagnosis of pervasive developmental disorders. There are no clearly established guidelines for measuring the severity of a person's symptoms. Therefore, the line between autism and PDD-NOS is often difficult to find.

Other rare, very severe disorders that are included in the Autism Spectrum Disorders are Rett syndrome and childhood disintegrative disorder.

Autism is a handicap that is difficult to grasp. This is reflected by the fact that even a consensus on the name of the handicap has proven to be difficult and is subject to changing scientific views.

"Autism related disorders" proves to be a confusing nomenclature. It suggests that it has nothing to do with autism. It is, in fact, a less pure form of autism in which it is possible that the disorder has not penetrated all development areas and is less acute. Yet this disorder is certainly part of the spectrum. The accompanying problems can be of a serious nature.

The disorders of Asperger and PDD-NOS rank among the group of autism-related disorders.

Summary
Autism is a name given to a severe form of Pervasive Developmental Disorders (PDD) or Autism Spectrum Disorders (ASD). These disorders include:
- Autistic disorder / Classic autism
- Asperger disorder
- PDD-NOS / Atypical autism

- Rett disorder
- Childhood disintegrative disorder

2.2 What does pervasive mean?

Pervasive means 'deeply penetrating.' It involves a disorder that digs deep into the development of a person in many areas of life. This denotes that the development of social relationships and skills, language and imaginative powers, the development of locomotion, self-image, feelings, play, fantasy, and knowledge of the ways of the world may evolve in a disorderly manner.

Pervasive Developmental Disorder (PDD) is not the same as a diagnosis, but only an indication of a group of disorders.

Among others, Dr. Bernard Rimland[viii] observes, however, that the term "pervasive" is particularly inappropriate. Rather than being a pervasive disorder, he is convinced autism is in fact a specific one, characterized by deficits in social and cognitive functioning contrary to severely retarded people, many of whom have chromosomal defects that affect every cell in their bodies. This is just an illustration of the controversies surrounding the various definitions of autism related disorders.

Summary
Pervasive means deeply penetrating into many areas of life.

2.3 Myths surrounding ASDs

Autism is puzzling even to experts, so it is little wonder that it has given rise to many myths and misconceptions. There are misconceptions prevalent among the public that do little to advance awareness and treatment of the disorders.

Here are some of the common myths, along with their accompanying realities:[ix]
- *Children with autism can perform amazing mental feats, such as memorizing the telephone book or multiplying large numbers in their heads.*
  Reality: A small number of children with autism have very high IQs and exhibit such "splinter skills," which relate only to one or two areas of extraordinary ability, as they are called, but most children with autism do not. Sadly, about eight out of ten children with autism also have some degree of mental retardation, without any extraordinary mental abilities.

- *Cold or distant mothering causes autism.*
  Reality: Autism is a biologically caused brain disorder. It does run in families, however, and some mothers and fathers of autistic children who seem extremely shy, socially awkward, or distant may themselves have very mild forms of autism.

- *Most children with autism never learn to talk; they have no language skills.*
  Reality: Individuals with a classic autism diagnosis are sometimes non-verbal or nearly non-verbal. But the autism spectrum also includes extremely verbal individuals with very high reading skills. With early identification and intensive intervention, as many as three-quarters of children with autism are able to talk. Children with autism who never acquire spoken language often have severe mental retardation in addition to their autism, which makes the learning of language especially difficult. With training, however, even these children can often learn to communicate non-verbally.

- *Autism can be caused by vaccinations.*
  Reality: At least two large studies have looked for a link between vaccinations and autism and did not find any evidence for it. Autism usually first appears within the first two years of life, at a time when children are receiving many immunizations. The appearance of autistic symptoms shortly after an immunization is bound to happen some of the time solely by chance.

- *Children with autism are completely cut off from human relationships.*
  Reality: Children with autism have abnormal social relationships, but they have relationships nonetheless. For example, a young child with autism may feel love and attachment for his mother and father, but still dislike being touched by them (unless they hug very firmly). While it's unlikely that an autistic child will be a cheerleader, it is very likely that they will have solid relationships with, at the very least, their closest family members. And many autistic people do build strong friendships through shared passionate interests. There are also plenty of autistic people who marry and have satisfying romantic relationships.

- *Autistic people cannot feel or express love or empathy.*
  Reality: Many – in fact, most – autistic people are extremely capable of feeling and expressing love, though sometimes in idiosyncratic ways! What's more, many autistic people are far more empathetic than the average person, though they may express their empathy in unusual ways.

- *Children with autism are all like the Dustin Hoffman character in the movie Rainman.*
  Reality: Autism is just one aspect of a child's personality and abilities. Children with autism differ in intelligence, sense of humor, interests, warmth, temperament, and many other qualities, just like all children. Autistic people are as different from one another as they could be. The only element that ALL autistic people seem to have in common is an unusual difficulty with social communication.

- **Autism is caused by chemical imbalances or allergies that can be cured by special diets or nutritional supplements.**
Reality: While these theories have undeniable appeal, no credible scientific evidence exists that diet or nutritional supplements can cure autism. Children with autism certainly can have allergies and nutritional deficiencies, and correcting these problems can help such a child to be healthier. This, in turn, may improve the child's behavior and general outlook, but special diets or vitamins are very unlikely to cure the autism itself, no matter what testimonials say.

- **Autistic are a danger to society.**
Reality: Violent behavior has led to fears about violence and autism. While there are many autistic individuals who exhibit violent behavior, their behavior is almost always caused by frustration, physical and/or sensory overload, and similar issues. It is very rare for an autistic person to act violently out of malice.

- **Autistic people can't do much of anything.**
Reality: Autistic individuals can achieve great things – but only if they're supported by people who believe in their potential. Autistic people are often the creative innovators in our midst. They see the world through a different lens – and when their perspective is respected, they can change the world.

- **ASDs are degenerative.**
Reality: Actually, people with autism who are receiving specialized services should improve over time rather than decline.

- **ASDs aren't inherited.**
Reality: More and more families are being identified as having more than one member with an ASD. In fact, since so little was known about ASDs for so long, some families have a parent with an ASD that was either misdiagnosed or never diagnosed at all. Many families also have more than one sibling with an ASD.

- **An autistic child's classmates shouldn't be told about his or her disorder because they won't notice something is wrong with the child if you don't mention it.**
Reality: ASDs are noticeable and children are more perceptive than we often give them credit for. Children as young as 5 notice differences in the children around them. Therefore, if they don't receive the correct information about the autistic child's disorder, they are forced to draw their own conclusions, which are likely to be wrong. Of course, confidentiality rules (where applicable) must be followed and parents must give their permission before the condition is discussed in a classroom setting.

- ***There are behavioral programs that can cure autism.***
  Reality: The fact is that autism is not curable. Behavioral programs may help the autistic person to better handle the disorder, but they will not cure it.

- ***Children with autism are unable to learn in a normal school environment and should be educated in a separate program.***
  Reality: Because one of the symptoms of ASDs is abnormal social interaction and the goal of any educational program is to develop a contributing member of society, isolating children with autism from children without the disorder may inhibit their ability to learn appropriate social behaviors. When individualized services are provided early, children with autism are able to benefit greatly from a normal school setting.

- ***ASDs are never present with other types of disorders.***
  Reality: ASDs can occur alongside any other disorder, such as Down syndrome, deafness, blindness, etc.

Chapter 3 What are the general symptoms of ASDs?

Though some of the developmental disabilities are easy to spot just by looking at somebody's physical appearance, autism is actually not that easy to distinguish because there are usually no physical deformities or distinguishing characteristics that accompany it.

So the only way to single out a person with autism is to know the symptoms or the characteristics of autism.

There are different signs and symptoms that accompany autism, but there are some symptoms that are easily distinguishable and there are minor symptoms that can be found only in some people and not all. There are main signs and symptoms of autism though, and they are common in most cases.

Communication is one of the most common skills that regress or underdevelop and it is also one of the most commonly noticed symptoms of autism. Communication skills that are affected are both verbal skills (spoken word or verbal communication) and non-verbal skills (unspoken which includes facial expressions, body language, pointing, smiling and other wordless forms of communication). It is easier to distinguish the symptom in children, especially children who are still in the early development stages. Children typically start learning their mother tongue by the age of one. Even if they have yet to actually utter words, children should employ other forms of communication at the age of one. Some of these non-verbal forms of communication are hand gestures, body movement, pointing, and smiling. If children at the age of one do not exhibit any knowledge of such skills, it may be a sign that they have autism.

A person with autism also exhibits a lack of **social skills**, although this could be partly because of the lack of communication skills. A person with autism is usually reserved and unsociable. Oftentimes people misconstrue shyness and reserve as symptoms of autism. But having autism means more than simply not talking. People with autism don't usually choose to be withdrawn. They are compelled by an unknown force to be solely attracted to their own world. Though they may engage people in conversation, the span of time that they are focused on the conversation can either be really short or fleeting on and off. There are other social skills such as sharing deep-seated emotions with people, comprehension of how others think and feel about a certain issue, and showing concern toward others. Though some of these symptoms can be associated with other developmental disabilities, their intensity and gravity can indicate autism.

Another distinct symptom of people with autism is evident in his or her habits, mannerisms, or cyclic behaviors, otherwise known as "**typecast behaviors**." Habits such as repeating terms or actions, fanatically following usual actions or plans, and playing in monotonous habits are clearly related to the development of autism.

The signs of autism can more often than not be observed by 18 months. There are a lot of likely crimson flags for autism – behaviors that may be ciphers or indications of autism. Some features might denote a holdup in one or other areas of improvement, while others could be more distinctive of autism spectrum disorders.

These are just some of the most common indicators or symptoms of autism but these are not the only ones. There other symptoms that are documented but sometimes they are associated with other developmental disabilities. Though some of them do occur in most developmental disabilities, these symptoms are some of the most common and are the most prevalent in the case of autism.

All children with ASD demonstrate deficits in:
  1. **Social interaction**
  2. **Verbal and nonverbal communication**
  3. **Repetitive behaviors or interests**

Social interaction means autistics generally have difficulty expressing emotions, exhibiting empathy, and conversing with others.

Verbal and nonverbal communication have to do with both speaking and non-verbal communication, such as eye contact, facial expression, body language, etc.

Repetition of certain phrases or strings of numbers characterize repetitive behaviors or interests. They may insist on following certain routines, playing in a repetitive fashion, or rigid organization of objects.

Thus ASDs are made of a **triad of impairments**. Each of these features can be represented on a continuum of severity, from a significant degree of impairment to a mild degree of impairment.

If a person has a severe degree of impairment in one of the features, it does not necessarily mean that they will be severely affected in the other areas. One can be affected severely to mildly in all three or any combination in between.

In addition, they will often have unusual responses to sensory experiences, such as certain sounds or the way objects look.

Each of these symptoms runs the gamut from mild to severe. They will present themselves in each individual child differently. For instance, a child may have little trouble learning to read but clearly exhibit extremely poor social interaction. Each child will display communication, social, and behavioral patterns that are individual but fit into the overall diagnosis of ASD.

Children with ASD do not follow typical patterns of child development.

In some children, indications of future problems may be apparent from birth. In most cases, the problems in communication and social skills become more noticeable as the child lags further behind other children of the same age. Some other children start off well enough. Often between 12 and 36 months old, the distinctions in the way they react to people and other unusual behaviors become apparent. Some parents report the change as being sudden, and that their children start to reject people, act strangely, and lose language and social skills they had previously acquired. In other cases, there is a plateau, or leveling, of progress so that the difference between the child with autism and other children of the same age becomes more noticeable.

ASD is defined by a particular set of behaviors that can range from the very mild to the severe. The following possible indicators of ASD were identified on the Public Health Training Network Web Cast 'Autism Among Us.[x]'

Possible indicators of autism spectrum disorders:
- Does not coo, babble, point, or make meaningful gestures by 1 year of age
- Does not speak one word by 16 months of age
- Does not combine two words by 2 years of age
- Does not respond to name
- Loses language or social skills
- Poor eye contact
- Doesn't seem to know how to play with toys
- Excessively lines up toys or other objects
- Is attached to one particular toy or object
- Doesn't smile
- At times appears to be hearing impaired

Whatever the case may be, when parents notice something is wrong, they are usually correct. Medical advice should be sought when any abnormal behavior is noticed.

Now we will take a closer look at the individual components forming the triad of impairments.

3.1 Social interaction ~ social symptoms ~ social relations

From the start, typically developing infants are social beings. Early in life, they gaze at people, turn toward voices, grasp a finger, and even smile.

In contrast, most children with ASD seem to have tremendous difficulty learning to engage in the give and take of everyday human interaction. Even in the first few months of life, many do not interact and they avoid eye contact.

They seem indifferent to other people, and often seem to prefer being alone. They may resist attention or passively accept hugs and cuddling. Later, they seldom seek comfort or respond to parents' displays of anger or affection in a typical way.

Research has suggested that although children with ASD are attached to their parents, their expression of this attachment is unusual and difficult to "read." To parents, it may seem as if their child is not attached at all. Parents who have looked forward to the joys of cuddling, teaching, and playing with their child may feel crushed by this lack of the expected and typical attachment behavior.

Children with ASD also are slower in learning to interpret what others are thinking and feeling. Subtle social cues – whether a smile, a wink, or a grimace – may have little meaning. To a child who misses these cues, "come here" always means the same thing, whether the speaker is smiling and extending his arms for a hug or frowning and planting his fists on his hips. Without the ability to interpret gestures and facial expressions, the social world may seem bewildering.

To intensify the problem, people with ASD have difficulty seeing things from another person's perspective. Most 5-year-olds understand that other people have different information, feelings, and goals than they have. A person with ASD may lack such understanding. This inability leaves them unable to predict or understand other people's actions.

Although not universal, it is common for people with ASD also to have difficulty regulating their emotions. This can take the form of "immature" behavior such as crying in class or verbal outbursts that seem inappropriate to those around them. The person with ASD might also be disruptive and physically aggressive at times, making social relationships still more difficult. They have a tendency to "lose control," particularly when they're in a strange or overwhelming environment, or when angry and frustrated. They may at times break things, attack others, or hurt themselves. In their frustration, some bang their heads, pull their hair, or bite their arms.

Unlike a person with classic autism, who often appears withdrawn and uninterested in the world around them, many people with Asperger's syndrome want to be sociable and enjoy human contact. They do still find it hard to understand non-verbal signals, including facial expressions, which makes it more difficult for them to form and maintain social relationships with people unaware of their needs.

Summary
Impairment of social relating:
- Appears to be unresponsive to people (does not imitate or respond to interaction with others)
- Unusual use of eye contact
- Difficulty using social smile

- May seem content when left alone
- Seeks social contact in unusual ways
- Uses adult's hands as tools
- Pays little or no attention to the needs and feelings of others

3.2 Verbal and nonverbal communication difficulties

By age 3, most children have passed predictable milestones on the path to learning language; one of the earliest is babbling. By his first birthday, a typical toddler says words, turns when he hears his name, points when he wants a toy, and when offered something distasteful, makes it clear that the answer is "no."

Some children diagnosed with ASD remain mute throughout their lives. Some infants who later show signs of ASD coo and babble during the first few months of life, but they soon stop. Others may be delayed, developing language as late as age 5 to 9. Some children may learn to use communication systems such as pictures or sign language.

Those who do speak often use language in unusual ways. They seem unable to combine words into meaningful sentences. Some speak only single words, while others repeat the same phrase over and over. Some ASD children parrot what they hear, a condition called echolalia. Although many children without ASD go through a stage where they repeat what they hear, it normally passes by the time they are 3.

Some children only mildly affected may exhibit slight delays in language, or even seem to have precocious language and unusually large vocabularies, but have great difficulty in sustaining a conversation. The "give and take" of normal conversation is hard for them, although they often carry on a monologue on a favorite subject, giving no one else an opportunity to comment. Another difficulty is often the inability to understand body language, tone of voice, or "phrases of speech." They might interpret a sarcastic expression such as "Oh, that's just great" as meaning it really IS great.

While it can be hard to understand what ASD children are saying, their body language is also difficult to understand. Facial expressions, movements, and gestures rarely match what they are saying. Also, their tone of voice fails to reflect their feelings. A high-pitched, sing-song, or flat, robot-like voice is common. Some children with relatively good language skills speak like little adults, failing to pick up on the "kid-speak" that is common in their peers.

Without meaningful gestures or the language to ask for things, people with ASD are at a loss to let others know what they need. As a result, they may simply scream or grab what they want. Until they are shown better ways to express their needs, ASD children do whatever they can to get through to others. As people with ASD grow up, they can become more and more aware of their difficulties in understanding others and in being understood. As a result they may become anxious or depressed.

People with Asperger's syndrome may speak fluently but they may not take much notice of the reaction of the people listening to them; they may talk on and on regardless of the listener's interest or they may appear insensitive to their feelings.

Despite having good language skills, people with Asperger's syndrome may sound over-precise or over-literal – jokes can cause problems as can exaggerated language, turns of phrase, and metaphors. A person with Asperger's syndrome may be confused or frightened by a statement like 'she bit my head off.' In order to help a person with Asperger's syndrome to understand you, keep your sentences short – be clear and concise.

A background on communication disorders associated with autism
One of the three major areas greatly affected in the development of autism is verbal and non-verbal communication. Along with this comes a deficiency in the child's imaginative play and social interaction.

By the age of 3 these symptoms will start to manifest. Children with autism develop normally prior to the onset of symptoms so parents usually do not find faulty areas until they become prevalent.

Ironically, the development of speech and language facilities begins intensively during the first 3 years of life. This is when a child learns to copy sounds from the environment, which he will later use as foundations for his talking abilities. This likely occurrence is best explained with the rapid development of the brain and the influence of his environment with his exposure to the speaking world. Many experts add that there is an innate desire for a child to communicate and to convey what his system tells him to do. A child will express this desire with cooing sounds, crying and facial expressions.

This may or may not be the case for children with autism. Some learn to develop speech and the basics of language but in time, regress into "forgetting" what they have first learned. Others totally fail to learn how to express themselves through properly structured sounds and syllables.

Gradually, children will learn to form new combinations of sounds until they advance into more complicated words that form sentences and then adapt themselves to the rules of language. They not only learn this technique but will also learn to associate things, actions, objects and symbols until they engage themselves into representational activities like pretend play.

Medical science is still not certain of the problems that cause people with autistic features to have deficiency in communication. Many experts believe, however, that something must have gone wrong during, after and before birth that has created adverse but gradual effects in the brain of the child. Such developmental hindrances impede the child from giving interpretations, both symbolic and non-symbolic, to what the world around him wants to convey. This also aggravates his impaired capacity to imagine another person's state of mind.

The effects of these impairments are best seen when a child with autism fails to give interest to what a person is telling him and in his obsession to details. Additionally, this is also manifested through showing no interest for pretend plays that usually characterize normal children.

Communication disorders among children with autism vary in intensity and in form. They largely depend on the social development of the child and his intellectual capacities. There are autistic children who cannot articulate simple words while there are others who have rich vocabularies and are able to go into in-depth discussion about their fields of interest which often lead people to misjudge them as intelligent.

Another significant communication disorder in children with autism is echolalia. This is characterized by repetitive saying of words that may or may not have meanings at all.

There are other communication disorders associated with autism like the delayed or advanced learning of words with or without the ability to interpret or provide proper meaning to them.

There is practically no treatment available for communication disorders in autism. The best thing to do is to start early in straightening what's wrong with your child by promoting social skills and improving what's left to be improved.

Summary
Impairment of communication:
- Uses very few gestures
- Uses little facial expression
- May have little or no speech, or be quite verbal
- Repeats or echoes words or phrases
- Does not appear to understand word meanings

3.3 Repetitive behaviors or interests

Although kids with ASD usually appear physically normal and have good muscle control, odd repetitive motions may set them apart from other children.

These behaviors might be extreme and highly apparent or more subtle. Some children and older individuals spend a lot of time repeatedly flapping their arms or walking on their toes. Some suddenly freeze in position.

As children, they might spend hours lining up their cars and trains in a certain way, rather than using them for pretend play. If someone accidentally moves one of the toys, the child may be tremendously upset. ASD children need, and demand, absolute consistency in their environment. A slight change in any routine – in mealtimes, dressing, taking a bath, going to school at a certain time and by the same route – can be extremely disturbing. Perhaps order and sameness lend some stability in a world of confusion.

Repetitive behavior sometimes takes the form of a persistent, intense preoccupation. For example, the child might be obsessed with learning all about vacuum cleaners, train schedules, or lighthouses. Often there is great interest in numbers, symbols, or science topics.

Summary
Repetitive, stereotyped and restricted interests and behaviors:
- Responds to objects in unusual and repetitive ways. For example they may line up cars, blocks, cups, and cutlery.
- Likes to listen to the same story or watch the same movie over and over again.
- Shows intense interest in one area. For example, they may show interest in toys, videos, pictures, etc. Relating to Bob the Builder or Sesame Street, etc.
- Unable to understand that an object can be used for different purposes.

In the next chapters we will zoom in on the different forms of Pervasive Development Disorder.

Chapter 4 'Classic' autism/autistic disorder

In the previous chapter we looked at the general characteristics of Autism Spectrum Disorders. In children with these pervasive developmental disorders there is substantial delay in communication and social interaction associated with the development of "restricted, repetitive and stereotyped" behavior, interests, and activities.

This implies that most people with an ASD will have difficulties in all aspects of life including learning, work, relationships, etc.

Autism affects each individual differently and at different levels of severity. Some individuals with autism are severely affected, cannot speak, require constant one-on-one care, and are never able to live on their own. Others have less severe ASD, can communicate, and eventually acquire the necessary skills to live on their own.

It is important to understand that autism is a disorder that affects not only the autistic individual, but has implications for family, caretakers, and educators as well.

In the next paragraph and in the following chapters, we shall take a closer look at the different forms Autism Spectrum Disorder can take.

First we will examine autism disorder.

The word 'autism' was coined by a psychiatrist named Eugen Bleuler in 1911, when he used the Greek word "autos," which means self. Bleuler also coined the term Schizophrenia, 3 years previously, in 1908.

Despite this, autism wasn't given any name until 1938, when a major breakthrough occurred. In that year a psychiatrist named Leo Kanner, for the first time ever, observed the behavior of 11 children at the Johns Hopkins Hospital in Baltimore, USA. They had previously, and incorrectly, been characterized as either emotionally disturbed or intellectually impaired. Although some of them seemed to fit into the latter category, there were also aspects of their behaviors and abilities that distinguished them from others in this category.

During the next few years Kanner studied the condition intensely. This research culminated in the 1943 publication called "Autistic Disturbance of Affective Contact." Kanner correctly wrote that autism appeared to be an inborn developmental disability that affects social and emotional understanding. Leo Kanner noticed that the children all had the same traits. We have listed most of them below.

Leo Kanner's Autistic Traits:

- *Extreme autistic aloneness*
  The children Kanner observed all failed to relate to people in a 'normal' fashion and appeared to be at their happiest when left alone. This lack of social responsiveness appeared to Kanner to start early in life as the autistic infant failed to put his arms out to the parent who was about to lift him up. An autistic child would disregard, ignore and shut out anything that came from outside the child.

- *Anxious and obsessive desire for the preservation of sameness*
  The children were extremely upset by changes of routine or surroundings. A different route to school, a rearrangement of the furniture, or moving of belongings would cause a severe tantrum. The child would not be calmed until the familiar order was restored. Some of the children would perform some of their rituals at the same time every day.

- *Excellent rote memory (rote memory involves repeating a concept or idea over and over again)*
  The 11 children Kanner observed all showed an ability to memorize large amounts of effectively meaningless material such as an encyclopedia index page. This ability was out of line with their apparent severe mental handicap, or so it was believed.

- *Delayed echolalia (involves repetition of a past utterance such as a past conversation or line from a video or TV commercial)*
  The children repeated language they had heard but failed to use words to communicate beyond their immediate needs. The echolalia probably explains the pronouns which Kanner remarked upon – that the children would use "you" when referring to themselves and "I" for other people. This usage would follow from a direct repetition of the other speaker's remarks.

- *Hypersensitivity to stimuli*
  Leo Kanner noticed that many of the children reacted strongly to certain noises such as voices, vacuum cleaners, banging and bus engines.

- *Limitation in the variety of spontaneous activity*
  This was shown in the children's repetitive movements, verbalizations and interests. Kanner felt that the children showed a good relationship to objects and often showed surprising dexterity in spinning objects or solving jigsaw puzzles. Other behavioral habits noticed by Kanner were a profound lack of emotion and a marked abnormality of speech. He was also struck by their alert, attractive and intelligent appearance.

Nowadays an autistic disorder is the classic form of autism and is distinguished by:

1. *Qualitative restrictions in contact with other people.*
   Some stand completely aloof from others. Others search for excessive contacts but it always remains one-way traffic. For either group of people with autism, others remain unpredictable beings which they cannot really understand or empathize with.

2. *Qualitative restrictions in communication and linguistic usage.*
   Many, especially the mentally handicapped, do not speak or hardly speak at all; others do speak but in a particular way (voice, choice of words, many repetitions). Some are deceptively eloquent but to those also contacts often remain one-way traffic. They all have difficulty putting their feelings into words. Understanding and manipulating sign language and facial expressions create problems and confusion.

3. *Restrictions of imagination powers.*
   People afflicted by autism have trouble correctly visualizing things not present: what happened before and what is going to happen in the future. They constantly need "images" or simple texts to conjure up something. They can, only with difficulty, prepare themselves for a future event or absorb it. They lack sufficient fantasy or have a surplus of it as a result of which they are carried away by illusions of the mind.

4. *A strikingly restrictive sphere of interest and activities.*
   People afflicted by autism are often only captivated by one or two objects, activities or notions. They remain stuck to them and can slip back into the same actions such as turning taps on and off, listening to the same music, or talking over and over about a specific subject (e.g. maps or dinosaurs).

Summary
Autism: By definition, autism must manifest delays in "social interaction, language as used in social communication, or symbolic or imaginative play," with "onset prior to age 3 years."

4.1 How to spot autistic disorder

Autistic disorder is a syndrome that results from the combination of certain traits in a child. Parents are usually the first to notice that something just isn't quite right with their child. They may notice differences right from birth, such as a dislike of physical contact, inability to make or maintain eye contact, or staring at objects for an unusually long time. Or, a child who has been meeting all milestones within the normal time frames may suddenly stop developing or even show a decline in skills. The child may stop verbalizing, begin exhibiting self-destructive behaviors, or avoid social contact.

Whatever the case may be, when parents notice something is wrong, they are usually correct. Medical advice should be sought when any abnormal behavior is noticed.

There are many ways to spot autistic disorder:

1. **Social impairment** – This is a child's inability to interact normally with other individuals. We all know that man is naturally social. An impairment of a child's social abilities can hamper many of his abilities. This sign of autistic disorder can be observed through the following symptoms:

    a.   No desire to make friends – Children are naturally very friendly individuals. When a child shows no inclination for friendship, it could very well point to an autistic disorder. However, you should not be alarmed if your child does not want to be friends with someone. After all, children have moods too.

    b.   Lack of eye contact – Eye contact is an important part of social interaction. A child who does not make any eye contact during conversations may be showing signs of autistic disorder.

    c.   Gullibility – Many people would realize that gullibility is a natural trait found in children. However, when coupled with other symptoms, this may point to autistic disorder.

2. **Language impairment** – We communicate through a variety of ways. However, all methods of communication can be referred to as a language. A child's inability to grasp the different idiosyncrasies of language can be a symptom of autistic disorder.

    a.   Monotonous speech – We use intonations and volume to convey our meaning together with words. A child with autistic disorder often speaks in a monotonous manner.

    b.   Overly formal speech – As humans, we are entitled to make small mistakes in grammar. The term 'slang' was invented for a reason. We often improvise words and change terminologies all the time. Someone with autistic disorder, however, will follow the proper form of language rigidly, not understanding the concept of colloquialism.

    c.   Taking phrases literally – Those who suffer from autistic disorder will not be able to grasp metaphors and take words at face value. Be careful what you say when they are around as they will take things literally.

    d.   Delayed response to questions – When being questioned, someone with autistic disorder will take a long time to respond.

3. **Impairment of imagination** – Imagination is a part of a human's everyday activities. In cases of those with autistic disorder, the imagination is

impaired and this means they are unable to take things beyond a literal level. It also limits their ability to improvise.

a. Poor understanding of abstract thought, metaphors and symbolism – Symbolic language is integrated into our everyday lives. We may not be able to imagine just how it would be to say things outright. A child with Autism Spectrum Disorder may interpret things differently.

b. Preference for routine – A child with Autism Spectrum Disorder has limited improvisational skills. This means they would rather stick to a good, solid routine. They will be confused when presented with an option to do something new.

If you suspect your child has an ASD, ask yourself these questions:
1. Does my child make good eye contact?
2. Does my child point at or draw my attention to things he/she is interested in?
3. Does my child speak as well as other children his/her age?
4. Does my child smile when others smile at him/her?
5. Is my child able to follow directions?
6. Does my child play with toys in a normal manner?
7. Would my child rather play alone than with others?
8. Does my child bring things he/she is interested in to me to show them to me?
9. Is my child able to appropriately tell me what he/she wants?
10. Does my child have extremely powerful or unusually long tantrums?
11. Does my child act as though he/she is in his/her own world and tune others out?
12. Is my child oddly attached to certain items, particularly hard things rather than soft?
13. Does my child over the age of 2 play imaginatively?

If you have answered "no" to one or more of the questions 1-9 or yes to one or more of the questions 10-13, discuss your concerns with your child's pediatrician.

Summary
If you or your doctor think there could be a problem, ask for a referral to see a developmental pediatrician or other specialist, or you can contact your local early intervention agency (for children under 3) or public school (for children 3 years old and older). More information on who to speak to can be found at the National Dissemination Center for Children with Disabilities.[xi]

Chapter 5 Asperger's syndrome

Asperger's syndrome was named after Dr. Hans Asperger, who is credited for discovering the disorder. Dr. Asperger referred to the autistic children he studied as "little professors" because, instead of having significantly delayed skills, they displayed highly developed intellectual functioning.

In children with this pervasive developmental disorder, language, curiosity, and cognitive development proceed normally while there is substantial delay in social interaction and "development of restricted, repetitive patterns of behavior, interests, and activities."

People with Asperger's syndrome generally function better in verbal, linguistic performance than in visual, three-dimensional and motor skills. This is in contrast to people with the classic form of autism.

Patients with Asperger's syndrome have normal speech development. This does not imply that communication is normal. It is characteristic that speech is often interpreted concretely. They will enter into lengthy discussions, introducing the most illogical arguments and succeed in talking the hind leg off a donkey. This often applies to people with a normal to supernormal intelligence who are motor disabled and have limitations under an 'autism disorder.'

Those with Asperger's syndrome often suffer a greater degree of difficulty being accepted in normal social situations because they are intellectually normal, but have unusual behaviors. Therefore, they're sometimes labeled as "odd" or "eccentric" rather than as individuals with a real medical disorder.

A short review of some distinguishing Asperger's syndrome characteristics:

- **Lack of imagination**
  While they often excel at learning facts and figures, people with Asperger's syndrome find it hard to think in abstract ways. This can cause problems for children in school where they may have difficulty with particular subjects such as literature or religious studies.

- **Special interests**
  People with Asperger's syndrome often develop an almost obsessive interest in a hobby or collecting. Usually their interest involves arranging or memorizing facts about a particular subject, such as train timetables, Derby winners, or the dimensions of cathedrals.

- **Love of routines**
  People with Asperger's syndrome often find change upsetting. Young children may impose their routines upon their families, such as insisting on always walking the same route to school. At school, sudden

changes, such as a correction to the timetable, may upset them. People with Asperger's syndrome often prefer to order their day according to a set pattern. If they work set hours, any unexpected delay, such as a traffic hold-up or a late train, can make them anxious or distressed.

People with Asperger's syndrome exhibit autistic characteristics like obsessive behaviors or lack of social and communication skills. Like all ASDs, the level and severity of these signs will vary from person to person.

Asperger's syndrome has been diagnosed more often during the last few years and has obtained its own place in the DSM-IV. The idea that Asperger's syndrome is only found in people with a normal to supernormal intelligence is under discussion.

Uta Frith, an authority in the field of Asperger's syndrome, is concerned about the fact that Asperger's syndrome may be prone to over-diagnosis. Not everybody showing clumsiness in making contact with others or behaving strangely has Asperger's syndrome.

Another danger is caused by the phenomenon that many people seem to indicate famous scientists or artists may have suffered Asperger's syndrome. Names like Newton and Einstein are offered as proof that Asperger's syndrome is a mild form of autism bordering on genius.

Asperger's syndrome, however, is not a mild form of autism. Although many people suffering Asperger's syndrome are able to cope well with the help of friends, family or a partner, others are prone to develop other disorders like an anxiety disorder or depression.

Summary
Asperger's syndrome is one of five pervasive developmental disorders (PDD) and is characterized by deficiencies in social and communication skills. It is differentiated from other PDDs in that a person with Asperger's syndrome also has normal to above normal intelligence and standard language development compared with classical autism. The diagnosis of Asperger's syndrome is complicated by the lack of a standard diagnostic screening instrument.

5.1 An overview of Asperger's syndrome and comparison with autism

Asperger's syndrome is a form of autism? But how does it differ?

Asperger's syndrome is also described as an autism spectrum disorder, in that it shares many of the same characteristics of more "classical" autism. Although they are both on the same continuum there are definite differences between children with Asperger's syndrome and children with autism. You can see this in their social interactions, language, and development over time.

Asperger's syndrome and autism display many similar features which may even cause the untrained eyes to see them as the same condition at times. However, experts clearly recognize significant differences which allow them to easily categorize them into different brackets.

Autism is basically a developmental condition that obstructs a child from proper communication. This deprives the person of social interactions and normal behavior. Asperger's syndrome, however, is said to be a high-functioning autism since it clearly shows many characteristics that place it above the level of autism. Let's make that clearer.

Like autism, Asperger's syndrome is grouped into a neurological disorder termed as Pervasive Developmental Disorder. Other disorders covered by this condition have one common denominator – poor social interaction.

Children with Asperger's syndrome develop normally, though, and may often be mistaken as "normal." However, as they age they gradually acquire various incapacities that separate them from normal children. They become unable to detect social clues like body language, facial expressions, and other non-verbal forms of communication. They interpret verbal communications literally and they lack empathy and interest in the interests of people they are talking with. However, they excel in language skills from their own perspective and may even have a wide spectrum of vocabulary that would lead others to conclude that they are bright. Some even have the ability to memorize extremely difficult items like the scientific names of animals and the capital cities of countries.

Their IQ level is good. Most score above average and average in IQ tests. In fact, one criterion for the diagnosis of Asperger's syndrome is a normal IQ. As a result, those with Asperger's syndrome are sometimes called "higher-functioning" autistics.

Children with Asperger's syndrome often display an obsession with some details while disregarding other details. This is why they are often observed collecting various materials that are meaningful to them. They are obsessed with seeking information on particular things and may even go on endlessly until their interest is filled. Thus, this behavior also manifests in their inability or unwillingness to change routines and focus of attention.

Though they may initially be perceived as advanced, compared to their peers, due to special skills that they may present, most of them experience a delay in acquiring self-help skills, including proper dressing and toileting.

Because of the difficulty in identifying what exactly causes the behavior of a person to become odd, many patients of Asperger's syndrome are diagnosed improperly. For instance, there are cases when they are thought to have Obsessive-Compulsive Disorder since a number of them suffer from a combination of the syndrome and this behavioral disorder.

Like many neurological and developmental disorders, there is still no cure for Asperger's syndrome since the roots from which it stems are still unclear. Most people who suffer from this condition grow up to be eccentric, odd or weird in other people's perception. However, help is of course always at hand. There are already developed techniques that can help tremendously with reducing the aggravation of this disorder. Such techniques include behavior modification, social skills training, psychosocial intervention, and parental training. The latter is helpful in helping parents to help their children with Asperger's syndrome.

If you suspect that your child displays features associated with Asperger's syndrome, it is best that you take him immediately to an expert to be diagnosed properly and to be given proper treatment. Never ignore symptoms; otherwise you might be too late to help save your child from potential troubles in the future.

For a parent who suspects their child may have Asperger's syndrome, what are the common symptoms to look out for?

Asperger's syndrome is a developmental disorder that affects a child's ability to socialize and communicate effectively with others. Children with Asperger's syndrome typically exhibit social awkwardness and an all-absorbing interest in specific topics.

Signs and symptoms of Asperger's syndrome include:
- Displaying unusual nonverbal communication, such as lack of eye contact, few facial expressions, or awkward body postures and gestures
- Showing an intense obsession with one or two specific, narrow subjects, such as baseball statistics, train schedules, weather or snakes
- Appearing not to understand, empathize with, or be sensitive to others' feelings
- Having a hard time "reading" other people or understanding humor
- Speaking in a voice that is monotonous, rigid or unusually fast
- Moving clumsily, with poor coordination
- Having an odd posture or a rigid gait
- They may also be overly sensitive to sounds, tastes, smells, and sights
- They have trouble understanding nonverbal cues (such as body language) and often a person with Asperger's syndrome has difficulty understanding proper body space (or "personal space")

Autism and Asperger's syndrome are difficult to diagnose, especially in young children where language and cognitive skills are still developing. All children are different, and many toddlers show a sign or symptom of Asperger's syndrome at some point. It's natural for small children to be egocentric, and many little ones show a strong interest in a particular topic, such as dinosaurs or a favorite fictional character. These alone aren't reasons to be alarmed!

However, if your child has frequent problems in school or seems unable to make friends, it's time to consult your pediatrician. These difficulties have many possible causes, but developmental disorders such as Asperger's syndrome shouldn't be ruled out.

It's important to remember that the person with Asperger's syndrome sees the world very differently.

Explaining Asperger's syndrome isn't easy no matter who you are talking to. It's not something that can be described in a single, snappy sentence. There are problems because you cannot tell by looking at someone if they have Asperger's syndrome's syndrome. Also because the causes of Asperger's syndrome are yet to be clearly identified it can sometimes be difficult convincing people that the condition actually exists.

You could try explaining to older children that people with Asperger's syndrome basically have problems in three major areas. These are usually part of the criteria for diagnosing Asperger's syndrome. They are:

1) **Social communication**
    This means knowing what to say to other people and understanding the meaning of what they are saying to you. Just imagine how many times a day the basics of social communication come into your child's life; at the shops, at home, at school, in the street.

    People with Asperger's syndrome can have problems when talking to other people as they can take things people say literally. For example, if you say to someone with Asperger's, "I laughed my head off," they may become alarmed, believing that your head really did come off your body.

    It can be very hard for people with Asperger's syndrome to understand when someone is joking, which is why they may become angry or upset by something you have said that wasn't meant to be hurtful.

2) **Social Understanding**
    This means knowing what to do when you are with other people. People with Asperger's syndrome have difficulty understanding social relationships. They do not understand all the rules involved in social relationships.

    As we grow up, we learn how to behave appropriately in certain situations. For example, we learn not to say things to people like "you look fat" (unless we are deliberately trying to be hurtful).

    A person with Asperger's syndrome usually doesn't meant to be rude, even though it can sometimes appear so, because their understanding of how to behave is confused.

3) **Imagination**
   This is the ability to think about things that aren't real.

   Children with Asperger's syndrome tend not to be interested in games that involve pretending to be someone else (like cops and robbers). Some children with Asperger's syndrome can be very interested in things that aren't interesting to other children or exclude social interaction.

   They may like collecting items that seem dull or unusual to us.

Chapter 6 PDD-NOS

Pervasive Developmental Disorder-Not Otherwise Specified (PDD-NOS) is also referred to as "atypical personality development," "atypical PDD," or "atypical autism."

Pervasive Developmental Disorder Not Otherwise Specified (PDD-NOS) is a diagnosis given to a child who has some signs of autism, but not all.

This designation, abbreviated NOS, can be used when the mental disorder appears to fall within the larger category but does not meet the criteria of any specific disorder within that category. The definition of "sub threshold" PDD (PDD-NOS) is essentially a negative one; i.e., for individuals with a disorder with some, but not all, features suggesting autism. Although probably relatively common, research on this condition is, paradoxically, highly limited.

In the present DSM-IV the condition PDD-NOS is very summarily described as follows: "There are serious defects in their social interaction, communication or stereotypical behaviors, interests and activities. The person, however, does not meet the criteria of the autistic disorder or related disorders."

This description has provoked many discussions among experts, because people who show disorders in one of three areas mentioned above might may be PDD-NOS classified.

According to experts, this leads to an irresponsible broadening of the notion of PDD-NOS. In the meantime experts have shown that PDD-NOS can be significantly distinguished from other disorders if the rules for classification are accentuated in such a way that at least three to five criteria in the three fields (social interaction, communication, and restrictive self-repeating stereotypical patterns of behavior) are met, with at least one being in the field of social interaction. While deficits in peer relations and unusual sensitivities are typically noted, social skills are less impaired than in classical autism.

The lack of definitions for this relatively heterogeneous group of children presents problems for research on this condition.

In the revised DSM-IV-TR, a revision of the 4th edition, published in May 2000, the description has, in spite of rumors circulating, not (yet) been adopted.

Children with PDD-NOS will show different symptoms. All children grow at a different rate so the symptoms vary with every child. Children with PDD-NOS could have problems with **social interaction** and issues **communicating** with parents and peers. These are two of the problems that children with PDD-NOS can show.

When a child has delays in social skills, they can show it at a very early age. Babies won't make eye contact or cuddle. This is hard for parents to deal with so you should talk to your child's doctor if you notice any of these problems. As the children get older they might enjoy playing by themselves and have no problems not interacting with children their own age. They will have no problem separating from their parents and no problem talking to strangers.

Children with a milder form of PDD-NOS can have different forms of social problems. Some children want friends, but don't know how to make them because of their social problems. As the children get older, they usually become closer to their parents and others that are around often, but don't know how to make new friends and interact with new people.

Speaking and communicating is a problem with some children with Pervasive Developmental Disorder Not Otherwise Specified. Unfortunately, this isn't something that is noticed until the child starts getting older. As babies, they may not babble and parents might find this a blessing not dealing with a noisy baby. However, as they get older they won't speak. On occasion a baby will pick up one word and just repeat it. This will be the only word they say and they won't learn anything new.

There are more problems than just learning how to speak. Children with PDD-NOS can have a tough time learning new words, but they will also have a difficult time picking up facial expressions and tone of voice. They won't understand when someone is joking or being sarcastic. They take words literally. Children with PDD-NOS have to learn the distinction between these issues.

Another problem in people with PDD-NOS is **dwelling on a certain subject**. They will keep talking about the thing they are into and not talk about anything else. If they like airplanes, they may learn everything they can. They will have pictures of them and stare at them in the sky. These obsessive behaviors usually only happen with one thing and the child won't care for much of anything else.

Emotions may be difficult for children with PDD-NOS to show. They tend to be indifferent, but when they do show emotions it's usually to the extreme. These children have outbursts and throw temper tantrums. However, this is also pronounced with sadness, happiness, and fear. Any emotion will be pronounced.

These are two of the main symptoms children will show if they have Pervasive Developmental Disorder Not Otherwise Specified. Talk to a doctor if you notice any these conditions to get further tests.

How PDD-NOS Is Diagnosed
Your child may show symptoms of autism, be diagnosed with Pervasive Developmental Disorder – Not Otherwise Specified (PPD-NOD).

A doctor will go through a list of criteria to determine if your child has PDD-NOS. Assessments will be done in a number of areas.

- **Medical Assessment**: If your child is showing any health problems, a doctor will do a physical to see if there are any other medical conditions present. Tests will include hearing, blood, and urine.

- **Educational Assessment**: Your doctor will check out your child's educational level based on where they are supposed to be. There are many different areas the doctor will check such as dressing, bathing, social interaction and other social skills. This can be assessed by interviewing parents, teachers and others who are with the child often. You can also keep a journal of everything your child does and how the child interacts to give to the doctor.

- **Psychological Assessment**: A psychologist will be on hand to interview the child to see if there are any mental disorders. Some of the symptoms your child is having could be from other conditions and your doctor will want to rule anything out.

- **Behavior Observation Assessment**: A doctor may want to observe your child in his or her natural setting. By watching the child, a doctor will be able to gauge what is going on. They will see firsthand how the child acts around other children their age and in the home environment.

- **Communication Assessment**: A doctor will test a child's communication skills because this is an important piece of information to see if a child has autism or PPD-NOD. This doesn't have to be just through words. The doctor will test body language, facial expressions and other forms of communication.

- **Occupational Assessment**: Your child's motor skills are an important way to determine if your child has autism or PDD-NOS. This will consist of tests that check the function of the child's motor skills and the child's senses. A child might dislike a certain texture or smell. This is important when figuring out what is wrong with the child.

Many of these assessments are done while interviewing the parents, teachers or anyone else who is close to the child. A child might exhibit different symptoms at different moments. That's why it's imperative to get as many people as you can to give information to the doctor or anyone else involved in the patient's care. These people will have plenty of knowledge to give the doctors. Don't be shy in finding anyone who can help.

After the assessments are complete your doctor or pediatrician will meet with other doctors to diagnose the problem. Here the doctors will decide if the child has autism or Pervasive Developmental Disorder-Not Otherwise Specified.

Once a child is diagnosed with PPD-NOS, a treatment plan will be given to help your child. This will help your child to have a normal life and communicate with people better. Getting a diagnosis is the first step in helping your child to have a better life.

Summary

PDD-NOS is a 'sub threshold' condition, in which some symptoms of autism or a similar pervasive developmental disorder can be identified, while other symptoms cannot. Especially common is difficulty interacting with peers.

Chapter 7 Rett's disorder (or Rett syndrome)

Rett's Disorder is included as a Pervasive Developmental Disorder because there is some potential confusion with autism – particularly in the preschool years. Otherwise the course and onset of this condition is very distinctive.

Children with this pervasive developmental disorder appear to develop normally at first, but their head growth slows, they lose social "engagement" and hand skills, and they develop stereotyped movements of the hands and poorly coordinated gait or trunk movements. There is also psychomotor retardation and impairment of language development.

Like CDD (see Chapter 8), Rett syndrome is also relatively rare, affecting almost exclusively females, 1 out of 10,000 to 15,000. After a period of normal development, some time between the age of 6 and 18 months, autism-like symptoms begin to appear. The little girl's mental and social development regress – she no longer responds to her parents and pulls away from any social contact. If she has been talking, she stops; she cannot control her feet; she wrings her hands. Some of the problems associated with Rett syndrome can be treated. Physical, occupational, and speech therapy can help with problems of coordination, movement, and speech.

Scientists sponsored by the National Institute of Child Health and Human Development (USA) have discovered that a mutation in the sequence of a single gene (a mutation in the gene encoding methyl-CpG-binding protein-2 (MECP2)) can cause Rett syndrome. This discovery may help doctors slow down or stop the progress of the syndrome. It may also lead to methods of screening for Rett syndrome, thus enabling doctors to start treating the children much sooner, and improving the quality of life these children experience.

Summary
Rett syndrome is a progressive neurological disorder. The symptoms of this disorder are easily confused with those of cerebral palsy. The clinical diagnosis specifies a small head and small hands and feet. Stereotypical repetitive hand movements such as mouthing or wringing of the hands are also included as diagnostic signs. Symptoms of the disease include learning disorders and a total inability to socialize. Girls with Rett syndrome are very prone to seizures and gastrointestinal disorders. They typically have no verbal skills, and about 50% of females are ambulatory.

Chapter 8 Childhood disintegrative disorder

Children with this pervasive developmental disorder appear to develop normally for the first two years of their lives, but then lose skills in areas such as language, play, and bowel control, and manifest impaired social interaction and communication associated with "restrictive, repetitive, stereotyped" behaviors.

Children with CDD develop a condition that resembles autism, but only after a relatively prolonged period (usually 2 to 4 years) of clearly normal development. This condition apparently differs from autism in the pattern of onset, course, and outcome. Although apparently rare, the condition probably has frequently been incorrectly diagnosed.

Very few children who have an Autism Spectrum Disorder (ASD) diagnosis meet the criteria for Childhood Disintegrative Disorder (CDD). An estimate based on four surveys of ASD found fewer than 2 children per 100,000 with ASD could be classified as having CDD. This suggests that CDD is a very rare form of ASD. Though it is rare, it was actually discovered in 1908, long before classic autism. However, it has only recently been 'officially' recognized. CDD most commonly occurs in boys and is generally noticeable around 3 to 4 years of age. Until this time, the child has age-appropriate skills in communication and social relationships.

The long period of normal development before regression helps differentiate CDD from Rett syndrome. The loss of such skills as vocabulary is more dramatic in CDD than they are in classical autism.

The diagnosis requires extensive and pronounced losses involving motor, language, and social skills. CDD is also accompanied by loss of bowel and bladder control and oftentimes seizures and a very low IQ.

The cause is unknown but several lines of evidence suggest that it arises as a result of some form of central nervous system pathology. Childhood disintegrative disorder is perhaps 10 times less common than more strictly defined autism.

Several different patterns of onset and course have been identified. Patterns of onset include gradual vs. spreading harmfully in a subtle manner, while patterns of course/development include progressive deterioration, developmental plateau with little subsequent improvement, and (much less frequently) marked improvement. The available data suggest that generally the prognosis for this condition is worse than that for autism.

Summary
Childhood disintegrative disorder (CDD), also known as Heller's syndrome and disintegrative psychosis, is a rare condition characterized by late onset (>3

years of age) of developmental delays in language, social function, and motor skills. Researchers have not been successful in finding a cause for the disorder.

CDD has some similarities to autism, but an apparent period of fairly normal development is often noted before a regression in skills or a series of regressions in skills. Many children are already somewhat delayed when the illness becomes apparent, but these delays are not always obvious in young children.

The age at which this regression can occur varies, and can be from ages 2 to 10, with the definition of this onset depending largely on the definition used.

Chapter 9 Other related syndromes/disorders

Ever since autism was first recognized, its continuity with schizophrenia has been a matter of debate. In fact, until the late 1970s, children with autism were often labeled as having "childhood schizophrenia." In the last 30 years, however, the term "childhood schizophrenia" has been displaced. Diagnostic criteria for autism have been established that rely solely on social, communicative and sensorimotor symptoms, without reference to the thought disorders typical of schizophrenia.

In a critical article, made in the DSM-III, about the choices concerning autism and autism related disorders (written by employees of Yale Child Study Center in 1986), Cohen et al. asked for attention to a proposal that got no hearing. It was about a group of children who were regularly seen in clinical practice, but in literature named very differently so far, namely:

- Atypical development
- Symbiotic psychosis
- Borderline disorders in childhood
- Schizoid personality disorders in childhood
- Schizotypical disorders

After investigating the literature, they came up with the idea that all those children matched the criteria summarized in three main categories:

1. Disorders in sensitivity for social signals and in the development of reciprocal social relations
2. Disorders in the regulation of affects
3. Disorders in thinking

At first this concept got the name Multiplex Developmental Disorder, but in 1993, the name was changed to Multiple-complex Developmental Disorder, because the initial abbreviation MDD caused too much confusion with the more naturalized abbreviation for 'Major Depressive Disorder.' The new abbreviation matches no predecessor.

Multiple Complex Developmental Disorder (MCDD) is now a proposed developmental disorder (or syndrome) designed to encompass preschool and early school-aged children who have consistent and enduring deficits in affect regulation, relatedness, and thought. Such children are thought to represent another variant in the spectrum of pervasive developmental disorders (PDDs).

Multiple Complex Developmental Disorder (MCDD) represents a distinct group within the autistic spectrum based on symptomatology. Unlike autistic children, some MCDD children develop schizophrenia in adult life. Despite the differences, patients of both disorders are mainly characterized by abnormal reactions to their social environment.[xii] Researchers found a specific difference between autistic and MCDD children in their cortisol response to psychosocial stress, which indicates that the disturbed reactions to social environment observed in these disorders may have different biological backgrounds.

Although the proposed syndrome of an MCDD appears to be a useful concept in diagnosing preschool children with developmental disabilities and comorbid emotional/behavioral disorders, there appear to be at least two distinct clusters of behavior seen in such children. One cluster approximates a borderline syndrome, while the other is more clearly in the PDD spectrum.[xiii]

The term MCDD signifies multiple complex developmental problems, meaning that normal development is impeded in many ways. MCDD is not a more serious form of ASD or a less serious form of autism. This disorder is not separately described in the DSM-IV classification system. It is defined[xiv] as a specific development disorder with, as a highlight, a problem in processing information. Apart from the ASD characteristics, MCDD afflicted people also have problems regulating their emotions. On top of that, they do not lack imaginative powers, but rather have them in excess.

The specific characteristics of MCDD were described by van der Gaag.
- Disorders in regulating emotions, in particular fear and aggression, e.g. fear degenerates into panic and anger in extreme fits of terrible tempers.
- Disorders in the susceptibility to social signals and disorders in social behavior toward contemporaries and adults, e.g. limitless in establishing contacts or steadfastly avoiding them, a lack of empathy.
- Disorders in thinking, in which fantasy and reality are intermingled, e.g. jumping from one subject to another, bizarre fantasies, being completely wrapped up in fantasies or having difficulties with the difference between fantasy and reality.

People with MCDD often have little hold of their emotions and thoughts and lack the feeling for social relations. They can react violently to events and know no restrictions. To them, the world is often a restless and unpredictable chaos. In addition, thinking disorders are often found in which these people are sidetracked into strange associations and runaway fantasies which can make them very terrified. They are unable to correct themselves or to set their minds at rest.

In this group within the PDD-NOS category other different psychiatric problems may play a part, such as fears or (in puberty) psychoses. Treatment is especially aimed at giving structure, preventing and diminishing fears, and stimulating health possibilities and skills. The emotions and thoughts of these people are to be regulated and determined.

Summary
MCDD: There are some children who display the severe, early-appearing social and communicative deficits characteristic of autism who also display some of

the emotional instability and disordered thought processes that resemble schizophrenic symptoms. Cohen et al. (1986) coined the term Multiplex Developmental Disorder (MDD) to describe these children, although they are often given a diagnosis of PDD-NOS by clinicians who may be unfamiliar with this terminology. Unlike schizophrenia, MCDD symptoms emerge in earliest childhood, often in the first years of life, and persist throughout development.

Chapter 10 What causes autism spectrum disorders?

Whenever a doctor informs the parents that their child is autistic, the first and foremost question they ask him is – How did it happen? How did my child get this disease?

Well, there is no definite answer to what are the exact causes of autism. Yet, there are various theories that researchers and doctors are working on. Interestingly, it is found that autism is more common in boys than girls.

Earlier, it was believed that autism occurred due to emotional trauma. Hence, bad parenting was added to its causes. The doctors said that mothers not giving their children enough attention and love were a problem. However, these factors were proved wrong with enough study and research.

So far, the following facts are known about the causes of autism. It is a consequence of a disorder, a malfunction of the mind.

There is however no specific cause of autism positively identified yet. The only widely accepted ideas concerning the causes of autism are that it is considered to be present at birth (though it appears later on in life), is caused by abnormalities in the brain, and may be genetic. However, what causes the brain abnormalities and which genes are affected by the disorder are still up for debate.

One other certainty concerning the causes of ASDs is that it is not a psychological disorder caused by poor parenting, unconsciously rejecting a child, or failing to bond emotionally. These theories have caused enormous guilt in parents and lack any scientific validity.

Listed are some possible causes of ASD.

- Biological Basis/Brain Structure/Neurotransmitters
- Hereditary/Genetic
- Pregnancy/Birth Injury
- Mercury/Toxins/Vaccinations

Medically speaking, autism is seen as a symptom, a phenomenon or a combination of phenomena with different causes. These causes cover a wide spectrum from genetic (chromosome related) disorders caused by Mendel's law of Independent Assortment (PKU) to infections and harmful substances like alcohol and thalidomide.

10.1 Biological basis

Autism is linked with some underlying health issues. It is said that children suffering with diseases like Fragile X Syndrome and Congenital Rubella have higher chances of being autistic.

Metabolic imbalance (when there is an excess of one over the other between tissue building up (anabolism) and tissue braking down (catabolism)) is another perception. Researchers say that metabolic imbalance in the child might also lead to autism.

Recent research shows that autistic brains grow and develop at an unusual rate between the ages of one and two and then, after that short period of ultra rapid growth, slow down again to a normal person's brain rate growth. Some of the images that doctors are studying suggest that there are certain areas in the brain noticeably larger than what is typical. Further study is ongoing to determine if the differences in brain size could cause autism.

Because of its relative inaccessibility, researchers have only recently been able to study the brain systematically. But with the innovative emergence of new brain imaging tools – computerized tomography (CT), positron emission tomography (PET), single photon emission computed tomography (SPECT), and magnetic resonance imaging (MRI) – study of the structure and the functioning of the brain can be done. With the aid of modern technology and the new availability of both normal and autism tissue samples for post-mortem studies, researchers will be able to learn much through comparative studies. Post-mortem and MRI studies have shown that many major brain structures are implicated in autism. This includes the cerebellum, cerebral cortex, limbic system, corpus callosum, basal ganglia, and brain stem.[xv]

It appears that in autism a disorder is found in the structure of the brain, e.g. the little brain (cerebellum). There is a disorder localized in the frontal lobes. Low blood flow to certain parts of the brain and reduced numbers of certain brain cells also seem to appear along with autism traits.

An exciting development is the Autism Tissue Program[xvi]. Studies of the post-mortem brain with imaging methods will help us learn why some brains are large, how the limbic system (interconnected system of brain nuclei associated with basic needs and emotions such as hunger, pain, pleasure, satisfaction, sex, and instinctive motivation) develops, and how the brain changes as it ages. Tissue samples can be stained and will show which neurotransmitters are being made in the cells and how they are transported and released to other cells. By focusing on specific brain regions and neurotransmitters, it will become easier to identify susceptibility genes.

Other research is focusing on the role of neurotransmitters such as serotonin, dopamine, and epinephrine. Problems are found in the general functioning of the brain as a result of a shortage or excess of neurotransmitters (dopamine and serotonin). As a result information entering the brain is not correctly processed.

Edwin Cook and his colleagues report that the first gene of autism relates to processing serotonin in the brain. In 1990, Dr. Cook said, "the most consistent finding has been over 25% of autistic children and adolescents are hyperserotonemic. After decades of investigation the mechanism of hyperserotonemia has not been determined." Hyperserotonemia is where you have high, elevated serotonin levels.

Researchers at the Yale School of Medicine have only recently discovered in the placenta what may be the earliest marker for autism, possibly helping physicians to diagnose the condition at birth, rather than the standard age of 2 or older. Current studies are searching for characteristics in children at risk for ASD so that the diagnosis can be made prior to age 1. The ideal time for diagnosis would be at birth, according to senior author on the study Dr. Harvey J. Kliman, research scientist in the Department of Obstetrics, Gynecology & Reproductive Sciences at the School of Medicine. They found that the placentas from ASD children were three times more likely to have trophoblast (the embryo's outer layer) inclusions. Kliman and the team identified trophoblast inclusions by performing microscopic examinations of placental tissues.

"We knew that trophoblast inclusions were increased in cases of chromosome abnormalities and genetic diseases, but we had no idea whether they would be significantly increased in cases of ASD," says Kliman. "These results are consistent with studies by others who have shown that ASD has a clear genetic basis." Trophoblast inclusions reflect abnormal folding of microscopic layers in the placenta and appear to result from altered cell growth.

10.2 Hereditary/Genetic

The best known theory regarding the causes of autism is that is it genetic. Some researchers feel that individuals are born with the predisposition to be autistic.

It is highly possible that autism has a genetic imprint or copy of sorts. Many researchers have discovered that parents from ancestries with autistic members are very likely to have autistic offspring. It is also possible that many families with a single autistic child are at heightened risk of having more than one autistic child. Autism therefore is concluded to have a genetic component: autism can be ruled as hereditary, which means children with autistic relatives in their family are more prone to becoming autistic than children with no autistic relatives. Researchers are on the right track when it comes to finding out more about genes playing a large part in having autism, but the final outcome is still pending.

Everyone knows genetics play a large part in our lives: what color hair you will have, how tall you will be, the color of your skin, basically your overall appearance. Scientists say the same goes for autism; there is not just one kind of autism. Some people have very mild autism, where you won't even notice they have it. During the past decades, scientists have made breakthroughs in finally beginning to understand the genetic bases of autism.

International research into the causes of Autism Spectrum Disorders (including the genetic aspects) is being fueled by recent developments. Evidence points to genetic factors playing a prominent role in the causes for ASD.

Twin and family studies have suggested an underlying genetic vulnerability to ASD.[xvii] To further research in this field, the Autism Genetic Resource Exchange is recruiting genetic samples from several hundred families.

Each family with more than one member diagnosed with ASD is given a two-hour, in-home screening. With a large number of DNA samples, it is hoped that the most important genes will be found. This will enable scientists to learn what the culprit genes do and how they can go wrong.

So it seems that congenital (existing at birth) factors play an important part. Some scientists believe that a cluster of unstable genes that adversely affects the development of the brain may cause autism. The first research results indicate that various chromosome spots are found where genomes could not possibly be. The most obvious spots are found on chromosomes 2, 7 and 16. Especially chromosome 7 stands out. However, the room on chromosome 7 is rather large and comprises a couple hundred genomes. The next problem to be investigated carefully is which genome(s) on chromosome 7 in fact is/are connected to autism.

"Children normally inherit one copy of a gene from each parent. We had the tools to see whether copy number changes found in kids with autism were causing the syndrome," CSHL Professor Alea Mills was quoted as saying. In 2007, Professor Michael Wigler, also at CSHL, revealed that some children with autism have a small deletion on chromosome 16, affecting 27 genes in a region of our genomes referred to as 16p11.2. The deletion – which causes children to inherit only a single copy of the 27-gene cluster – is one of the most common copy number variations (CNVs) associated with autism.[xviii]

Recent neuroimaging studies have shown that a contributing cause for autism may be abnormal brain development beginning in the infant's first months. This "growth dysregulation hypothesis" holds that the anatomical abnormalities seen in autism are caused by genetic defects in brain growth factors. It is possible that sudden, rapid head growth in an infant may be an early warning signal that will lead to early diagnosis and effective biological intervention or possible prevention of autism.[xix]

For detailed information on Autism Spectrum Disorders research, see the NIMH website, Autism Spectrum Disorders Research.[xx]

Some scientists believe in a genetic theory called "complex inheritance." What scientists mean by "complex theory" is that many different factors are probably included in this inheritance. While an autistic person must have the right genes to have autism, environmental factors may add to the development of autism. Here is an example: let's say you have a specific type of gene which makes a special type of chemical and which causes a chain reaction with another type of chemical. By studying autistic people, scientists may be able to find out the exact environmental issue, like chemicals in paint, that could contribute to causing autism.

Prof. Dr. R.B. Minderaa[xxi] points out that in autism, as a rough estimate, between 80 to 90% of hereditary factors play a part. Autism can be hereditary in three ways.

- In most people with an ASD hereditary factors play a part. This is a combination of (hereditary) risk factors and coincidence.
- In a very small percentage (1 to 1.5%) autism shows up as a part of a syndrome existing at birth (i.e. Tuberous sclerosis, Williams-Beuren Syndrome, Landau Kleffner Syndrome, Lennox Gasteau Syndrome, Lujan Frijns Syndrome).
- In a very small percentage (1 to 1.5%) autism is the result of a specific chromosome deviation (i.e. Fragile X-syndrome, Klinefelter, Turner). In these syndromes it can, from a medical point of view, be clearly indicated where the cause originates. In these cases heredity research can be conducted.

The hereditary factor
It appears that autism may run in families, since families with multiple children often have more than one child exhibiting signs on the autistic spectrum. In addition, parents may show signs of autism.

The chance that in a family with an ASD child another child with ASD is born lies between 2 and 5%. Therefore, parents with an ASD child have a chance up to 100 times greater to have another child with ASD than parents who have 'normal' children.

Studies of twins also indicate a hereditary factor in the occurrence of autism.

Family researches have proven that in families where autism is found, disorders are more common than in families without autism. It then involves disorders such as reading, spelling, language and/or motor disorders or other development disorders such Attention Deficit and Hyper Activity Disorder (ADHAD) or a tic disorder and also milder forms of autism.

10.3 Pregnancy/Birth Injury

The idea that autism is caused by difficulties occurring during the pregnancy or birth process is also being investigated. Only in very exceptional cases can illness during pregnancy be a secondary cause of autism.

Prenatal environment[xxii]
The risk of autism is associated with several prenatal risk factors. Autism has been linked to birth defect agents acting during the first eight weeks from

conception, though these cases are rare. Other potential prenatal environmental factors do not have convincing scientific evidence.

Maternal infection
Prenatal viral infection has been called the principal non-genetic cause of autism.[xxiii] Prenatal exposure to rubella or cytomegalovirus activates the mother's immune response and greatly increases the risk for autism. Congenital rubella syndrome is the most convincing environmental cause. Infection-associated immunological events in early pregnancy may affect neural development more than infections in late pregnancy, not only for autism, but also for other psychiatric disorders of presumed neuro developmental origin, notably schizophrenia.

The maternal antibody theory hypothesizes that immunoglobulin G (IgG) in a mother's blood can cross the placenta, enter into the fetus's brain, react against fetal brain proteins, and cause autism. The theory is related to the autoimmune disease hypothesis, except it focuses on maternal antibodies rather than the child's. A 2008 study found that these antibodies bind to fetal brain cells, most commonly in mothers of children with regressive autism. A 2008 study found that rhesus monkeys exposed during gestation to IgG from mothers of children with ASD demonstrated stereotypies, one of the three main symptoms of autism.[xxiv]

Gestational diabetes
Diabetes in the mother during pregnancy is a significant risk factor for autism; a 2009 meta-analysis found that gestational diabetes was associated with a twofold increased risk. Although diabetes causes metabolic and hormonal abnormalities and oxidative stress, no biological mechanism is known for the association between gestational diabetes and autism risk.[xxv]

Teratogens
Teratogens are environmental agents that cause birth defects. Some agents that are known to cause other birth defects have also been found to be related to autism risk. These include exposure of the embryo to thalidomide, valproic acid, or misoprostol. These cases are rare[xxvi]. Questions have also been raised whether ethanol (grain alcohol) increases autism risk, as part of fetal alcohol syndrome or alcohol-related birth defects, but current evidence is insufficient to determine whether autism risk is actually elevated with ethanol[xxvii]. All known teratogens appear to act during the first eight weeks from conception, and though this does not exclude the possibility that autism can be initiated or affected later, it is strong evidence that autism arises very early in development[xxviii].

Pesticides
A 2007 study by the California Department of Public Health found that women in the first eight weeks of pregnancy who live near farm fields sprayed with the organochlorine pesticides dicofol and endosulfan are several times more likely to give birth to children with autism. The association appeared to increase with dose and decrease with distance from field site to residence. The study's

findings suggest that on the order of 7% of autism cases in the California Central Valley might have been connected to exposure to the insecticides drifting off fields into residential areas. These results are highly preliminary due to the small number of women and children involved and lack of evidence from other studies[xxix]. It is not known whether these pesticides are human teratogens, though endosulfan has significant teratogenic effects in laboratory rats[xxx].

A 2005 study showed indirect evidence that prenatal exposure to organophosphate pesticides such as diazinon and chlorpyrifos may contribute to autism in genetically vulnerable children[xxxi]. Several other studies demonstrate the neuro developmental toxicity of these agents at relatively low exposure levels[xxxii].

It has been suggested that exposure during pregnancy to pyrethrin, a common ingredient in antiflea and antitick pet shampoos, can cause autism in the child. One retrospective study suggesting an association has been conducted, but has not been published[xxxiii].

Thyroid problems

Thyroid problems that lead to thyroxine deficiency in the mother in weeks 8–12 of pregnancy has been postulated to produce changes in the fetal brain leading to autism. Thyroxine deficiencies can be caused by inadequate iodine in the diet, and by environmental agents that interfere with iodine uptake or act against thyroid hormones. Possible environmental agents include flavonoids in food, tobacco smoke, and most herbicides. This hypothesis has not been tested[xxxiv]. A related untested hypothesis is that exposure to pesticides could combine with suboptimal iodine nutrition in a pregnant mother and lead to autism in the child[xxxv].

Stress

Prenatal stress, consisting of exposure to life events or environmental factors that distress an expectant mother, has been hypothesized to contribute to autism, possibly as part of a gene-environment interaction. Autism has been reported to be associated with prenatal stress both with retrospective studies that examined stressors such as job loss and family discord, and with natural experiments involving prenatal exposure to storms; animal studies have reported that prenatal stress can disrupt brain development and produce behaviors resembling symptoms of autism[xxxvi].

Perinatal environment

Autism is associated with some perinatal and obstetric conditions. A 2007 review of risk factors found associated obstetric conditions that included low birth weight and gestation duration, and hypoxia during childbirth. This association does not demonstrate a causal relationship; an underlying cause could explain both autism and these associated conditions[xxxvii]. A 2007 study of premature infants found that those who survived cerebellar hemorrhagic injury (bleeding in the brain that injures the cerebellum) were significantly more likely to show symptoms of autism than controls without the injury[xxxviii].

There are different opinions about the possible effects of a laborious delivery. In recent years opinions tend to suppose that laborious pregnancies are a consequence of autism in the child rather than the cause of it. After all, if heredity plays a role then autism comes into the picture at conception and symptoms may reveal themselves at pregnancy and birth.

Birth demands a lot of every baby. A baby suddenly has to breathe on its own. This requires great adaptation and gearing, the very thing that causes a lot of trouble in babies with a disorder in the autism spectrum. Hence problems can be indicated around the birth.

10.4 Mercury/Toxins/Vaccinations

Environmental factors are thought to make a great impact on autism. Studies show that there are several cases of autism in small towns that are exposed to high levels of toxins & chemicals.

Toxins ingested by the mother during pregnancy are another cause currently being investigated, as well as environmental factors: some researchers are investigating the idea that autism may be caused by environmental factors such as viruses.

During the past few years, there has been public interest in a theory that suggested a link between the use of thimerosal, a mercury-based preservative used in the measles-mumps-rubella (MMR) vaccine, and autism. Some suppose, as autism was first diagnosed near the same time as vaccines were given, autism was caused due to the mercury content in the vaccines.

The primary theory implies that the MMR (Mumps-Measles-Rubella) vaccine may be the reason for intestinal troubles leading to the development of autism. The second theory mentions that a mercury-based preservative called thimerosal, found in quite a few vaccines, could be associated with autism. Though these theories are plausible, the actual effects of the vaccines may still vary in the long run.

The MMR vaccine theory of autism is one of the most extensively debated theories regarding the origins of autism. The supposition that vaccinations cause autism has little real proof, but originated when a British researcher, Dr. Andrew Wakefield, reported that a small number of children who just happened to be autistic had indications of a measles infection in their intestines after getting their MMR vaccinations. The increase went up along with the autism increase so the coincidence was hard to ignore. As some parents started becoming more concerned they made reports. They recorded that their kids seemed normal until getting a triple vaccination DPT shot. Since the autism increase, the Autism Research Institute has been flooded with parents asking for help with their children.

In 2004, the interpretation of a causal link between MMR vaccine and autism was formally retracted by 10 of Wakefield's 12 co-authors.[xxxix] The retraction followed an investigation by The Sunday Times, which stated that Wakefield "acted dishonestly and irresponsibly."[xl] The Centers for Disease Control and Prevention,[xli] the Institute of Medicine of the National Academy of Sciences,[xlii] and the U.K. National Health Service[xliii] have all concluded that there is no evidence of a link between the MMR vaccine and autism.

In 2009, the US Federal Vaccine Court rejected "speculative and unpersuasive" claims that the MMR vaccine caused autism.[xliv]

Rather high levels of mercury can result from eating a lot of fish, or being exposed to industrial emissions. Research says that there might be a certain link between expecting mothers who are exposed to high mercury levels and autistic children. Researchers are currently testing pregnant women's exposure to mercury and will further study their babies at birth to determine the validity of this theory.

Although mercury[xlv] is no longer found in childhood vaccines[xlvi] in the United States, some parents still have concerns about vaccinations. Keep in mind there could be several other risks if these vaccines are not given to the child. So, there is no reason to blindly blame the vaccines and hence avoid them in order to prevent Autism. Many well performed large-scale studies have now been done that have failed to show a link between thimerosal and autism. A panel from the Institute of Medicine is now examining these studies, including a large Danish study which has concluded that there was no causal relationship between childhood vaccination using thimerosal-containing vaccines and the development of an Autism Spectrum Disorder.[xlvii]

Research into Causes and Treatment of Autism Spectrum Disorders
Research into the causes, diagnosis, and treatment of Autism Spectrum Disorders have advanced in tandem. With new well-researched standardized diagnostic tools, ASD can be diagnosed at an early age. And with early diagnosis, the treatments found to be beneficial in recent years can be used to help the child with ASD develop to his or her greatest potential.

Summary
Causes of ASD. There is no single known cause for autism. There are many theories about potential causes and it appears that multiple factors are involved. Autism Spectrum Disorders are physical disorders of the brain that are neurologically based and are not emotional disorders. Parents do not cause autism. The exact cause remains unclear, as we still do not understand how autism affects the structure of the brain, the brain function, or brain chemistry. Diagnosis of autism is difficult as there is no definitive biological test that confirms it, and so there are people who may be well into adulthood before autism is diagnosed. The biological basis for ASD is unclear although there does seem to be a genetic component. Autism has also been associated with a wide range of pre-, peri-, and postnatal difficulties.

10.5 Autism Risk Factors

As you now know, one of the most effective means of managing autism in the family is early intervention through diagnosis. Autism diagnosis may include two stages, the initial "well child" checkup with a physician and an extensive developmental and behavioral screening. In the initial screening, doctors can determine the range, level, and type of autism.

Children may be diagnosed with PDD-NOS if they show several symptoms of autism but not exactly the symptoms found in classical autism; Asperger's syndrome if they exhibit distinct autistic behaviors but have strong language skills; childhood disintegrative disorder if the child grows up normally but deteriorates when he or she reaches an age between 3 and 10 years; or Rett syndrome in girls who withdraw from social interaction, regress in speech patterns, and severely wring their hands.

If the child exhibits grave tendencies related to autism in the initial examination, the physician will require more thorough assessment and extensive evaluation such as the Comprehensive Diagnostic Evaluation, which is the second stage of diagnosis conducted by a multi-disciplinary team composed of professionals such as a psychologist, a speech therapist, a neurologist, and a psychiatrist.

In order to diagnose if a child indeed suffers from autism or any other type of ASD, this multidisciplinary group must conduct a scrupulous, painstaking, and conscientious neurological evaluation as well as an extensive mental and speech assessment.

Autism's risk factors

The term "risk factor" refers to an element(s) that may increase the possibility of having a specific condition or disease. The following are just some of the risk factors for autism.

- **Pregnancy**. Many studies indicate that autism can greatly be connected to the condition and development of the fetus during the mother's pregnancy because. Risk factors include the baby's breech presentation, a low Apgar score for the baby after the first few minutes of birth, and being born on or before 35 weeks. Problems during pregnancy or after delivery such as the presence of a mild yet highly contagious illness usually caused by a virus called "rubella" increases not only birth defects but increases the risk of autism.

  Genetic factors and parental psychiatric histories. The parents' history of mental conditions or affective disorder such as various forms of schizophrenia, depression, bipolar disorder, and psychosis contributes to the possibility of producing a child with autism.
  Families who have one child with autism have an increased risk of having another child with the disorder. It's also not uncommon for the

parents or relatives of an autistic child to have minor problems with social or communication skills themselves or to engage in certain autistic behaviors.

- **Age.** Babies aged 3 and below can suffer from autism if they show symptoms of the disorder in the earlier years of their life and are not able to overcome these symptoms.

- **Parents' ages.** Having an older father (being 40 or older) may increase a child's risk of autism. There may also be a connection between children being born to older mothers and autism, but more research is necessary.

- **Gender.** Studies show that boys suffer from autism more commonly than girls. However, girls who are affected by autism are prone to more serious cases of autism.

- **Existing medical conditions.** Experts say that children who have existing medical conditions such as rare and uncommon genetic disorders are more prone to suffer from autism. Diseases that increase the possibility of autism in children include Tuberous Sclerosis, Cytomegalovirus, Fragile X Syndrome, Neurofibromatosis, Herpes Encephalitis, Phenylketonuria (PKU), and Moebius Syndrome.

- **Conditions such as epilepsy.** People who suffer from a disorder that involves recurring seizures called "epilepsy" have a greater chance of developing autism. Epilepsy is characterized by loss of consciousness, convulsions or unusual jolting muscles and abnormalities in an emotional state or in the absence of sensation. Experts say that the aftermath of epilepsy contributes to autism.

There is no known cure for autism. This is why parents are encouraged to be observant and mindful of their child's development and behavior, especially in the first 3 years of life. Pregnant women are also advised to take the necessary and extra effort before, during, and after the pregnancy to ensure that the fetus develops well inside the womb before birth. Parents with children who suffer from various medical conditions, especially those with rare diseases, should also prepare themselves for the possibility of autism in their child.

Summary
Autism's risk factors include your child's sex, family history, other disorders and parents' ages.

Chapter 11 Scientific theories on autistic thinking

A relatively new hypothesis in the field of autism has been labeled 'Theory of Mind.' This idea has received much attention, including a recent book in 1995 by Dr. Simon Baron-Cohen (Mindblindness, Cambridge, Mass.: The MIT Press) and an article by Dr. Uta Frith in Scientific American in 1993.

Theory of mind refers to the notion that many autistic individuals do not understand that other people have their own plans, thoughts, and points of view. Furthermore, it appears that they have difficulty understanding other people's beliefs, attitudes, and emotions.

Many of the tasks used to test this theory have been given to non-autistic children as well as children with mental retardation, and the theory of mind phenomenon appears to be unique to those with autism. In addition, theory of mind appears to be independent of intelligence even though people with Asperger's syndrome exhibit this problem to a lesser degree.

Interestingly, people with autism have difficulty comprehending when others don't know something. It is quite common, especially for those with savant abilities, to become upset when asking a question of a person to which the person does not know the answer.

By not understanding that other people think differently than themselves, many autistic individuals may have problems relating socially and communicating to other people. That is, they may not be able to anticipate what others will say or do in various situations. In addition, they may have difficulty understanding that their peers or classmates even have thoughts and emotions, and may thus appear to be self-centered, eccentric, or uncaring.

Although this is an egocentric view of the world, there is nothing in the theory of mind to imply that autistic individuals feel superior to others.

The vital question which must be asked is: How does one teach individuals with autism to understand and acknowledge the thoughts and feelings of others? One of the methods used to teach autistic children and adults this concept is an intervention developed by Carol Gray called 'social stories.' These short stories describe different scenarios which allow autistic individuals to understand themselves and others better. These stories may motivate them to start asking questions about other people and at least recognize that different individuals think in unique ways.

Another hypothesis is the theory of weak central coherence.

Autism is characterized by a series of strengths as well as weaknesses. Tests that tap factual knowledge and focused attention to detail can lead to peak performances, whereas tests tapping common sense comprehension can be surprisingly poor. Some of these features are explained by the theory of 'central coherence.' This theory refers to an information processing style, rather than a deficit. This cognitive style relates to the tendency to process incoming information in its context.

In the case of strong central coherence, this tendency would work at the expense of attention to and memory for details. In the case of weak central coherence, piecemeal processing is favored at the expense of contextual meaning. For example, when retelling a story, typical individuals find it easier to recall accurately the gist of the story rather than its specific details.

People with autism show the opposite profile. Thus, individuals with autism are described as exhibiting 'weak central coherence.'

An important extension of the central coherence account postulates not poor integration of information in a gestalt, but rather enhanced discrimination of individual elements.

The brain basis of central coherence has been little explored, although preliminary suggestions are that the early stages of sensory processing (where emphasis is paid to the local features of a stimulus) are intact in autism whereas the top-down modulation of these early processing stages (requiring the extraction of the global features of a stimulus) is not functioning appropriately.

Summary
"Theory of mind" is a fairly new hypothesis, which states that autistic individuals are unaware that other people have different thoughts and feelings than they do. Another hypothesis, "weak central coherence," posits that autistic individuals process individual details rather than the overall picture, or context, of an event. More research is needed to determine whether either of theories, neither of these theories, or a combination of these theories is correct.

Chapter 12 Conditions comorbid to autism spectrum disorders

There are many conditions existing simultaneously but independently in patients with autism spectrum disorders, such as Fragile X Syndrome and epilepsy.

Autism and other autism spectrum diagnoses, including Asperger's syndrome, are diagnosed strictly as a cognitive disability, as a brain disorder that begins in early childhood, persisting throughout adulthood, and affecting three crucial areas of development: communication, social interaction, and creative or imaginative play.

Other conditions that often coincide with autism are:

Anxiety, depression & anger[xlviii]
Many people with autism have clinically diagnosable problems with anxiety, depression and anger. These issues seem to be more common among people with high functioning autism and Asperger's syndrome. This may because people with high functioning autism and Asperger's syndrome are more aware of their differences and more likely to feel the effects of being ostracized by peers. But some experts believe that mood disorders that go along with autism may be caused by physical differences in the autistic brain. Mood disorders can be treated with medication, cognitive psychology, and behavior management. If the issues are caused by external issues, though, it makes the most sense to change the environment to suit the needs of the patient.

Bowel disease[xlix]
Children with autism are more likely than other children to have stomach and bowel issues. Some researchers believe that the relationship between autism and gastrointestinal problems is a clue to the cause of autism. Others simply note that many kids with autism have stomach troubles. Either way, it makes good sense to treat the symptoms while also ensuring proper nutrition. Whether changes in diet and nutrition can really help cure autism is still debatable. But no child with chronic diarrhea, stomach cramps and nausea will learn, behave or socialize well. By treating GI problems, parents can help their children become more receptive to school, therapy, and social interaction.

ADHD
The Diagnostic and Statistical Manual of Mental Disorders (4th edition) prohibits the co-diagnosis of an ASD and attention-deficit hyperactivity disorder (ADHD). However, clinically significant symptoms of these two conditions commonly co-occur, and children with both sets of symptoms may respond poorly to standard ADHD treatments, and may benefit from additional types of medications or from behavioral or other therapies[l].

Amazingly, attention deficit, aggressive behavior and difficulty with focus are not included in the diagnostic criteria for autism. This is very strange, since they're all extremely common. That being the case, many children with autism also have ADD or ADHD diagnoses. Sometimes, medications that help with ADHD (such as ritalin) can help children with autism to improve behavior and focus. Just as often, however, they make little difference. More likely to be helpful are changes in the environment that lessen sensory distractions and annoyances and support focus. Other tools to help include social stories, hands-on learning methods, and sensory integration therapy.

Sleep Problems and Autism[li]
While there is little research on the subject, it's clear that many people with autism also have sleep problems. Some have a tough time falling asleep; others wake frequently during the night. Of course, lack of sleep can make autistic symptoms much worse: few people think, behave or socialize well when they're exhausted. Parents, too, can be overwhelmed when they're sleep deprived. Studies show that melatonin, a hormone-based supplement, can help people with autism get to sleep. It's not clear, however, that melatonin can make much of a difference in helping people with autism to sleep through the night.

Motor clumsiness
The initial accounts of Asperger's syndrome and other diagnostic schemes include descriptions of motor clumsiness. Children with ASD may be delayed in acquiring motor skills that require motor dexterity, such as bicycle riding or opening a jar, and may appear awkward or "uncomfortable in their own skin." They may be poorly coordinated, or have an odd or bouncy gait or posture, poor handwriting, or problems with visual-motor integration, visual-perceptual skills, and conceptual learning. They may show problems with proprioception (sensation of body position) on measures of apraxia (motor planning disorder), balance, tandem gait, and finger-thumb apposition[lii].

Obsessive-compulsive disorder
Obsessive-compulsive disorder is characterized by recurrent obsessional thoughts or compulsive acts.

Obsessional thoughts are ideas, images or impulses that enter the individual's mind again and again in a stereotyped form. They are almost invariably distressing (because they are violent or obscene, or simply because they are perceived as senseless) and the sufferer often tries, unsuccessfully, to resist them. They are, however, recognized as the individual's own thoughts, even though they are involuntary and often repugnant.

Compulsive acts or rituals are stereotyped behaviors that are repeated again and again. They are not inherently enjoyable, nor do they result in the completion of inherently useful tasks.

It must be recognized that this is different from the obsessions that are a feature of autism spectrum disorders in that the obsessions are not enjoyable or in any way beneficial, which can sometimes be the case with autism, for instance an obsession to study an interest.

Tourette syndrome
The prevalence of Tourette syndrome among individuals with autism is estimated to be higher than the prevalence for the general population. Several hypotheses for this association have been advanced, including common genetic factors and dopamine, glutamate or serotonin abnormalities[liii].

Seizures
One in four children with autism has a seizure disorder. Seizures can range from full-scale convulsions to blackouts or brief staring spells. This spectrum of symptoms can make it hard to spot seizures, which can also be diagnosed through the use of electroencephalograms that measure changes in brainwaves. Unlike most autistic symptoms, seizures do have a medical solution. Anticonvulsants can usually control seizures effectively. It's important to be sure that the right anticonvulsant is selected, since some can have serious side effects.

Sensory problems
Unusual responses to sensory stimuli are more common and prominent in autistic children, although there is no good evidence that sensory symptoms differentiate autism from other developmental disorders[liv]. The responses may be more common in children: a pair of studies found that autistic children had impaired tactile perception while autistic adults did not. The same two studies also found that autistic individuals had more problems with complex memory and reasoning tasks such as Twenty Questions; these problems were somewhat more marked among adults[lv]. Several studies have reported associated motor problems that include poor muscle tone, poor motor planning, and toe walking; ASD is not associated with severe motor disturbances[lvi].

Most people with autism have sensory problems. They may over-respond to noise, light and touch. Or, on the other hand, they may crave deep pressure and physical sensation. Either way, hyper- or hyposensitivity can make everyday activities extremely difficult. What child learns well when they're overwhelmed by intense light, constant sound, and scratchy clothes? While there are treatments to improve sensory issues, the best solutions usually involve changing the environment to suit the child.

Summary
Conditions comorbid to autism spectrum disorders include a wide variety of problems adding to the complexity of accurate diagnoses and successful interventions.

Chapter 13 How many people suffer from autism?

There have always been people with ASDs. Yet for the past few years, the subject has been more in the limelight.

This is also caused by the fact that the autistic way of thinking and acting is less adapted, or not adapted, to the demands of a modern society. As a consequence more and more people with an ASD fall by the wayside. In earlier times they may perhaps have behaved a bit strangely but they could still keep up with society.

Add to this that the knowledge of autism has increased and that autism is often recognized at an earlier stage. Furthermore, nowadays more types of autism are described than 30 years ago. At that time only classic autism was brought up; now PDD-NOS and Asperger's syndrome are acknowledged as well.

Autism Spectrum Disorders are more common in the pediatric population than some better-known disorders such as diabetes, spinal bifida, or Down syndrome[lvii].

Prevalence studies have been done in several countries. Prevalence estimates range from 2 to 6 per 1,000 children.

This wide range of prevalence points to a need for earlier and more accurate screening for the symptoms of ASD. The earlier the disorder is diagnosed, the sooner the child can be helped through treatment interventions. Pediatricians, family physicians, daycare providers, teachers, and parents may initially dismiss signs of ASD, optimistically thinking the child is just a little slow and will "catch up."

Although early intervention has a dramatic impact on reducing symptoms and increasing a child's ability to grow and learn new skills, it is estimated that only 50 percent of the children are diagnosed before kindergarten.

It is worldwide agreed that 4 to 5 in 10,000 people come within the classic category of autistic disorder.

If we include autism-related disorders, the complete spectrum of autistic disorders comprises 58 of every 10,000 people (Lorna Wing).

Prof. Dr. M. Haveman[lviii] and his team have investigated the occurrence of autism among the population and whether this incidence has increased of late. They investigated more than 30 prevalence studies and concluded that 0.6 per cent of the examined population in the age group from 3 to 18 have (or suffer from) a pervasive development disorder. The sub-division they found: for autism a prevalence of 8.1 in 10,000 applies, for Asperger's syndrome 38.4 in 10,000 applies, and for PDD-NOS the prevalence is 12 in 10,000[lix].

Many professionals assume that the percentages are in fact higher.

Simon Baron-Cohen, an English clinical psychologist at Cambridge University, states that present studies suggest that 1 in 200 children have a disorder within the autism spectrum.

ASD is found more often in men than in women. In normally talented people the relation of men and women thus diagnosed is about 6 to 1. However, in different examinations these values differ strongly (from 3 to 1 and 10 to 1). Generally speaking boys are more sensitive than girls in developing developmental, learning and behavioral disorders. Biologically speaking they are the stronger sex. It is possible girls are less prone due to hormonal factors during pregnancy of the mother, different development of the brain, or hereditary factors. This means that girls compared with boys usually have several and/or more severe causes leading to the development of autism. As a result girls, when they suffer from autism, often have a more severe form accompanied with developmental disabilities or below average intelligence.

Although it has not been established unequivocally, some scientists believe that the recent reported rises in the incidence (number of new cases) and prevalence (total number of cases) of ASD do not reflect a true increase in autism or ASD.

The determination of whether autism and/or ASD rates are increasing or not may be complicated by several issues:

- *Methodological differences:*
  Study design differences complicate comparing rates from newer studies with older studies.

- *Changes in diagnostic criteria:*
  Variable diagnostic criteria have added to the difficulty in comparing rates over time.

- *Reporting errors:*
  Prevalence rates for infantile autism and ASD, although very different, may be incorrectly combined or delineated, resulting in under- or over-reporting, which has also made it difficult to evaluate actual temporal increases.

- *Misclassification:*
  Early epidemiology studies may have misclassified autism as mental retardation; some forms of mental retardation may be misclassified and confused with more extreme ASD, which may also involve retardation.

- *Misdiagnosis:*
  Similarity of symptoms of ASD to other pervasive developmental disorders or learning disabilities could result in misdiagnosis and over-reporting of ASD.

- *Reproductive risk factors:*
  Older maternal age and lower birth weight have been associated with ASD; national trends suggest these concerns are becoming more significant.

- *Socioeconomic factors:*
  Affluent school systems may have increased awareness of developmental disorders and may have more resources available to assist these children if they are diagnosed.[lx]

Summary

With the increasing awareness and prevalence of ASDs, it has become easier to track statistics such as occurrences, costs involved, and other significant information. Currently autism-related disorder research shows a wide range of ASD prevalence rates, estimated somewhere between 2 and 6 per 1,000. Approximately 1 in every 250 babies born has an ASD. Families with one autistic child have a higher chance of having another autistic child. Boys are more likely to be diagnosed with an ASD.

DIAGNOSIS

Chapter 14 Diagnosis

14.1 Classification

Autism Spectrum Disorder (ASD) is an increasingly popular term that refers to a broad definition of autism, including the classical form of the disorder and closely related disabilities that share many of the core characteristics. People who suffer from an Autism Spectrum Disorder (ASD) form a diverse group. No two people with ASD are the same. Just like all people, people with ASD are unique. They have their own personalities, temperaments, experiences, limitations and qualities. While one might make eye contact, another will not. One might sit still for hours on end in a corner of a room; another might seek contact with people in an easygoing manner.

Experts all over the world try to use the same classification system, encompassing all disorders and symptoms of mental illness. For psychiatric disorders, experts use The Diagnostic and Statistical Manual of Mental Disorders (DSM). The DSM is published by The American Psychological Association (http://www.apa.org). The DSM Classification system is based on mutual agreement between scientists and practitioners. Because the psychiatric field is very dynamic, this classification system is updated regularly. The fourth edition of The DSM (DSM-IV) has been in use since 1994. In the meantime the DSM-IV-TR (2000) has been released. The DSM-IV-TR does not supply us with a re-editing of the criteria, but has updated the text related to the different disorders.

The diagnosis of autism can't be made by any clinical method like laboratory research (blood tests), scanning (MRI), or hereditary research (chromosomes). Autism remains a diagnosis based on subjective information.

Classifying is not the same as diagnosing. However, it can be an important aspect of making a diagnosis. In daily practice different names for the disorder of people with ASD can be found:
- Autism
- Autism Spectrum Disorder
- Disorder of Asperger
- Multiplex Development Disorder or Multiple (Complex) Development Disorder (M(C)DD)
- Pervasive Developmental Disorder – Not Otherwise Specified (PDD-NOS)

All these different names belong to the autism spectrum. When an "Autism Spectrum Disorder" is mentioned, one of these forms is referred to. Internationally, "Pervasive Development Disorder" is often used, as well as the name "Autism Disorders Spectrum."

Lorna Wing
Lorna Wing, an autism researcher, came up with a different classification that concerns the manner in which people with ASD behave. She distinguishes:
- Aloof group
- Passive group
- Active but odd group
- Over-formal, stilted group

The aloof group: Behavior may include: Behaving as if other people do not exist; Little or no eye contact made; No response when spoken to; Faces empty of expression except with extreme joy, anger or distress; No response to cuddling; If something is wanted, a person's hand may be pulled toward the object; May respond to rough and tumble play well, but when this stops, returns to aloof pattern; Seem to 'be in a world of their own.'

The passive group features include: The child willingly accepts social approaches; May meet the gaze of others; May become involved as a passive part of a game.

The active but odd group. Children of this group make active approaches to others but make that contact in strange ways, including: Paying no attention to the other party; Poor eye contact although sometimes may stare too long; May hug or shake hands too hard.

The over-formal, stilted group. Seen in later life, this behavior is common in the most able person with autism. The following characteristics tend to be displayed: Excessively polite and formal; Have a good level of language; Try very hard to stick to the rules of social interaction without really understanding them.

Behavior of people with ASD can differ from context to context. For instance at home, in a safe environment, somebody might be "active but odd" and at school "aloof." During the course of one's lifetime different emphasis on one of the groups may occur. Lorna Wing does not look upon these groups as easy to distinguish and unchangeable.

Simon Baron-Cohen
A British psychologist, Simon Baron-Cohen, developed the ES (empathizing–systemizing) Theory in an effort to understand why the cognitive difficulties in autism appeared to lie in domains in which on average females outperformed males and why cognitive strengths in autism appeared to lie in domains in which on average males outperformed females.

Baron-Cohen had previously proposed the mind-blindness theory in 1985, which argued that children with autism are delayed in their development of a theory of mind, that is, the ability to keep track of the thoughts and feeling of themselves or others. A strength of this theory lies in its power to explain one of the core features of autism (the social and communication difficulties), but a limitation of the mind-blindness theory is that it ignored the other main domain in autism (unusually narrow interests and highly repetitive behaviors, also called 'resistance to change or need for sameness'). To address this, Baron-Cohen put forward the E-S theory in the late 1990s.

Baron-Cohen developed the hypothesis that typical sex differences may provide a better understanding of autism (the empathizing–systemizing theory). The theory proposes that autism is an extreme of the male brain. The extreme male brain (EMB) theory of autism sees autism as being on a continuum with individual differences in the general population (sex differences). Baron-Cohen proposes that the cause of autism at a biological level may be hyper-masculinization. This hypothesis posits that certain features of autism ('obsessions' and repetitive behavior, previously regarded as 'purposeless') as being highly purposive, intelligent (hyper-systemizing), and a sign of a different way of thinking. He wrote a popular book on the topic of sex differences and its relationship to autism (The Essential Difference, 2003).

The empathizing–systemizing (E-S) theory[lxi] classifies people on the basis of their scores along two dimensions: empathizing (E) and systemizing (S). It measures a person's strength of interest in empathy (defined as the drive to identify a person's thoughts and feelings and to respond to these with an appropriate emotion); and a person's strength of interest in systems (defined as the drive to analyze or construct a system). A system in turn is defined as anything that follows rules. Key classes of systems include mechanical systems, natural systems, abstract systems, and collectible systems. Rules in turn are defined as repeating, lawful patterns.

The E-S theory generates 5 different 'brain types.' The E-S theory is a better predictor of who goes into STEM (Science, Technology, Engineering and Mathematics) subjects than is gender. The E-S theory has been extended into the 'Extreme Male Brain' (EMB) theory of autism to show deficits and delays in cognitive empathy (also called 'theory of mind') alongside intact or superior systemizing.

Research on relatives of people with Asperger's syndrome and autism has found that their fathers and grandfathers are twice as likely to be engineers as the general population. Natural science students have more relatives with autism than humanities students. Asperger's syndrome is found more often in mathematicians and their siblings than in the general population. Both mothers and fathers of children with Asperger's syndrome tend to score high on systemizing. Both mothers and fathers of children with autism or Asperger's syndrome often have fathers who worked in systemizing occupations. Both mothers and fathers of children with autism have a strongly masculine pattern of brain activity when doing systemizing activity.

Summary

There is a wide variety of people who suffer from ASD, and there are a number of methods for classifying them. The Diagnostic and Statistical Manual of Mental Disorders (DSM), which is published by The American Psychological Association, is the industry standard. Lorna Wing has created a different classification system based on observed behavior. Simon Baron-Cohen created yet another one. They all have their merits. Classifying is not the same as diagnosing, but it can be a useful step in diagnosis.

14.2 Diagnosis

There are people who do not like to diagnose their child because they are afraid this will stigmatize the child and that a classification or diagnosis doesn't pay tribute to the child's unique characteristics. These critics mention two main points of criticism.

1. A diagnosis labeling your child with autism might hinder the child in its development because people might react overprotectively or might have the wrong notions about autism and thus make the wrong decisions.
2. The label may replace somebody's true identity. The child is no longer acknowledged. It's no longer Peter or Robert but 'the autistic.'

These concerns are legitimate. But it is not the diagnosis that is responsible, but the people who wrongly use the labels or diagnosis.

Regarding the first point of criticism, of course you can deny the child certain liberties knowing he is labeled with autism. On the other hand the diagnosis might free resources he would otherwise have no connection with. For instance the child may receive specialized education and adequate housing.

The second point of criticism is primarily the result of the way many people misuse the label. Your child does not change after the diagnosis. It's the way some people look at your child that changes. A sound diagnosis gives a thorough profile of your child, with his or her weak traits and strong traits. This can be very helpful in maximizing the child's quality of life.

There are signs to look for if you think your child might suffer from autism.

If you witness any of these problems or abnormal behavior, call your doctor.

- If your child is showing speech regression, there might be a reason for concern. Also, if your child is taking a long time to start talking, longer than most children at that age.
- Another problem you might see is the way your child interacts with other children. Perhaps your child refuses to play with other children or doesn't seem to respond well in social settings. If so, you should visit a doctor to get more information.

If a doctor suspects a problem, they will perform a battery of tests. Every child is different, so one test will not show if a child has autism. Every child has different symptoms and responds to the disorder differently. Your family doctor will do a full work-up with a family history. If your doctor does suspect any problems, your doctor may refer you to a specialist in autism and similar disorders to get a proper diagnosis.

If your child does get diagnosed with autism, it's important to give your child structure. This is going to start with the doctor. Don't drag your child around to three or four doctors hoping the diagnosis is going to change. Get one doctor who is going to give your child a uniform treatment. Seeing the same face all the time will help your child to trust other people.

Detecting Autism

Autism Spectrum Disorders can often be reliably detected by the age of 3 years, and in some cases as early as 18 months. Studies suggest that many children eventually may be accurately identified by the age of 1 year or even younger. The appearance of any of the warning signs of ASD is reason to have a child evaluated by a professional specializing in these disorders.

Parents are usually the first to notice unusual behavior in their child, although they may not realize the specific nature or degree of the problem. In some cases, the baby seemed "different" from birth, unresponsive to people or focusing intently on one item for long periods of time. The first sign of an ASD can also appear in children who seem to have been developing normally. When an engaging, babbling toddler suddenly becomes silent, withdrawn, self-abusive, or indifferent to social overtures, something is wrong.

The Diagnosis of Autism Spectrum Disorders

Diagnostics is the process of finding the strengths and weaknesses of a person, his or her abilities and disabilities. Diagnostic investigation eventually must lead to advice for care at home, at school, at work, for spending leisure time and making it through the day. Diagnostics should not be confined to making a diagnosis, a classification.

People with ASD have, from early youth, a disorder in processing information. They do have sensory perceptions but they lack the overall view and relationship. Their eyesight and sense of hearing, feeling, taste and smell are fine, but they cannot associate their senses properly. They mostly select a detail and ascribe a very literal meaning to it. They observe the world as if it were as loose particles. They often stick to small unimportant details without surveying the connection and the whole. They often fail to understand the meaning of a specific event or make wrong associations so they cannot react well. In a world obscure to them, they search for order and safety by clinging to fixed habits and patterns. When changes are abrupt they can easily be seized by panic.

Among other things, these problems in processing information can be recognized by the following characteristics:

- Deals with stimuli in a different way and, as a result, reacting differently to situations
- Over-reacts to sensory stimuli from the environment such as sounds, smells, visual details and touch stimuli
- Not (or differently) associating various events, thus experiencing the world as a jumble of impressions
- Unable to apply knowledge and experience acquired in a specific situation to another comparable situation (generalization problems)
- Not being able, or with difficulty, to make a distinction between important and unimportant information
- Receives all information from outside with equal loudness (irrelevant side issues as well)
- Unable to cut oneself off from noise or background noises
- Observes surroundings in details and insufficiently surveys the whole
- Digests language literally and finds it difficult to look beyond the observation itself
- Rigid, black and white thinking with little flexibility
- Lack of imagination, fantasy and imaginative powers
- Has trouble projecting themselves into the thoughts and feelings of others
- Difficulty recognizing and expressing emotions, or doing so in other ways
- Fails to have insight in social situations and understanding insufficiently the social conduct of others, resulting in insufficient gearing
- Sticks to familiar habits and patterns for need of safety
- Shows a restricted field of interest and patterns of behavior
- Has difficulties coping with changes or sudden events
- Violently acts emotionally to obviously trifling affairs and has the tendency to get stuck in them

Although there are many concerns about labeling a young child with an ASD, the earlier the diagnosis of ASD is made, the sooner the necessary interventions can begin. Evidence over the last 15 years indicates that intensive early intervention in optimal educational settings for at least 2 years during the preschool years results in improved outcomes in most young children with ASD.

In evaluating a child, clinicians rely on behavioral characteristics to make a diagnosis. Some of the characteristic behaviors of ASD may be apparent in the first few months of a child's life, or they may appear at any time during the early years. For the diagnosis, problems in at least one of the areas of communication, socialization, or restricted behavior must be present before the age of 3.

The diagnosis requires a two-stage process. The first stage involves developmental screening during "well child" check-ups; the second stage entails a comprehensive evaluation by a multidisciplinary team.

Screening (First Stage)

A "well child" check-up should include a developmental screening test. If your child's pediatrician does not routinely check your child with such a test, ask that it be done. Your own observations and concerns about your child's development will be essential in helping to screen your child. Reviewing family videotapes, photos, and baby albums can help parents remember when each behavior was first noticed and when the child reached certain developmental milestones.

Several screening instruments have been developed to quickly gather information about a child's social and communicative development within medical settings. Some of these are the Checklist of Autism in Toddlers (CHAT[lxii]), the modified Checklist for Autism in Toddlers (M-CHAT[lxiii]) , the Screening Tool for Autism in Two-Year-Olds (STAT), and the Social Communication Questionnaire (SC Q [lxiv]) (for children 4 years of age and older).

Some screening instruments rely solely on parent responses to a questionnaire, and some rely on a combination of parent reports and observation. Key items on these instruments that appear to differentiate children with autism from other groups before the age of 2 include pointing and pretend play. Screening instruments do not provide individual diagnosis but serve to assess the need for referral for possible diagnosis of ASD. These screening methods may not identify children with mild ASD, such as those with high-functioning autism or Asperger's syndrome.

During the last few years, screening instruments have been devised to screen for Asperger's syndrome and higher functioning autism. The Autism Spectrum Screening Questionnaire (ASSQ[lxv]), the Australian Scale for Asperger's Syndrome[lxvi], and the most recent, the Childhood Asperger's Syndrome Test (CAST)[lxvii], are some of the instruments that are reliable for identifying school-aged children with Asperger's syndrome or higher functioning autism. These tools concentrate on social and behavioral impairments in children without significant language delay.

If, following the screening process or during a routine "well child" check-up, your child's doctor sees any of the possible indicators of ASD, further evaluation is indicated.

Screening Tools for Autism [lxviii]

Tool
Childhood Autism Rating Scale (CARS)
Description
First used in the early 1970s, this system was created by Eric Schopler. It uses a 15-point scale to evaluate the child's:
- Ability to relate to other people.

- Use of his/her body
- Ability to adapt to change
- Listening abilities
- Verbal communication skills

Tool
Checklist for Autism in Toddlers (CHAT)
Description
This system was created by Simon Baron-Cohen in the early 1990s to evaluate children for autism as young as 18 months. Both the parents and the child's physician complete a short form.

Tool
Autism Screening Questionnaire (SCQ)
Description
40 items are used to evaluate children ages 4 and older.

Tool
Screening Test for Autism in Two-Year-Olds (STAT)
Description
This method is under development by Wendy Stone. Using this method, children under 2 are directly observed for three skill areas:
- Play
- Motor Imitation
- Joint Attention

Screening Tools for Asperger

Tool
The Autism Spectrum Screening Questionnaire (ASSQ)
Description
The ASSQ is designed for completion by parents or teachers to screen for Asperger's syndrome and other high-functioning Autism Spectrum Disorders in school-aged children.

Tool
Childhood Asperger Syndrome Test (CAST)
Description
The Childhood Asperger Syndrome Test (CAST) is a 37-item parental self-completion questionnaire to screen for autism spectrum conditions in research. Good test accuracy was demonstrated in studies with primary school-aged children in mainstream schools.

Comprehensive Diagnostic Evaluation (Second Stage)

The second stage of diagnosis must be comprehensive in order to accurately rule in or rule out an ASD or other developmental problem. This evaluation may be done by a multidisciplinary team that includes a psychologist, a neurologist, a psychiatrist, a speech therapist, or other professionals who diagnose children with ASD.

Because ASDs are complex disorders and may involve other neurological or genetic problems, a comprehensive evaluation should entail neurological and genetic assessment, along with in-depth cognitive and language testing. In addition, measures developed specifically for diagnosing autism are often used. These include the Autism Diagnosis Interview-Revised (ADI-R)[lxix] and the Autism Diagnostic Observation Schedule (ADOS-G)[lxx].

The ADI-R is a structured interview that contains over 100 items and is conducted with a caregiver. It consists of four main factors – the child's communication, social interaction, repetitive behaviors, and age-of-onset symptoms. The ADOS-G is an observational measure used to "press" for socio-communicative behaviors that are often delayed, abnormal, or absent in children with ASD.

Still another instrument often used by professionals is the Childhood Autism Rating Scale (CARS)[lxxi]. It aids in evaluating the child's body movements, adaptation to change, listening response, verbal communication, and relationship to people. It is suitable for use with children over 2 years of age. The examiner observes the child and also obtains relevant information from the parents. The child's behavior is rated on a scale based on deviation from typical behavior of children of the same age.

Two other tests that should be used to assess any child with a developmental delay are a formal audio logic hearing evaluation and a lead screening. Although some hearing loss can co-occur with ASD, some children with ASD may be incorrectly thought to have such a loss. In addition, if the child has suffered from an ear infection, transient hearing loss can occur. Lead screening is essential for children who remain in the oral-motor stage in which they put any and everything into their mouths for a long period of time. Children with an autistic disorder usually have elevated blood lead levels.[lxxii]

Customarily, an expert diagnostic team has the responsibility of thoroughly evaluating the child, assessing the child's unique strengths and weaknesses, and determining a formal diagnosis. The team will then meet with the parents to explain the results of the evaluation.

Although parents may have been aware that something was not "quite right" with their child, when the diagnosis is given, it is a devastating blow. At such a time, it is hard to stay focused, but the best opportunity parents will get to ask questions and get recommendations on what further steps they should take for the child is when the members of the evaluation team are together. Learning as much as possible at this meeting is very important, but it is helpful to leave this meeting with the name or names of professionals who can be contacted if the parents have further questions.

Summary
Autism Spectrum Disorders can often be reliably detected by the age of 3 years, and in some cases as early as 18 months. Generally, evaluation involves a range of screening tools or methods over a period of time since no specific observation is likely to definitively yield results.

Chapter 15 After the Diagnosis

Each of us will cope differently with the news that a cherished one is, or you yourself are, diagnosed with an ASD. When you hear that your child has been diagnosed with autism, the worst thoughts come to your mind. You can feel scared, lonely and overwhelmed. One matter we all have in common is the overall feeling that you are alone as you face the emotional stress and anxiety of the situation. Particularly, the fear of the unknown.

All of these feelings are natural when dealing with a new situation, but it doesn't have to be terrifying.

You need to allow yourself to grieve. You cannot help yourself or your child until you can come to terms with the diagnosis. Be upset. But understand you will have better days than the present. Find out what is most important. Focus on that. Take one step at a time. Write down your feelings and questions. That often helps.

Many people find it easy to see the weaknesses in others and themselves. The stimulating challenge is to focus on the abilities. There lies the greatest reward.

No story will ever be the same. Everybody is unique. But there will be noticeable similarities in experience.

During the process of coping with the diagnosis of autism, you may go through a mixture of feelings. There is no right or wrong way to grieve. All your feelings are normal. It is useful, however, to understand that human grief is a routine that often follows a healing pattern. We have listed the phases people generally go through below. But it is important to realize it is not a scientific fact that everybody goes through the phases in a chronological way. The feelings may come and go. Here is what to expect and the stages of dealing with the diagnosis.

- **Shock**: Shock is the first stage. It is accompanied by disbelief and numbness. People who experience emotional numbness say they have a sense of being paralyzed, distant, and removed from their feelings of grief.

- **Denial and Isolation**: This is common and usually follows quickly after you hear the diagnosis. Thinking "I don't believe it," or "It can't be." In this stage, the person experiencing grief and bereavement has significant difficulty accepting the reality of their loss. While complete acceptance is part of the work of the entire grief process, the initial more acute difficulties with acceptance are included in this phase. You could think "Not *my* child" or "The doctors have to be wrong." There is nothing wrong with getting a second opinion but if a second opinion confirms what has been told, don't keep dragging your child from doctor to doctor hoping for something different. It's important to move past this stage of the process because denying the existence of autism isn't going to help anyone, especially the child. The quicker parents accept the diagnosis of autism, the quicker treatment can begin.

- **Anger**: Getting angry is a natural human emotion. Anger is another big factor, which seems to be necessary in order to face the reality of life and then to get beyond it. We must all heal in our own ways. Anger is a natural stage through which we must pass. There are different ways to go through this anger. In this phase, the grieving person feels anger with the world, fate, God, or people in their lives. He or she may ask, "Why me?" and/or "Why not someone else?" during this phase. You can get mad at yourself, thinking you did something wrong. You may even get mad at other parents with healthy children, wondering why they don't have to deal with autism. The key when dealing with anger is speaking to someone about it. Speak to someone you trust. Your doctor might be able to refer you to a counselor who can help with these issues.

- **Depression**: Depression is a stage of grief that comes and goes. Grief is a very strong emotion, but a natural one in dealing with bad news. Knowing this, be prepared to give yourself time to heal. Feeling sad is not a bad thing though, so you should never feel guilty about feeling heartbroken. However, don't let this emotion overwhelm you because you might transfer this onto your child who might blame themselves, thinking they did something wrong. Working past grief is important, but it's also a natural process. If you notice you are sitting in this stage too long or people around you think you have been grieving too long, seek the help of a counselor. Resignation is a late stage. It comes when finally you accept the truth. As time passes, grieving individuals experience acknowledgement and acceptance of loss.

- **Acceptance**: It may have taken some time to get to this stage, but this is the end result in coping with the diagnosis of autism. At this point, you can finally move on and get the best care. The bereaved person comes to terms with the loss, and is able to move on to re-invest in the different life that lies ahead. He or she will experience fewer extremes of emotion and will understand that things will never be the same but that life goes on and a new meaning and purpose will eventually be found.

Where do we go after grieving?
Autism can be difficult to manage, especially depending on the severity of the case. When the acceptance stage has set in, it is very important to find out all you can about autism until you have your questions answered. Don't sit back and let others take control. Don't be afraid to ask your pediatrician or GP everything that's on your mind. If they don't have the answers, look for somebody qualified who can answer your questions.

You can also visit your local library for information on this topic. And of course don't forget the Internet. That surely is a great source of information.

Remember that others in similar circumstances can be a great source of information just like (local) support groups or Early Childhood Intervention Centers. There are people to help you, so you never have to feel overwhelmed.

Coping Mechanisms
A coping skill is a behavioral tool that may be used by individuals to offset or overcome hardship, disadvantage, or disability without correcting or removing the underlying condition. Coping skills are also sometimes called workarounds.

Virtually all living beings routinely use coping skills in everyday life. These are perhaps most obvious in response to physical disabilities. An easy example of the use of coping skills in the animal kingdom are three-legged dogs, which typically learn to overcome the obvious disability to become as agile and mobile as their four-legged counterparts, whether born with the impairment or having received it due to an injury.

When helping humans deal with particular problems, trained counselors have found that focusing on coping skills (with or without remedial action) often helps individuals. The range of successful coping skills varies widely with the problems to be overcome. However, the learning and practice of coping skills are generally regarded as very helpful to most individuals. Even the sharing of learned coping skills with others is often beneficial.

When coping methods are overused, they may actually worsen one's condition. Alcohol and cocaine, for example, may provide temporary escape from one's problems, but, with excess use, ultimately result in greater hardship.

One group of coping skills are coping mechanisms, defined as the skills used to reduce stress. In psychological terms these are consciously used skills, and defense mechanisms are their unconscious counterpart. Overuse of coping mechanisms (such as avoiding problems or working obsessively) and defense mechanisms (such as denial and projection) may aggravate one's problem rather than remedy it.

In psychology, coping is the process of successfully managing difficult circumstances, expending effort to solve personal and interpersonal problems, and seeking to master, minimize, reduce or tolerate stress or conflict.

In dealing with disease, people tend to use one of the two main coping strategies: either problem focused or emotion focused coping.

People using **problem focused strategies** try to deal with the cause of the problem. They do this by finding out information on the disease, learning new skills to manage it, and rearranging their lives around the disease.

Emotion focused strategies occur when the person modifies the way they think, for example employing denial or distancing oneself from the problem. People may alter the way they think about a problem by altering their goals and values, such as by seeing the humor in a situation.

People may use a combination of these different types of coping, and coping mechanisms will as a rule change over time. All these methods can prove useful, but some claim that those using problem focused coping strategies will adjust better to life.

Generally speaking I would advise the following mechanism:
- Share your feelings with someone.
- Discuss those feelings openly and honestly.
- Show interest and solid support to those who need your help.
- Get professional assistance!

Everyone will cope differently, and where you are will also affect how your cope. You need to ensure that you start the setting up of YOUR coping mechanisms – no one is going to do it for you. To make it manageable, a good way to help you cope is to look at the different places and people that surround you.
- Your home
- Immediate family
- Close friends
- Local support groups

Your home
The first place you need to consider is under your roof and those who live in it. If there are older children, they need the current situation explained to them. They could feel excluded at times as you will definitely find yourself spending more time with your autistic child. You need to be aware of this and make sure that you set aside precious time to spend with all your children so that they don't get jealous of their sibling. For kids who are not yet old enough to comprehend, they will grow up accepting the child for who they are and as they get older it can be explained to them.

You and your partner need to thoroughly discuss the situation openly and honestly. Chances are one of you will be coping better than the other or maybe one of you hasn't accepted the reality yet. You need to make sure that you unreservedly support each other and make time to be together.

Don't try to do this on your own. The more support you can get the easier it will be and the best place is to start at home.

Immediate family
My advice would be to only tell your immediate family on an as needed basis. Unfortunately not everybody will understand or accept what you tell them but others will, and it may startle you who will and who won't. Don't waste too

much time trying to get them to understand if they won't. You need to concentrate on you, your child and your immediate family.

Close friends
Only tell them on an as needed basis. You need to be able to discuss your situation with someone, but if they are not going to support you or be there when you need them then find someone else.

The people you decide to confide in/trust need to be good listeners, make a good cup of tea or maybe be able to 'walk with you.' You don't want someone to feel sorry for you – you require someone who can support you and 'hold you up' when you need it.

But don't isolate yourself. It is the worst thing you can do. If going to others' homes is stressful – throwing, running, no barriers or whatever – then invite your friends to your home. Isolation is a dangerous thing. Don't turn your back on your trusted friends. You are still you and true friends will always be there for you.

Local support groups
Ask your doctor or pediatrician. Have a look on the Internet. You have to feel your way. No one is going to walk up and tell you.

A support group can help in many ways. Here you can hear about problems other families face and talk to people in the same situation as you. People who will understand and are willing to listen and help. They are an invaluable resource.

Summary
Fear can prevent a parent from wanting to diagnose his or her child with ASD, but ignoring its presence won't make it go away. If your child has ASD, you need to know this so that you can come to terms with your feelings – they will of course be powerful – and do what you can to maximize your child's quality of life. There are a number of strategies you can use to help you, your child, your spouse, and other members of your family to adjust. Look at the places and people that surround you in your home, your immediate family, your close friends, and local support groups. You also can (and should) get professional assistance. There are others who have been through what you are going through. Find them.

15.1 The Grief Cycle

Since autism is not a simple condition, more help and resources are available not only for the child but also for those people around him or her such as parents, siblings, and other family members.

The following are just some of the first few steps to recovery after knowing the result of the autism diagnosis. These are simple steps but can aid parents and siblings alike to pass through the grief cycle and overcome all challenges it will bring to the entire family.

1. Don't be terrified. Although the thought of autism is quite terrifying, parents should learn to be more level headed once they have read all the diagnosis results. It is only common to feel dizziness and weakness over the diagnosis but there is nothing left to do but to accept it and face the situation with a positive attitude. Yes, life with a child or a sibling who suffers from autism will not be easy but it can be better. This happens when the parents and siblings do not panic and stick together to think of ways to adjust to the situation.

2. Nothing's changed. It will be better if the family thinks that the child that has been diagnosed with autism is still the same child they love and care for. Thinking that the child is different will lead parents and siblings to treat him or her differently. The diagnosis only states the medical condition of the child but it does not mean that she or he should be left behind. Remember that all the good qualities the child exhibits will always be there. Some things and behavior might change in the future because of the child's condition. What parents and siblings can do is to help the child use his or her good qualities to compensate for the condition.

3. Again, be level-headed, especially when it comes to taking any action. Although early intervention is vital, experts say that parents should not rush into action because this can worsen the condition of the child. Although it seems appealing to try any therapeutic treatments, don't jump into immediate action until you have consulted with a professional about what is best for the child.

4. Enrich your knowledge about the condition. Having enough knowledge and deep understanding about the disorder can help you accept and adjust to the situation easier. You can do this by reading various resources such as books and magazines and by asking questions about what you don't understand regarding the condition. By using the Internet, parents and siblings can also now browse for different websites and find a support group where they can share and exchange ideas on how to manage the situation.

5. Be aware of the needs of the special child. Determining the child's needs above all else should be the topmost priority of families who have member(s) diagnosed with the condition. Depending on the level of the child's autism, the family should be able to list all he or she might need and provide it.

6. Allot enough time to research possible resources. After determining what the child needs, parents can now determine what are the possible treatments that can be used and how accessible they are for the family.

You can do research into the immediate resources and programs offered by the local government to support your needs.

7. Know the basics and start with those. Today, there are many treatment options available for children diagnosed with autism. Don't be overwhelmed with the more expensive and complex ones hoping that these are better because they might not be. The most practical thing to do is start with simple treatment options that are already available, appropriate, and well-funded. These basic treatment options involve speech, physical and occupational therapy and other home-based therapeutic programs, especially for young ones.

8. Take it slowly. The burden of autism can only be alleviated by a series of therapies. But, this does not mean that you should try each and every treatment and therapy there is at the same time. What you can do is add therapies and treatments slowly so you can give yourself and the child time to adjust to each session.

9. Try to be positive. The situation is already here and there's nothing you can do to change it. What you can do is try to be positive about it and live each day as normally as possible, especially for the child.

Summary

For many families, a diagnosis of autism in a child brings about a profound sense of loss. The grief process, for a parent coming to terms with having a child with special needs involves cycling through the different parts of the loss, depending on what is going on developmentally with the child, and what is going on within the family or the community.

TREATMENT & INTERVENTION

Chapter 16 Treatment and intervention

Caution: No single mode of treatment is ever likely to be effective for all children and families. Intervention should be based on individual needs. But whatever you decide, keep a keen eye on the strengths of the person with the ASD. Making use of these strengths in a certain area is good for his or her self-confidence and self-esteem.

Discovering that your child has autism can be an overwhelming experience. For some, the diagnosis may come as a complete surprise; others may have suspected autism and tried for months or years to get an accurate diagnosis. In either case, you perhaps have many questions about how to go on.

The behaviors associated with autism can be trying to those around the autistic person. The autistic child may insist on organizing the items on his or her desk in a particular manner before being able to concentrate on a lesson. Or, he or she may repeat a phrase or behavior over and over to calm down in stressful situations. There may also be instances when the autistic's emotional reaction to a situation seems extremely disproportionate to the situation itself. Indeed, the cause of an outburst may be completely non-apparent to non-autistics.

The treatments used to lessen the signs and behaviors associated with ASDs are as varied as autistics themselves. Because so little is known about the cause of ASDs, there is still much discussion about the best way to treat them.

One thing is certain; at present there is no cure for autism. Treatments may improve behaviors and enable the autistic to better function in educational and social settings, but the disorder itself will not go away. Thus there are treatment and education approaches that may reduce some of the challenges associated with the disability. Intervention may help to lessen disruptive behaviors, and education can teach self-help skills that allow for greater independence. But just as there is no one symptom or behavior in particular that identifies autistic children, there is no single treatment. Children can learn to function within the limits of their disability, but treatment must be tailored to the child's own behaviors and needs.

When considering treatments for autistic children, the Autism Society of America recommends asking the following questions about treatment programs:
- Could my child be harmed by this treatment?
- If the treatment fails, how will my child and my family be affected by the failure?
- Has scientific research been conducted to validate the effectiveness of the treatment program?
- Are there specific methods used to determine the success of the treatment for my child?

- How will the treatment be integrated into my child's current program?

Further, the National Institute of Mental Health recommends these questions:
- What success rate does the treatment have?
- Are data available showing the percentage of children that have gone on to be mainstreamed in a regular school? How successful has the program been for other children?
- How well have those children done in a regular school setting?
- Do staff members have training and experience in working with children and adolescents with autism?
- Which methods are used to plan and organize activities?
- Will my child follow a daily schedule and certain routines?
- How much individual attention will my child receive? How many hours per day?
- Which steps are taken to measure the success of the treatment?
- Will my child's behavior be closely observed and recorded?
- Are activities and positive reinforcements individualized to my child's interests? Will my child be given tasks and rewards that are personally motivating?
- How are distractions minimized within the learning environment?
- Will I receive assistance to carry out the therapy at home? Will the program prepare me to continue the therapy at home?
- What costs are involved in the program?
- Where will treatment take place?
- How much time will my child be required to put into the program?

Most people agree that whatever treatment is used, it must be individualized to the autistic person. This is because no two autistics are alike. And, since the child has his or her own personality and sets of likes and dislikes in combination with a unique set of autistic behaviors, it's important that the child's interests be incorporated into the treatment program so that learning remains a positive experience and the child is motivated to continue.

Because of the great variances from one autistic to another, it's difficult to determine exactly which techniques and interactions will work best for the individual. Treatment programs needn't be carried out separately. There may be great benefit to combining treatment methods in a manner that is most effective for your child.

Summary
There is no cure for autism or ASDs. Your child has a permanent disability, but there are strategies your child can learn to handle the challenges that come with that disability. Likewise, knowledge will make life less trying for those who are around the autistic. There are a number of treatment programs and strategies. Learn about them all, and determine what is most effective for your child.

Chapter 17 Documenting. What and why?

You will need to keep all reports and documents that doctors, child care centers, Early Intervention, etc. give you – you never know when you may need them again. For example, if you move to another town or change doctors, it is easier if you have everything to show the new doctor.

Documenting is always useful when you have to decide what worked best and whether for instance problematic behavior has worsened. If you are going to follow a diet you need to document everything. It is best to document everything for a couple of weeks before you start the new diet, as this will help you see the results.

What do you need to record?
- The date
- What your child eats for each meal – and how much, e.g. little bit, seconds
- Any snacks they have during the day
- The times they eat
- Any drinks they have
- Toileting – when they go to the toilet/nappy changes – is their feces solid?
- Sleep patterns – any sleep through the day – times and duration
- How long do they sleep at night and how late do they wake up
- Behaviors – good and bad, when and possibly why
- If they have little or no speech you may want to record the new words they say or sign
- Anything else that may affect their day – doctors' appointments, visitors, holidays, etc.

You can use a cheap lined book for your record keeping or more sophisticated electronic journal possibilities. Whatever suits you best.

Summary
You will find that you must remember more about your child with ASD than you've been asked to remember about any other child you've raised, anyone else you've cared for, or perhaps even yourself. In fact, it'll be more than you can remember, so always keep good records. You never know which information you'll need in the future.

Chapter 18 Early intervention services

Note: A large part of this chapter will be USA specific when institutions or programs are mentioned. If you live outside the USA you can always ask your doctor or pediatrician for help.

Childhood intervention programs for the disadvantaged focus on the benefits that accrue to the children. Programs may influence the parents (typically the mother), as most programs provide services to the mother as well as the child.

To be eligible for services, children must be less than 3 years of age and have a confirmed disability or established developmental delay, as determined by the state, in one or more of the following areas of development: physical, cognitive, communication, social-emotional, and/or adaptive.

The Early Intervention Program[lxxiii] offers a rich variety of therapeutic and support services to eligible infants and toddlers with disabilities and their families, including:

- family education and counseling, home visits, and parent support groups
- special instruction
- speech pathology and audiology
- occupational therapy
- physical therapy
- psychological services
- service coordination
- nursing services
- nutrition services
- social work services
- vision services
- assistive technology devices and services

Early intervention applies to children of school age or younger who are discovered to have or are at risk of developing a handicapping condition or other special need that may affect their development. Early intervention consists of the provision of services to such children and their families for the purpose of lessening the effects of the condition. Early intervention can be remedial or preventive in nature – remediating existing developmental problems or preventing their occurrence.

Early intervention may focus on the child alone or on the child and the family together. Early intervention programs may be center-based, home-based, hospital-based, or a combination. Services range from identification – that is, hospital or school screening and referral services – to diagnostic and direct intervention programs. Early intervention may begin at any time between birth and school age; however, there are many reasons for it to begin as early as possible.

Why Intervene Early?

There are three primary reasons for early intervention with an exceptional child: to enhance the child's development, to provide support and assistance to the family, and to maximize the child's and family's benefit to society.

1. Child development research has established that the rate of human learning and development is most rapid in preschool years. Timing of intervention becomes particularly important when a child runs the risk of missing an opportunity to learn during a state of maximum readiness. If the most teachable moments or stages of greatest readiness are not used, a child may have difficulty learning a particular skill at a later time. Karnes and Lee (1978) have noted, "only through early identification and appropriate programming can children develop their potential."

2. Early intervention services also have a significant impact on the parents and siblings of an exceptional infant or young child. The family of a young exceptional child often feels disappointment, social isolation, added stress, frustration, and helplessness. The compounded stress of the presence of an exceptional child may affect the family's well-being and interfere with the child's development. Families of handicapped children are found to experience increased instances of divorce and suicide, and the handicapped child is more likely to be abused than a non-handicapped child. Early intervention may result in parents having improved attitudes about themselves and their child, improved information and skills for teaching their child, and more release time for leisure and employment. Parents of gifted preschoolers also need early services so that the supportive and nourishing environment needed by the child is provided in a better way.

3. A third reason for intervening early is that society will reap maximum benefits. The child's increased developmental and educational gains and decreased dependence upon social institutions, the family's increased ability to cope with the presence of an exceptional child, and perhaps the child's increased eligibility for employment, all provide economic as well as social benefits.

When your child is participating in an early intervention program, you must get involved. Accompany them to the sessions. Ask lots of questions. Participate in therapy sessions so you can see what the staff is doing so you can continue the work at home.

Do whatever you can to ensure that you are available to help your child. They only get one shot at life – help them get the best shot.

Available Aids

When your child has been assessed and diagnosed with an Autism Spectrum Disorder, you may feel inadequate to ably help your child develop to the fullest extent of his or her capacity. As you start to look at treatment options and at the sorts of aid available for a child with a disability, you will discover that there is help for you. It is going to be tough to learn and remember everything you need to know about the resources that will be most helpful. Write down everything. If you keep a journal, you will have a foolproof method of recalling information. Keep a record of the doctor's reports and the evaluations your child has been given so that his or her capacity for special programs will be documented. Learn everything you can about special programs for your child; the more you know, the more effectively you can advocate.

For every child eligible for special programs, each state guarantees special education and related services. The Individuals with Disabilities Education Act (IDEA) is a federally mandated program that assures a free and appropriate public education for children with diagnosed learning deficits. Usually children are placed in public schools and the school district pays for all necessary services. These will include, as needed, services by a speech therapist, occupational therapist, school psychologist, social worker, school nurse, or aide.

By US law, the public schools must prepare and carry out a set of instruction goals, or specific skills, for every child in a special education program. The list of skills is known as the child's Individualized Education Program (IEP). The IEP is an agreement between the school and the family on the child's goals. When your child's IEP is developed, you will be asked to attend the meeting. There will be several people at this meeting, including a special education teacher, a representative of the public schools who is knowledgeable about the program, other individuals invited by the school or by you (you may want to bring a relative, a child care provider, or a supportive close friend who knows your child well). Parents play an important part in designing the program, as they know their child and his or her needs best. Once your child's IEP is developed, a meeting is scheduled once a year to review your child's progress and to make any alterations to reflect his or her changing needs.

If your child is under 3 years of age and has special needs, he or she should be eligible for an early intervention program; this program is available in every state. Each state determines which agency will be the lead agency in the early intervention program. The early intervention services are provided by workers qualified to care for toddlers with disabilities and are usually in the child's home or a place familiar to the child. The services provided are written into an Individualized Family Service Plan (IFSP) that is reviewed at least once every 6 months. The plan will describe services that will be provided to the child, but will also describe services for parents to help them in daily activities with their child and for siblings to help them adjust to having a brother or sister with ASD.

Summary

You are eligible for assistance programs which you should take advantage of, and early intervention is crucial. Children do their most rapid learning and development in their preschool years. As the family of an ASD child, you will face stresses that other families do not, so you and your family also need the support of early intervention services, and the fulfillment of seeing your ASD child succeed early. Not only is this support better for your well-being, but the happier home life that results will be better for your ASD child. You must get involved in an early intervention program. As you reach out to various support groups, this doesn't mean you're inadequate as a parent. You're simply consulting with others who have more training and/or experience. Let them help you, but always be aware of who and how. Stay involved, and help them help you.

Chapter 19 Treatment options

There is no single best treatment package for all children with ASD. One point that most professionals agree on is that early intervention is important; another is that most individuals with ASD respond well to highly structured, specialized programs.

Before you make decisions on your child's treatment, you will need to gather information about the available options. Learn as much as you can, look at all the options, and make your decision on your child's treatment based on your child's needs. You may want to visit public schools in your area to see the type of program they offer to special needs children.

An effective treatment program will build on the child's interests, offer a predictable schedule, teach tasks as a series of simple steps, actively engage the child's attention in highly structured activities, and provide regular reinforcement of behavior. Parental involvement has emerged as a major factor in treatment success. Parents work with teachers and therapists to identify the behaviors that need changing and the skills that need to be taught. Recognizing that parents are the child's earliest teachers, more programs are beginning to train parents to continue the therapy at home.

As soon as a child's disability has been identified, instruction should begin. Effective programs will teach early communication and social interaction skills.

In children younger than 3 years, appropriate interventions usually take place in the home or a child care center. These interventions target specific deficits in learning, language, imitation, attention, motivation, compliance, and initiative of interaction. Included are behavioral methods, communication, occupational and physical therapy, and social play interventions. Often the day will begin with a physical activity to help develop coordination and body awareness; children string beads, piece puzzles together, paint, and participate in other motor skills activities. At snack time the teacher encourages social interaction and models how to use language to ask for more juice. The children learn by doing. Students, behavioral therapists, and parents who have received extensive training are working with the children. In teaching the children, positive reinforcement is used.[lxxiv]

Children older than 3 years usually have school-based, individualized, special education. The child may be in a segregated class with other autistic children or in an integrated class with children without disabilities for at least part of the day. Different localities may use different methods but all should provide a structure that will help the children learn social skills and functional communication. In these programs, teachers often involve the parents, giving useful advice on how to help their child use the skills or behaviors learned at school when they are at home.[lxxv]

In elementary school, the child should receive help in any skill area that is delayed and, at the same time, be encouraged to grow in his or her strengths. Ideally, the curriculum should be adapted to the individual child's needs. Many schools today have an inclusion program in which the child is in a regular classroom for most of the day, with special instruction for a part of the day. This instruction should include such skills as learning how to act in social situations and in making friends. Although higher-functioning children may be able to handle academic work, they too need help to organize tasks and avoid distractions.

During middle and high school years, instruction will begin to address such practical matters as work, community living, and recreational activities. This should include work experience, using public transportation, and learning skills that will be important in community living.[lxxvi]

All through your child's school years, you will want to be an active participant in his or her education program. Collaboration between parents and educators is essential in evaluating your child's progress.

The adolescent years
Adolescence is a period of stress and confusion; and it is no less so for teenagers with autism. Like all children, they need support in dealing with their budding sexuality. While some behaviors improve during teenage years, some get worse. Increased autistic or aggressive behavior may be one way some teens express their new-found tension and confusion.

Teenage years are also a time when children become more socially sensitive. At an age when most teenagers are concerned with acne, popularity, grades, and dates, teens with autism may become painfully aware that they are different from their peers. They may notice that they lack friends. And unlike their schoolmates, they aren't dating or planning for a career. For some, the sadness that comes with such realization motivates them to learn new behaviors and acquire better social skills.

Summary
There is no single best treatment for all children with ASD. Early intervention is important, and most individuals with ASD respond well to highly structured, specialized programs. Each step in the child's education should build on what he or she has learned before, beginning with communication and social skills, working through strengths and abilities, and progressing to practical matters such as work and community living. Adolescence may be an especially difficult time for teenagers with autism.

Chapter 20 Family life after autism diagnosis

Being a lifelong disorder that affects human development, autism can change the life of the entire family in just a snap. Why is that? Because the emotional and physical demands needed in taking care of the special child will eventually take their toll on all family members which can make daily living difficult for everyone.

To be able to maintain a normal functioning family despite the condition of one of its members, experts say that each and every family member should have a deep understanding of the disorder and should be willing to accept and adjust to the demands of the situation.

Since autism is a complex disorder, living with somebody who is diagnosed with it can be challenging and very hard for the parents and other family members as well. Studies show most parents with autistic children show signs of withdrawal from their circle of friends and other relatives because they need to devote the majority of their time and energy to taking care of the child.

There are also cases in which one of the parents needs to stop working to be able to tend to the needs of the autistic child. Although dealing with autism can be tiring, draining, and exhausting to the family members physically, mentally, and emotionally, this is not enough reason to give up on the child. If help is needed, parents can rely on various support groups to face the challenges brought by the disorder.

Statistics show that one of the challenges parents face after their child has been diagnosed with autism is explaining the condition to other family members, especially to the siblings in order to get support.

Below are just some approaches you can use to explain the condition to other family members.
1. Accept and understand the situation wholeheartedly.
   Although it is difficult to accept that your child's life can never be normal like others, the best way to cope after an autism diagnosis is to recognize the needs of the child. By admitting that caring for a child diagnosed with autism is devastating is more practical than making yourself believe it is not because this will only bring about more stress.

2. Help them understand everything about the disorder.
   Experts say that one of the reasons why families cannot function properly after one member has been diagnosed with autism is that they don't have enough understanding of the condition. For the parents, they should understand and accept the condition first so other family members will follow their lead. By making other children or members of the family understand the disorder, they will also know how to adjust

to the situation and adapt to the autistic child's needs emotionally and physically.

3. Give them breathing space.
   After breaking the news to the family, it is best that you give them time to absorb the information on their own.

4. Don't force members of the family to take care of the autistic child if they don't want to.
   Each family member has a life of their own so don't force them to dedicate all their time to the autistic child. What you can do is designate a schedule or task for them in taking care of the child. By doing this, they will learn to care more about the autistic child without being forced to do so.

5. Everybody needs a break.
   Taking care of an autistic child is draining physically, mentally, and emotionally. Give yourself or a family member a break by rewarding them with a special dish or a treat to the movie theater.

6. Join a support group.
   By doing this, you can share experiences with others and vice versa so you can get help. You can also ask other members of the family for a counseling session.

7. Remind everybody to breathe and relax when the going gets tough.

8. Ask everybody to keep a journal of their own.
   Here, they can write down everything they feel and can relieve the stress of taking care of an autistic child.

Summary
Dealing with autism isn't about rushing to a cure. Instead, it's about finding a set of supports and a way of life that will work, with tweaks and adjustments, over time. If you can, take time to enjoy your child, your mate, your family, your life.

Chapter 21 Most common autism treatments

Over the years and after painstakingly studying the different kinds of autism and their gravity, researchers, doctors and experts have come up with different kinds of treatments to help people with autism.

Some of the therapies and treatments include medication and work from different sensory devices that people have. Other treatment options many include different techniques such as a biomedical approach, behavioral approach, and an arts-based approach. You can try these treatments and therapies but make sure that you discuss them first with your physician to avoid further complications.

Although there are many treatment and therapies available out there, it's sad to say that there is no definite "cure" for the disease. But this does not mean there's no hope for improvement. Parents can help their children diagnosed with autism to increase their skills and try to have a life as normal as possible.

There are many studies that suggest different treatments for autism spectrum disorders. First we will provide a short overview of the treatments for childhood autism and some information about them. Later on we will consider several treatment types in depth.

Autism Treatments
1. ABA (Applied Behavior Analysis) Treatment
2. Positive Behavior Support (PBS)
3. Relationship Development Intervention (RDI)
4. Occupational therapies
5. Visual and auditory therapy
6. Sign Language
7. Speech Therapy
8. Computers, toys & stimulation
9. Physical exercise
10. Floor Time
11. Neurofeedback
12. Mindfulness
13. Treatments for Asperger's syndrome

21.1 ABA Treatment

This is the first scientifically validated treatment for autistic children. It normally involves intervention at a very young age. The autistic child is paired with a therapist who uses the following procedure:

1. The therapist requests or directs the autistic child for an action.

2. The child responds with a behavior that may be classified as a success, a noncompliance or no response.
3. The therapist reacts with a consequence that ranges from strong positive reinforcement to strong negative response.

Among the many methods available for treatment and education of people with autism, ABA has become widely accepted as an effective treatment. Mental Health: A Report of the Surgeon General states, "Thirty years of research demonstrated the benefit of applied behavioral methods in reducing inappropriate behavior and in improving communication, learning, and appropriate social behavior.[lxxvii]"

The basic research done by Ivar Lovaas and his colleagues at the University of California, Los Angeles, calling for an intensive, one-on-one child-teacher interaction for 40 hours a week, laid a foundation for other educators and researchers in the search for further effective early interventions to help those with ASD live up to their potential. The goal of behavioral management is to reinforce desirable behaviors and reduce undesirable ones.[lxxviii]

Behavioral therapy is used to treat many different types of disorders, including ASDs. Many people are familiar with the work of B.F. Skinner who, in 1938, coined the term "operant conditioning." Operant conditioning is the idea that the response a teacher gives to a behavior may be directly responsible for changing the behavior. (In the case of treatments for autism, the teacher may literally be an educator, but may also be a therapist, parent, or other caregiver.) In other words, if performing a certain behavior earns the child a reward, the behavior is likely to increase. Conversely, if the behavior doesn't produce a desired effect (perhaps the teacher simply ignores it, redirects, or tells the child "no") the behavior will decrease.

Skinner and others further defined the science of behavioral therapy by identifying principles of behavior such as reinforcement, fading, prompting, shaping, etc. These principles make up the science of behavioral analysis. Applied Behavioral Analysis refers to the application of these principles and actually encompasses several different strategies for treatment.

History of ABA and Autism
The most recognized name associated with ABA when it comes to autism is Dr. Ivar Lovaas, a professor at the University of California, Los Angeles. He is credited with developing ABA for use in treating autistics. In the 1960s, Dr. Lovaas conducted research involving children who participated in a concentrated intervention program while another group of children participated in a control group who followed a less demanding treatment program. At the close of the study, significantly fewer children in the control group were able to attend a regular school than those in the intensive treatment program.

Published results claimed that 30-50% of autistics who receive early and intensive treatment in the form of behavior therapy using discrete trial training show improvement in both behavioral and intellectual skills, and are able to attend school normally without special assistance.

In 1993, McEachin, Smith, and Lovaas conducted follow-up research of the children involved in the original study. This follow up showed that the benefits of the intensive therapy program continued to at least the age of 11.

ABA and Autism Research
Several studies on ABA have been published in the last 30 years. These studies show that ABA is effective for a variety of populations, teachers (parents, educators, therapists, caregivers), environments, and behaviors. Some of the research is detailed below.

Year: 1972 **Conducted By:** Hingtgen & Bryson
Description of Study: More than 400 research articles concerning autism that were published between 1964 and 1970 were reviewed.
Findings: Researchers concluded that behavior interventions showed consistent results.

Year: 1981 **Conducted By:** Hingtgen & Jackson
Description of Study: Review of more than 1,100 studies from the 1970s including both behavior therapies and other methods.
Findings: Intensive behavior programs yielded the best results for improving behaviors in autistic children.

Year: 1996 Conducted By: *Hingtgen & Jackson*
Description of Study: 251 studies published between 1980 and 1995 concerning behavior therapies for children with autism were reviewed.
Findings: Discovered that the research surrounding behavioral therapy for autistics has significantly improved and that ABA consistently yields positive results.

ABA Basics
ABA is centered on the theory that behaviors can be increased or reduced based on the reaction the behavior produces. Specific behaviors that are reinforced in using ABA to treat autism are those deemed "socially significant behaviors."

These include:
- Literacy
- Educational skills
- Social skills
- Communication skills
- Adaptive living skills (motor skills, food preparation, personal care, cleaning, time, money, work skills, etc.)

Prior to beginning an ABA program, the child must undergo a behavioral assessment so that the program can be specifically tailored to meet the child's behavioral needs.

The behavioral assessment usually encompasses four steps:

1. Defining the behavioral problem: In this step, determinations are made concerning which behaviors are undesirable and need to be changed. For example, perhaps the child exhibits a self-destructive behavior like banging his or her head.

2. Determining how often the behavior problem occurs: A baseline measurement is taken that will enable the therapist and parents to measure achievements, and determine where the program is working and where it needs revision.

3. Noting when the behavior occurs: Those involved in the program will keep a journal of what occurs before the undesired behavior. For example, if a child bangs his head when asked to put his toys away, the direction given is considered an "antecedent behavior" and is noted as such.

4. Noting the consequences of behaviors: In this step, the outcome of the situation is journaled. In the above example, if a parent ends up picking up the toys to stop the head banging, this is a consequence of the child banging his head.

Once the initial assessment has been completed, a specific program is designed to address behavior problems and develop needed skills. To ensure that children can learn new skills, Dr. Lovaas' method has two main objectives, to help the children want to learn and to empower children to believe they can learn.

To accomplish these goals, skills are taught in very small steps. For example, if the skill being taught is to dress independently, the teacher (i.e., parent, educator, therapist, or caregiver) might start with something as small as putting on socks. Skills are taught in very short increments, which are called "trials" in some ABA methods.

The trials themselves have four components:

1. Instruction: The child is told what to do as clearly as possible given the child's level of communication. This may mean that the instruction consists of just a few short, simple words, like "put the socks on your feet." Later, when the child has become more comfortable with the skill, the instruction may become more complex and more like natural conversation. So, the instruction might be, "It's time to put your socks on."

2. Prompts: When necessary, the child is given a boost toward performing the desired action. The teacher might hand the child his socks if he doesn't perform the task after being given the instruction. However, the goal for the child is to eventually perform the action without the use of prompts.

3. Response: The child should perform (or begin to perform) the desired action within five seconds of being given the instruction. If the action doesn't occur, the trial is over and the teacher begins a new one. Now, this could be the same action. In other words, the teacher might again say, "Put the socks on your feet." Or, the teacher may move on to another task and come back to this one later.

4. Feedback: The child must be provided feedback immediately with each trial. The feedback must be specifically motivational for the child. If the child values hugs or treats, the teacher might tell him that he did a fantastic job when the action is performed correctly and give him a hug or treat. However, there may also be situations when it is appropriate to give positive feedback even when the action isn't performed correctly, such as when the child has worked particularly hard. If the child doesn't perform the action correctly or if he exhibits an undesirable behavior, the teacher may provide negative feedback, such as a firm "no." However, emphasis should always remain on making learning fun so that more intense negative feedback is seldom necessary and is usually inappropriate.

To determine if the "socially significant behaviors" are being taught effectively, they must be performed in settings other than the program and using language other than the memorized instruction. If the child is only able to put his socks on in the therapy setting and when given the instruction, "Put your socks on your feet," the behavior isn't generalized and the program has not been successful for that skill. If, however, the child can be told while sitting in his kitchen after eating breakfast, "Okay, it's time to get your socks," and he gets up from the table, goes upstairs, and puts his socks on, the skill has been successfully learned and generalized.

Children Best Suited to ABA
Many people believe that ABA is successful regardless of the age of the child. In fact, Dr. Lovaas' original research included children from 5 to 12 years of age. Studies have also been conducted with children under the age of 5, and research shows improvement for children falling all along the spectrum of autism.

As children with autism usually like the structured nature of an ABA program, most are likely to respond favorably to the routine. However, children who experience anxiety in highly structured situations, where they feel trapped and unable to control what comes next, may experience negative outcomes, such as further avoidance of social contact.

The Pros and Cons of ABA
One of the more positive aspects of ABA is the emphasis placed on parental involvement. Parents are encouraged to carry out aspects of the program at home to help reinforce learned skills and allow for generalization. And, when carried out at home, daily activities such as naptime may be included in the program.

The program is quite intensive, and when performed to its fullest potential, it may take up to 40 hours per week. This is often a daunting challenge for parents and sometimes results in further stress for the family. However, ABA isn't an "all or nothing" approach. If 40 hours per week is too time-consuming and stressful for the family, the program may be implemented for 20 hours per week or whatever amount of time works well for the family. Results may not occur as quickly, but improvement is usually seen.

Opponents to ABA cite the idea that the treatment produces robotic children, instead of children who think independently. Sometimes, though, this opinion is a result of the inexpressive quality of many autistic children's voices. It may not be an accurate assessment of the treatment itself.

Perhaps the biggest obstacle in implementing a successful ABA program is the lack of qualified providers specializing in the treatment. Parents may spend a good deal of time finding a provider who is capable of carrying out the program and who meets their individual needs. They will need to review the provider's formal training, areas of competency, and experience.

Parents should look for providers with a master's degree or doctorate in behavior analysis, psychology, or special education. The provider should have attended classes relevant to learning, behavior, and behavior analysis. He or she should have completed an internship or a supervised practicum, or have demonstrated experience directly related to ABA. Providers should show skills in behavioral fields (description, analysis, change procedures, etc.), ethics, emergency management, and other areas of significance.

Parents should look for providers who have proven success with ABA. Some specific things to look for are:
- A minimum of 12 months of hands-on training with ABA for people with autism
- Successful creation of individualized programs
- Formal training or self-study in ASDs
- Proof of qualifications
- References from employers and families they've developed ABA programs for
- Proof of any certifications or licenses
- Copies of any published papers they've authored or research they've conducted

Applied Behavioral Analysis includes the following treatment strategies:
- Positive Behavioral Interventions and Support (PBS)
- Pivotal Response Training (PRT)
- Incidental Teaching
- Milieu Therapy
- Verbal Behavior

- Discrete Trial Teaching (DTT)
- Others

21.2 Positive Behavior Support (PBS)

Fighting, biting, hitting, scratching, kicking, screaming – as well as extreme withdrawal – are behaviors that challenge even the best educators and families. For years, researchers and practitioners alike have asked the question: Why does a particular child act that way?

Unlike traditional behavioral management, which views the individual as the problem and seeks to "fix" him or her by quickly eliminating the challenging behavior, positive behavioral support (PBS) views systems, settings, and lack of skills as parts of the "problem" and works to change those. As such, PBS is characterized by long-term strategies to reduce inappropriate behavior, teach more appropriate behavior, and provide contextual supports necessary for successful outcomes.

Positive Behavior Support (PBS) is a broad approach for resolving problem behaviors that are displayed by people with disabilities. Problem behaviors may include: (1) self-injury, aggression, and other destructive acts, (2) tantrums and other disruptive responses, and (3) excessively repetitive or irritating behaviors including actions that interfere with a person's learning or social interactions.

Some Important Features of PBS
- PBS is based on person-centered values. A PBS plan requires that procedures be positive and respect the dignity of the person.
- PBS interventions are individualized and based on an understanding of the person and his or her environment.
- PBS interventions usually consist of more than one strategy. They involve collaboration among more than one caregiver and support provider.
- PBS goals should include improvements in social relationships and other "lifestyle" enhancements, as well as reductions in problem behavior.

Support Team
The process of PBS begins with the identification of a support team, which consists of the most relevant individuals in the person's life. The team may include family members, teachers, friends, and/or others who are involved and concerned with the person and the problem behavior. The team members are usually responsible for implementing the positive support plan.

Vision
The next step is to establish a vision, an agreement on the broad goals that a support plan should seek to achieve. The vision is developed through a process known as "person-centered planning."

Once the support team defines its common vision, a "functional behavioral assessment" is conducted to gather information about the problem behavior. One tool for this is the Motivation Assessment Scale – MAS (Durand and Crimmins – See Suggested Readings).

Based on the person-centered plan and the functional behavior assessment, the team writes a positive behavior plan.

Positive Behavior Plan
The behavior support plan should include strategies for:
- Teaching and increasing skills that are intended to replace problem behaviors
- Preventing the problems before they occur
- Dealing with the problems in case they do occur
- Monitoring progress

As time goes on, the support team meets more often to evaluate progress and make adjustments to the plan as necessary.

Background
PBS evolved out of applied behavior analysis, and many of the intervention procedures derived are from this discipline. PBS is a rapidly growing approach that is based on extensive research. New York and other states are making an effort to provide training and information about PBS.

How is PBS different from traditional behavior management?
The differences between PBS and traditional approaches are vast and have been discussed in detail over many years[lxxix]. Here follows a paraphrase of some of the underlying assumptions and potential consequences of PBS and traditional approaches, as identified by Radler & Cook (2002):

Traditional approaches
Assumptions:
- Adults are responsible for children learning to control their feelings and behaviors, to conform to the world of adults, to become well behaved.
- Adults need to teach children what they should not do.
- Adults will need to control some children until they develop self-control themselves.

Strategies:
Historically, the following rewards and punishments have been used:
- Positive and negative consequences
- Token economies, charts, e.g. tick charts, sticker charts

- Withdrawal of attention, which may include time out or warning systems
- Avoiding opportunities for recognition and acknowledgment

Possible Consequences:
- Children are taught to do whatever an adult tells them.
- Children learn that people with difficult behaviors are 'less worthy.'
- Development of the self-concept of being good at being 'bad.'
- Teaches some children that they can gain more power and influence with inappropriate behavior.
- Some children may use similar ignoring/excluding/punishment/reward approaches with others.

Positive Behavior Support
Assumptions:
- Some children require different levels of support as they learn to self-regulate their feelings and behavior. By nature, some children are likely to feel more anxious or stressed than others.
- Children can rely on teachers to acknowledge their feelings and the message of their behavior. They will provide personal support and affirmation for the student, and give specific acknowledgment for behavioral learnings.
- Teachers help children develop understandings of 'what to do' and provide feedback on what has been done well. Teachers support and lead children toward more appropriate ways of interacting.

Strategies:
PBS emphases the need for responsiveness to children's feelings and needs by:
- Acknowledging and trying to interpret what the child may be communicating through his/her behavior
- Gently supporting and leading the child to a calmer state
- Attending to the messages and analyzing the functions of behavior
- Teaching the child other ways to meet a need or communicate a feeling
- Providing encouragement and feedback about personal successes along with aspects of difficult situations the child may have handled well
- Deliberately building a sense of self worth, valuing the person and acknowledging all attempts at positive interaction
- Creating situations where the child is at 'best advantage'

Possible Consequences of PBS:
- Children learn that their feelings will be noticed and acknowledged, and will not be directly escalated by adults.
- Children learn where and when behaviors are appropriate and valued, and how to manage situations and emotions that have previously led to difficult behaviors.
- Children learn that considerate and cooperative behavior is acknowledged, gets things achieved, and leads to good feelings.

- Children learn that they can make a difference, and influence others in ways that are mutually pleasing, potent and positive.

So positive behavior support can help you evaluate the challenging behaviors, look at why/when the behavior is exhibited, and possibly stop that behavior from reoccurring. See the example below.

Behavior Support Plan Example
Step / Task
1. List all the behaviors that are causing concern.
2. Prioritize the behavior you feel is of most concern.
3. What is the function of the behavior?
4. Describe the behavior that you want.
5. Identify strategies you could use to teach alternatives to the challenging behavior.
6. What environmental factors can be altered?
7. List the ways the appropriate behavior will be reinforced.
8. List the consequences of unacceptable behavior.
9. List the people responsible for each task.
10. How is this plan going to be distributed to all the people involved?

Now we will go through each step one at a time:

Step 1. List all the behaviors that are causing concern.
Fairly self-explanatory – Behaviors like tantrums, door banging, throwing objects, pushing everything off the tables, head banging.

Step 2. Prioritize – Which behaviors are causing you the most concern?

Step 3. What is the function of the behavior?
- When does the behavior occur and when doesn't it?
- Is it an attempt at communication?
- What occurred before the incident?
- What were they doing during the incident?
- What happened after the incident?

This is a very important step. Here you need to really understand the behavior.

Included is a checklist to help you with this step.

A. Before the incident
Possible triggers
New person – Change in routine – Crowded place – Teasing
Bullying – Excluded – New activity – Expressing a need
Noise – Lack of choice – Smell – Room temperature
Weather – Assembly time at school

Where did the behavior occur?
Own room – Another room – Classroom – Library
Playground – Backyard – Shopping center – Car

Who was present?
Were they agitated or anxious before the incident?
Yes – No

B. During the incident
Behaviors
Offensive language – Confrontational – Run away – Upset
Demanding – Not following directions – Self injure – Rocking
Physical withdrawal – Hurt others – Damage objects – Staring
Lining up/ordering objects – Yelling – Screaming
Duration of the behavior
Intensity of behavior

C. Things that happened after the incident
Punished – Excluded – Time-out – Sent away
Mediate – Removal of desired object – Ignored – Peer approval
Redirection – Victimized – Attention – Left alone
Self injure – Received desired object – Injured others – Damaged property

Change in the person
Happy – Upset – Angry – Aggressive
Same – Withdrawn – Nervous – Isolated
Distant – Agitated

These lists are by no means complete but hopefully they will help you to start understanding where you need to look for answers. You will need to form a hypothesis regarding the behaviors and then test them. This will help with the next steps.

Step 4. What is the behavior that you want?
Be realistic. You may need to gradually get to the desired behavior.

Step 5. Identify strategies you could use.
This is where a good understanding of the disorder helps.

Step 6. Environmental factors.
Such things as placement of furniture, an area where they can be alone, or fencing. It must be workable.

Step 7. How will the positive behavior be supported?
How the child will benefit by doing the desired behavior – rewards, positive reactions – will differ from child to child, as each child will respond to different rewards – for some it may be food, others a cuddle or trip to the park – it must be workable for you, your child and the immediate family.

Step 8. List the consequences.
Why? So the same consequence can be issued each time. If the consequence is the same each time, the child will soon learn what happens if... However, if you find that the consequence isn't working, change it and keep adjusting it until you find something that does work.

Step 9. List the people responsible.
If the child is with you all the time, you are responsible. But if there are behaviors that you and the childcare center are working on together to eliminate, then they will need to be on the list. It may be that you issue the consequence, but there should be a talk before leaving the center where the teacher is able to tell you and the child of the incident.

Step 10. How will everyone know about it?
It could be as simple as writing it down and giving everyone a copy.

21.3 Relationship Development Intervention (RDI)

Preliminary research[lxxx] indicates that a Relationship Development Intervention (RDI™) program may help children with Autism Spectrum Disorder (ASD) achieve improvements on the Autism Diagnostic Observation Schedule (ADOS), a standardized protocol for observation of social and communicative behavior associated with autism.

The RDI program is a parent-based clinical treatment that addresses the core problems faced by all individuals with ASD, such as learning friendship, empathy, and a love of sharing their world with others. The RDI program is based on extensive research in typical development and translates research findings into a systematic clinical approach. Dr. Steven Gutstein, author of the study, called the findings encouraging.

RDI is a relatively new treatment program for ASD. Dr. Steven Gutstein, who has written several books on the subject, created it. It is based on the idea that autism is primarily a social disorder that affects other skills within the autistic's life. Gutstein believes that autistics are as capable of developing real and meaningful relationships as non-autistics if they are introduced to them in a slow, purposeful manner. They must be taught to want to willingly share their ideas and experiences with others as well as wanting to learn about those people surrounding them.

RDI is effective for autistics of all ages, but, like most treatments, works best when implemented early. It also helps children improve regardless of their position on the autism spectrum.

RDI is a parent-based program in which parents are taught the necessary skills and given the appropriate tools to work with their children. The emphasis throughout the program is on the emotional benefits the autistic and his or her family will receive through learning to connect with one another and the world around them. Parents and children participate in activities that encourage communication and working together.

An example of one of the "games" participants might play involves the use of a tray and a glass of water. The object of the game is for a parent and the autistic child to move across the room without speaking or spilling the water. While this might be relatively easy for a non-autistic child who is able to pick up on nonverbal cues such as body posture, an autistic child often has difficulty reading non-verbal cues. The idea is for the child to interact with the parent by observing facial expressions, body posture, and other forms of non-verbal communication. This helps the child to be more aware of other people and assists them in learning non-verbal communication.

Published studies on RDI state that of 17 children ages 2 to 10 on an RDI program, 70% of the children achieved a better diagnostic category using the Autism Diagnostic Observation Schedule (ADOS). In addition, the percentage of children in the study who were successful in a regular classroom setting increased from 12% to 82%.

21.4 Occupational therapies

This treatment for childhood autism involves trying to filter out the different sensory stimuli experienced by an autistic child in order for him or her to process the information better. This involves the use of different devices to help a child with autism focus one or more senses.

Developmental neurologists have discovered that autistic children have a tendency to be hyposensitive and/or hypersensitive to one or more than a few sensory stimuli, and that their gross and fine motor skills are more often than not impaired to unstable levels.

Occupational therapists specialize in assisting individuals with disabilities such as autism to learn ways to complete common and necessary tasks. In many cases, the tasks themselves and the conditions surrounding the tasks are modified to make them more manageable for the autistic. This might mean that the therapist helps to find specialized equipment to assist the autistic with communication, or teaches him or her ways to communicate without speaking. The tasks taught are relevant to the life of the autistic and the developmental stage he or she is at.

In the case of autistics, there are problems with interacting socially and communicating with others. An occupational therapist will first perform a thorough evaluation of the child to determine skills that are lacking or completely non-existent. The therapist will then develop a plan for overcoming the disabilities.

In addition to interaction and communication problems, autistics often suffer from sensory integration problems. An autistic can be either under-sensitive or oversensitive to sensory stimulation. He or she may feel pain when hearing noises that seem normal to non-autistics. Or, the autistic may not experience pain in the same way as non-autistics, which can lead to self-destructive behaviors.

An occupational therapist can develop a Sensory Integration (SI) program to help the child's central nervous system to appropriately process sensations. In developing an SI program, the therapist will focus on three key senses:

Tactile:
This system includes the nerves that send information about pain, pressure, and temperature to the brain. Signs of difficulties with the tactile system include unwillingness to be touched, refusal to eat foods of a certain texture, avoidance of substances on the hands (dirt, paints, glue, etc.), and using only the fingertips to work with objects.

Vestibular System:
The vestibular system involves the inner ear, which helps the person to be aware of movement and head position changes. Autistics with vestibular issues might be afraid of things like swinging or going down slides. Parents might notice they have difficulty learning to walk up or down stairs. Or, at the other end of the spectrum, these children might engage in high-movement activities such as spinning or jumping.

Proprioceptive System:
This is the system that enables a person to be aware of his or her body position. It is also responsible for allowing us to perform fine motor movements. Children with difficulties in this area may appear very clumsy, fall easily, hold their bodies in an unusual manner, have trouble handling small objects, and resist performing new activities.

As with any occupational therapy program, the therapist will conduct a thorough evaluation of the child prior to developing an SI program. The program will seek to enable the child to appropriately deal with sensations, which means the central nervous system must be taught to organize the input it receives and allow the child to produce an appropriate response.

In the case of vestibular system problems, the child may be placed in a swinging hammock for short periods of time to help acclimate his system.

For tactile problems, the child will be provided textured toys.

Proprioceptive problems might be overcome by providing the child small, interesting objects to manipulate in a specific manner, such as stringing beads.

Occupational therapy has demonstrated triumph in helping autistic children deal more effectively with sensory images, use their five senses more successfully and productively, and become more conscious of their bodies. Probably the most effectively therapy and treatment for autism, it employs all of the senses rather than using just one. The advantage of this is that the patient learns that there should be interaction between the other senses to make sure that a task can be accomplished.

21.5 Visual and auditory therapy

Visual therapy
Colored lenses were popularized by autistic writer Donna Williams in her book Like Color To The Blind and went on to be extensively used by people with autism for the visual perceptual disorder of Scotopic Sensitivity Syndrome. Visual rehabilitation as established by Melvin Kaplan and others makes use of prism lenses that warps the child's mental picture, forcing him/her to use his/her focal vision more prolifically.

Auditory therapy
Auditory therapies center on teaching the child to use his/her sense of audible ranges more successfully in the course of techniques such as auditory incorporation education. This helps a great deal in making the child more familiar with the variety of sounds that they will come across and how they interact with them. The patient randomly listens to sounds and matches them with their sources. It's like a game of matching. Though the theory is quite simple the application is difficult due to the minimal attention span of most patients.

21.6 Sign language

Sign language was first developed as a means of communication for hearing-impaired individuals. Sign language has also been used to teach people with developmental disabilities who have little or no communication skills. Teaching autistic children how to use sign language is not as common a practice today as in previous years, possibly due to an increase in the use of computerized communication systems. However, research suggests that teaching sign language along with speech will likely accelerate a person's ability to speak.

Sign language is useful for those who have little or no verbal abilities or communication skills. It is not recommended for those who have a relatively large vocabulary. Furthermore, people with a variety of functioning levels can be taught to use sign language. Many aberrant behaviors associated with autism and other developmental disabilities, such as aggression, tantrums, self-injury, anxiety, and depression, are often attributed to an inability to communicate with other people. Signed speech may, at the very least, allow the person to communicate using signs and may stimulate verbal language skills. When teaching a person to use sign language, another possible benefit may be the facilitation of their attentiveness to social gestures of others as well as their own.[lxxxi]

A sign language (also signed language) is a language which uses manual communication instead of sound to convey meaning – simultaneously combining hand shapes, orientation and movement of the hands, arms or body, and facial expressions to express a speaker's thoughts fluidly. Sign languages commonly develop in deaf communities, which can include interpreters and friends and families of deaf people as well as people who are deaf or hard of hearing themselves.

Makaton
Makaton™ is a system of communication that uses a vocabulary of "key word" manual signs and gestures to support speech, as well as graphic symbols to support the written word. It is used by and with people who have communication, language or learning difficulties. This includes people with articulation problems (such as cerebral palsy), people with cognitive impairments such as autism or Down syndrome, and their families, colleagues and carers. Adults can use it to help the development of speech and language in children, or as a means of functional communication for every day use.

Communication using Makaton involves speaking (where possible) while concurrently signing key words. The sign vocabulary is taken from the local deaf sign language (with some additional 'natural gestures'), beginning with a 'core' list of important words. However, the grammar generally follows spoken language rather than sign language. Makaton does make limited use of the spatial grammatical features of directionality and placement of signs. As Makaton is used in over 40 countries world wide, Makaton Keyword Signing varies from country to country and can even vary from state to state within each country.

Makaton was developed in the early 1970s in the UK for communication with residents of a large hospital who were both deaf and intellectually disabled. The name is a blend of the names of the three people who devised it: Margaret Walker, Kathy Johnston and Tony Cornforth.

Helping your child to communicate will totally change their lives. It will mean that you can understand them – this will help boost their self-esteem. Then the circle sets in. Once one word and sign is understood, they will learn more because they can communicate better. Their self esteem improves and they keep learning and using the signs. They know you can understand them so they will keep going.

21.7 Speech therapy

The purpose of speech-language therapy is to enhance intentional communication via expression of ideas, obtaining desires, sharing information, and interpersonal interaction. Language is the means by which communication is achieved.

Speech is a troubling issue in Autism Spectrum Disorders. Some children develop speech in time according to milestones, and then regress, losing all speech. Some children develop speech in time, but talk so much you'd like to pull your hair out, and some children never develop speech and are completely nonverbal. Every child is different in the "speech" part of the Autism Spectrum

Disorder disability. Whether your child is verbal or nonverbal, don't give up hope. Many children with Autism Spectrum Disorders begin to speak with one-on-one speech therapy. Others make incredible strides with PECS (Picture Exchange Communication System) and other visual cues.

Speech therapy will help both verbal and nonverbal children with autism. Before you begin therapy, you will likely have to complete a speech evaluation from a licensed speech language pathologist. After completing a series of tests with your child, the therapist should be able to tell you whether your child would benefit from speech therapy or qualifies for speech therapy. Remember, vocabulary isn't the only part of speech.

Children with autism have a severely limited ability to speak in social settings, also known as pragmatic speech. Pragmatics is knowing how to use language appropriately in social settings. As children with autism already have social deficits, speech is impaired more by their limited social skills, which makes for very awkward and odd speech patterns. The ability to converse is severely limited in most cases.

Speech therapy can help autistic children with any level of speech disorder – from the completely non-verbal to the child who talks incessantly. Before beginning a speech therapy program, you and your child will work with a trained speech therapist to complete an evaluation. Your child will undergo testing and the therapist will report on ways he or she believes speech therapy will help your child.

As with any treatment program, early intervention is best. However, speech therapy is also effective with older children. Some areas addressed in speech therapy for autistic children may include:
- Helping the child to understand social interaction and ways he or she can affect his or her environment
- A desire to communicate
- Paying attention and listening skills
- Play skills
- Understanding verbal communication
- Social skills
- Improved speech rate and rhythm

21.8 Computers, toys & stimulation

The use of computers has actually been found to be beneficial as a treatment for childhood autism. Interaction with a computer may help children develop their interaction skills because the fact that they are actually in direct control of the computer means that interaction may not be as intimidating as a face-to-face interaction with another person. In 2007 an interesting feature film was released in Belgium. In this movie called BenX a boy with Asperger's syndrome plays his favorite online computer game Archlord avidly, trying hard to train himself for the real world he lives in.

Toys that provide the individual with an immediate reward are ideal.

You need to understand your own child. What achievable things stimulate them best? Some children are quiet and fairly withdrawn. Some need to be constantly on the move. Others need their whole day mapped out and regimented. Every child on the autism spectrum is different and will respond differently to stimuli.

Choosing Toys for a Child with Autism
Buying toys for your child is one of the most exciting things you can do as a parent. However, for parents with a child with autism, it is an entirely different story.

Since a child with autism has a different mindset on the things he likes and the things he doesn't, he also has a different mindset on the toys he can enjoy and the toys he can't. Somehow, choosing toys for a child with autism may prove to be a difficult task to parents. The excitement of picking among the thousands of toys lined up is replaced by a careful consideration of the toys that are proper for his mental age as well as his condition.

There are no special toys for children with autism, so you cannot find a special section in the toy store that offers toys only for autistic children. You need to know how to choose.

Basically, children's toys are labeled with the age bracket. Do not take this into consideration. What you should look for is a toy that is right for his mental age. If the box says "age 4 – 6" but your child's mental age is only 3, he might not be able to enjoy such toys. Of course, the choking hazard should also be considered. You always have to ensure that your child cannot swallow small parts of the toy you would buy.

Another thing you should keep in mind is his interest. Autistics have a particular inclination for specific objects. You should remember that he decides what he likes, and what he likes should be respected. Selecting the right toys for him should be based on his interest and not on yours. You may ask, "How will I know if he likes a particular toy or not?" Observation is the best way to know. Another is trial and error. This is much more difficult since it can be a never-ending process. But somehow, you will stumble upon the toys he will enjoy.

If you are puzzled by toys to buy, consider the educational ones. Toys that develop your child's imagination are your best bet. Puzzles, building blocks, and alphabets may not be as appealing for them as other toys, but it is better to gamble on these things than on other toys that may further impair their development.

Also, choose a toy that develops his motor skills. Bicycles and other similar toys will provide them with both fun and exercise. Since motor skills should be developed at an early age, especially in the case of children with autism, you must ensure that you have given the proper tools for developing this skill.

Do not rely on the opinion of other people, even those who have a child with autism. Your child's needs may be different from other autistic children. Thus, the toys that your child would enjoy can be different from others, even if they both suffer from autism. You know your child better than anybody else and you know what he likes and what he enjoys.

Base your selection on these guidelines and you are almost certain that what you buy will be enjoyed. Of course, there is a margin of error but it is worth taking the risk rather than doing nothing at all.

Some toys/stimulation to consider:
- Trampolines
- Large exercise balls – about 50 cm diameter
- Jigsaw puzzles
- Visual learning
- Play-Doh
- Train sets
- Books (pop-up books)
- Music
- Bubble makers
- Marble tracks

21.9 Physical exercise

A major problem encountered with autistic children is their characteristic self-stimulatory behavior, which frequently interferes with on-task responding and other appropriate behaviors. However, the experimental literature suggests that with many populations, increased physical activity[lxxxii] might positively influence subsequent responding.

One of the most under-used yet effective treatments for autistic individuals is exercise. Obviously, exercise is important for everyone, especially for people with autism. Several research studies have shown that vigorous or strenuous exercise is often associated with decreases in stereotypic (self-stimulatory) behaviors, hyperactivity, aggression, self-injury, and destructiveness. These benefits have also been observed in the mentally impaired population.

In general, vigorous exercise refers to a 20-minute or longer aerobic workout, 3 to 4 days a week. However, mild exercise has little effect on behavior.

In general, exercise is important for both physical and mental health. A number of studies have shown that vigorous exercise is one of the best treatments for depression. Exercise can reduce stress and anxiety as well as improve sleep, reaction time, and memory. Many autistic individuals gain weight because of their relatively inactive lifestyle.

Since stereotypic behaviors interfere with teaching, a physical exercise program may also improve the student's attention in the classroom. Parents and teachers should seriously consider including a rigorous exercise program in the student's Individualized Education Program (IEP). One should not assume that the student receives an adequate amount of exercise during recess.

Since physical exercise is inexpensive, safe, and healthful, it makes more sense to try an exercise program to reduce behavior problems in the classroom and at home rather than to use more expensive and harmful treatments, such as drugs.

21.10 Floor Time

Floor Time (also known as Developmental Individual-Difference, Relationship-Based Model, or DIR) is a treatment method that was developed by Dr. Stanley Greenspan, a child psychiatrist who has conducted copious research in the area of child development and published numerous articles on the subject.

According to Greenspan, there are six developmental milestones. He states that appropriate emotional experiences during each stage will help develop critical cognitive, social, emotional, language and motor skills as well as a sense of self-respect.

These milestones are:
- Having the ability to notice the things around him and be interested in them while also being able to calm himself. During this stage the manner in which infants modulate and process sensations is an important contributor. Children may either be hypersensitive (too easily stimulated) or hyposensitive (need a lot of sensory input to be stimulated). Children's sensitivities may vary with each sense (touch, smell, and hearing) or from day to day (sometimes hyposensitive, sometimes hypersensitive).

- Being able to enter into relationships with other people. At this stage children start to recognize sounds and sources of speech. They begin to scan the world for familiar faces and objects, and pay attention for 30 seconds or more. This ability to be intimate forms the basis of all future relationships and cements motor, cognitive, and language skills.

- Communicating with others, including gestures (this must be a two-way conversation – not simply talking "at" someone else). During this phase, the child first realizes that his actions cause reactions. This is the beginning of gestural dialogues that lead to the opening and closing of circles of communication. The experiences of two-way communication help children form a basic sense of intentionality. This leads to learning fundamental emotional, cognitive, and motor lessons.

- Creating a complex problem solving process. At this stage the child starts to link gestures into complicated responses. The number and complexity of closed circles begins to increase. Growing gestural dialogues become preludes to speech. The child develops the ability to create complex gestures and to string together a series of actions into an elaborate and deliberate problem-solving sequence. This growth in expressiveness and complex gestures also increases creativity.

- Developing ideas. During this stage the child learns that symbols represent things and that each symbol is an idea, an abstraction of the concrete thing, activity or emotion with which the world is concerned. The ability to create ideas begins, which leads to pretend play. The more the child experiments with pretend play, the more comfortable he becomes with the world of ideas.

- The ability to take ideas and make them real and logical. At this stage, the child begins to express feelings, using words instead of actions. The cause of their feelings becomes linked to specific actions or events., i.e. I am happy because I am playing with Mommy. These links between feelings and actions help the child to predict future occurrences. The child also starts to build bridges during play and link them into logical sequences. The child starts to understand the emerging concepts of space and time in a personal and emotional way. There is also an increase in verbal communication and problem-solving skills.

Children achieve these milestones at different ages. Each milestone is mastered and is a foundation for the next stage. Greenspan discusses all of these stages in great depth in his book, The Child with Special Needs. The book also has many useful strategies and examples.

Floor Time is less time intensive than is ABA, which requires two to five hours per day. The idea is to develop a relationship with the child to help draw him or her into a desire to interact with the world. The relationship is created by devoting Floor Time to the child's interests and by the caregiver joining in the child's activities, initially on his or her level and performing the same actions as the child.

Later, when the child has accepted the relationship and is comfortable with having someone join in the activity, the caregiver will introduce changes designed to initiate communication or other desired actions. By doing so, the child's behavior is shaped in small steps and allows him or her to begin meeting the six milestones.

For example, if the child is sitting on the floor lining up plastic animals, the caregiver will sit on the floor with the child and join in the lining up of the animals in the same manner as the child. Once the child has accepted this, the caregiver might place one of the animals out of order or line them up in a way the child will want to change. The purpose of this is to get the child to communicate in some manner what he or she wants you to do with the animal.

There are **five steps involved in a successful Floor Time program**. They are:

1. *Observe:*
   Watch the child and listen to what he or she says. Look at expressions, patterns of movement, gestures, and anything else that will help you to interact with the child at his or her level.

2. *Open the Circle of Communication:*
   This simply means to pay attention to the child and to follow along with his or her interests. In the example above, this would refer to lining up the animals. In this step, it's important to pay attention to the child's mood and to come in with an approach that takes that mood into consideration.

3. *Follow the Child's Lead:*
   Once you've approached the child, just act as a play partner. Do what he or she is doing and allow the child to lead you. Doing so builds the child's confidence and allows room for assertiveness on the child's part. A further benefit of this step is that the child begins to sense that a warm relationship is developing and that he or she is being understood, and begins to enjoy having someone to play with.

4. *Extend and Expand Plan:*
   Eventually, during Floor Time you'll begin to increase the child's area of interest through supportive comments without imposing your own ideas on the play. The child will begin to express his or her own ideas. Encourage him to direct the activity. You should also begin to ask questions about the activity in a positive, non-critical manner.

5. *The Child Closes the Circle:*
   When the child responds to your comments and builds on them, he or she is closing the circle. This does not mean Floor Time ends, it simply means that you open another circle and allow circles to overlap, which will begin to feel more like normal social interaction and two-way communication.

Floor Time focuses on the emotional development of the child, which Dr. Greenspan believes is critical to the developmental ladder. It does not treat each behavior or set of behaviors, such as delayed speech or fine motor skills, individually. For that reason, it is often used in conjunction with other treatment methods[lxxxiii].

21.11 Neurofeedback

This involves attaching electrodes to the scalp and teaching an autistic child to control his or her brainwaves. This treatment for childhood autism shows promising results, based on a pilot study with eight children.

Neurofeedback (NFB), also called neurotherapy, neurobiofeedback or EEG biofeedback, is a therapy technique that presents the user with real-time feedback on brainwave activity, as measured by electrodes on the scalp, typically in the form of a video display, sound or vibration. The aim is to enable conscious control of brainwave activity. If brain activity changes in the direction desired by the therapist, a positive "reward" feedback is given to the individual, and if it regresses, either a negative feedback or no feedback is given (depending on the protocol). Rewards can be as simple as a change in a tone's pitch or as complex as a certain type of movement of a character in a video game.

Neurofeedback is training in self-regulation. It is simply biofeedback applied to the brain directly. Self-regulation is a necessary part of good brain function. Self-regulation training allows the system (the central nervous system) to function better.

Training sessions last about 40 minutes to an hour, and are conducted from one to five times per week. Some improvement is generally seen within 10 sessions. Once learning is consolidated, the benefit appears to be permanent in most cases.

The EEG biofeedback training is a painless, non-invasive procedure. One or more sensors are placed on the scalp, and one on each ear. The brainwaves are monitored by means of an amplifier and a computer-based instrument that processes the signal and provides the proper feedback. This is displayed to the trainee by means of a video game or other video display, along with audio signals. The trainee is asked to make the video game go with his brain. As activity in a desirable frequency band increases, the video game moves faster, or some other reward is given. As activity in an adverse band increases, the video game is inhibited. Gradually, the brain responds to the cues that it is being given, and a "learning" of new brainwave patterns takes place. The new pattern is one which is closer to what is normally observed in individuals without such disabilities.

21.12 Mindfulness

Current research suggests that mindfulness practice could be beneficial to those on the higher functioning end of the autistic spectrum, for example Asperger's syndrome[lxxxiv]. Stress and anxiety can be major problems for individuals on the autism spectrum. For all of us, modern life can be overwhelming, pressured, fast-paced and demanding. For those on the spectrum, the stresses can be even greater, because they may include social anxiety, sensory problems, career difficulties, or managing repetitive thoughts.[lxxxv]

Mindfulness is the trait of staying aware of (paying close attention to) your responsibilities. Jon Kabat-Zinn [lxxxvi]defines it as "paying attention in a particular way: on purpose, in the present moment, and non-judgmentally." It is cultivated by formal practices of meditation and by informal practice in daily life. As a result, you show up for what's happening with and in you, become more accepting of what you cannot change, and become more aware of what you can change. So mindfulness is the art of staying in the moment. Accepting what is. Because it is already here.

Mindfulness practice can be beneficial for treating inattention, restlessness, and impulsivity. It is also closely tied to cognitive-behavioral interventions that seem to work well with clients on the autistic spectrum. Because autism is a deficit in connections of all kinds, emotional, social, and neurological, it would make sense that there would be room for a mindfulness protocol that would encourage new connections to be made. Mindfulness practice could include a guided meditation practice, or a relaxation practice in which the client interacts with the therapist to create a social connection with another person. It can lead to decreased *anger* behavior and reduced stress.

Mindfulness for parents
Having a clear, calm, and focused mind (mindfulness) can help parents work with their children with autism.

Summary
The most common treatments for autism are ABA; Positive Behavior Support; Relationship Development Intervention; Occupational, visual and auditory therapies; Sign Language; Speech Therapy; Computer Use; Toys and Stimulation; Physical Exercise; Floor Time; Neurofeedback; and Mindfulness. All share the goals of increasing the child's education, social, communication and living skills. Through instruction, prompts and feedback, undesirable behaviors and responses are eliminated or at least attenuated. Any treatment, or combination of treatments, must be customized to best suit the individual autistic's needs.

Chapter 22 Treatments for Asperger's syndrome

Asperger's syndrome is one of several autism spectrum disorders. It is characterized with problems in social interaction, although bad motor skills are also a common condition of Asperger's syndrome. Treatment for Asperger's syndrome varies with each child. There is no medication to treat a child with Asperger's syndrome, but there are treatments to help with the symptoms of the condition.

The treatments can vary because different things will work for different children. Just because one treatment works for one child who has Asperger's syndrome doesn't mean it will work for another.

Here is a short overview of the different treatments a child with Asperger's syndrome can have:

Social Skills Training: Children with Asperger's syndrome have a hard time distinguishing facial expressions and tone of voice. They don't understand the different meanings and will take everything said literally. These children will be taught the differences between facial expressions and tone of voice and how to understand jokes and sarcasm. Children with Asperger's syndrome usually have a difficult time making eye contact. Giving them training in social skills will help them interact with other people and other children better, making social settings a lot easier for them.

Cognitive Behavior Therapy: This type of therapy helps children recognize a bad situation before it happens. Many children with Asperger's syndrome usually have high anxiety and this type of therapy will teach them how to reduce stress. Normally, the child will have a meltdown or throw a temper tantrum when something doesn't go their way. This type of therapy helps children to cope and handle situations better, reducing the number of outbursts.

Medication: There isn't a specific medicine that will treat Asperger's syndrome, but there are prescriptions to treat symptoms. Children can take anxiety or depression medication. Unfortunately, these pills may have side effects, so you have to monitor your child closely. Check to see how they are responding and if their behavior is more unusual. Some children may also have a difficult time sleeping. Children with Asperger's syndrome can be given sleeping pills or some type of sedative to help them at night.

Parental Education: Children aren't the only ones who can go through training. Parents can also take training classes to learn how to deal with their children who have Asperger's syndrome. Tips that parents learn include using a reward system with their children. The reward system shows the child that remaining calm will have its benefits. This training also shows parents how to handle children when they have outbursts.

Positive Reinforcement: Children with Asperger's syndrome can do well when parents and other authority figures give positive reinforcement. By showing them what they need to do and supporting them through their endeavors, parents can teach children with Asperger's syndrome to maintain independent lifestyles.

Summary

Children with Asperger's syndrome don't have to be left behind. They have can have normal lives, and with proper treatments they don't have to suffer. There are no magic pills or treatments that are going to cure Asperger's syndrome, but there are ways to help reduce the symptoms. Talk to your doctor about the different treatment options to help your child in social settings.

Chapter 23 Alternative autism treatments

There is still much work to be done toward the improvement of treatments for autism. New theories are introduced frequently and it's tempting for parents to try anything with even a remote chance of helping their children. Certainly, since there is still so little known about autism, there's nothing wrong with trying some alternative treatments as long as they pose no threat of harm to the child.

Parents should carefully consider introducing new treatment methods and should speak to their child's physician before doing so. Many treatments for autism are complementary to one another and can be used in conjunction. However, it's a good idea to make certain that everyone who takes care of the child, or is involved in his or her treatment, is aware of all treatment methods being used.

Even though you know as a parent that autism isn't curable, many keep hoping for a miracle or a happy ending. Many take advantage of this fact.

Over the years many alternative treatments for ASDs have been introduced. It has become big business if you view the money that sometimes is involved. They are considered alternative because no scientific proof exists (this is very expensive and time consuming research) that they are effective. This does not necessarily mean, however, that they do not work.

Parents should review any available information about alternative treatments and speak with other parents who have tried the method with their own autistic child. There are many autism support groups and discussion boards available on the Internet that provide parents from all over the world the opportunity to ask questions and gather information from others who have tried some of these methods.

1. Facilitated Communication
2. Holding Therapy
3. Auditory Integration Therapy
4. Dolman/Delacato Method
5. Snoezelen

The chance of best results is increased when:
- The treatment is based on extensive research into the child's individual needs, handicap and strengths, and adapts itself to these
- The treatment actively asks involvement of the parents when goals are set and when goals are evaluated
- The treatment doesn't try to minimize the autism but is primarily focused on learning new skills

- The treatment is imbedded in a climate of full predictability and clarity for the child

23.1 Facilitated communication

Facilitated communication (FC) is a method intended to help people with severe neurological impairment to use communication aids with their hands.

In the 1970s, Rosemary Crossley, who worked as an aide in an institution for individuals with multiple disabilities, began working with a woman who had cerebral palsy. She encouraged the woman to communicate by using Ms. Crossley as her facilitator. This was the beginning of the use of Facilitated Communication for people with disabilities, including ASDs.

Advocates of Facilitated Communication believe that autistics have the mental capacity required for communication, but lack the physical capacity to do so. Therefore, they say that if a facilitator supports the autistic's arm or hand, they are able to type or use other types of boards to communicate. The immediate aim of FC is to allow the user to make choices and to communicate in a way that has been impossible in the past. The ultimate goal of the method is to enable the person to use an augmentative communication device independently.

In 1986, Ms. Crossley founded the DEAL Communication Center in Melbourne, Australia. The Center's objective is to "assist people without or with dysfunctional speaking abilities to find alternative means of communication." The prevalent theory at the Center is that autism is not a social or communication disorder, but a physical deficit that prevents communication.

A qualitative study conducted by Biklen in 1990 asserted that 90% of children with autism would be able to communicate using Facilitated Communication and that once they were able to communicate, they would display normal to high intelligence levels. However, other research studies have not been able to duplicate these findings.

People who question the validity of Facilitated Communication wonder whose thoughts are really being communicated – the facilitator's or the autistic's. Is there really any way of knowing whose thoughts are coming through? Even Biklen concurs that the facilitator may be responsible for influencing the communicator.

Research conducted by Wheeler et al. in 1993 reviewed the responses of 12 autistics who used a facilitator. The responses were typed in response to pictures the communicators were familiar with. The conclusion of the research was that there wasn't just some level of influence, but that the communication was entirely controlled by the facilitators.

Another question brought up by skeptics is how the physical contact made between the facilitator and the communicator enables communication. In 1997, a study conducted by Kezuka used a mechanical device to support the arm rather than a facilitator. The research showed that people who used a mechanical arm were not able to respond to questions without their human facilitator. Proponents of Facilitated Communication contend that the physical contact provides emotional support and forges a bond that gives the individual the confidence to communicate.

Yet, despite the controversies surrounding Facilitated Communication, it has been used in intelligence tests.

Individuals who had previously been tested as severely mentally impaired and later used facilitators tested in the normal range and, based on the testing using a facilitator, have been placed into regular classroom settings. And, Facilitated Communication has also been used within the legal system to provide testimony in criminal, domestic, and custody cases.

In fact, Facilitated Communication has been used as evidence to remove disabled people from homes and to fire staff accused of abuse.

Facilitated Communication has become widely popular since it first came on the scene. It's only recently that people have begun to question whether or not the treatment method holds any real scientific value.

23.2 Holding therapy

Holding therapy is a practice described and recommended in the book Holding Time, by Martha Welch.

It consists of forced holding by a therapist or parent until the child stops resisting or until a fixed time period has elapsed; sometimes the child is not released until there is eye contact. Although this technique was initially intended for autistic adults, it has also been used for autistic children, teenagers and younger children with "attachment disorders," and infants with "residual birth trauma."

Holding Therapy had its beginnings in the late 1970s when child psychiatrist Dr. Martha Welch began using it as treatment for children with ASD. She later published a book titled Holding Time.

Holding Therapy stems from the idea that a primary problem in children with ASD is the lack of a bond between parent and child. During Holding Therapy, the parent hugs the child, even if the child fights the therapy, for extensive periods of time. The contact is usually made face to face in either a sitting or lying position. During this time, the parent also tries to make and maintain eye contact with the child and speak to the child about feelings. It is the parent's duty to stay calm throughout the session and to comfort the child when he or she stops struggling. This time together in close physical contact is thought to create a parent-child bond. Further, there is some discussion about whether or not the holding triggers the part of the brain in which the child senses the boundaries of his or her own body.

As with most alternative treatments, Holding Therapy has its supporters and its opponents. Those who support the treatment claim to have seen incredible improvements in children undergoing Holding Therapy. But, those who oppose the treatment say it borders on abuse. Many believe that forced holding is not only no 'therapy,' it is a form of abuse because many, if not most people with autism have tactile defensiveness and/or tactile hypersensitivity. This claim is grounded in the fact that so many children with autism have sensory integration problems and experience touch as painful, and many others with autism become extremely agitated by forcible restraint.

23.3 Auditory integration therapy

Auditory Integration Therapy (AIT) was designed to normalize hearing. Distortions in hearing can sometimes be a significant contributing factor for individuals diagnosed with autism or pervasive developmental disorders (PDD). Developed by Dr. Guy Berard, an Ear, Nose, and Throat doctor, Auditory Integration Therapy is meant to correct distortions in hearing, hypersensitive hearing, and difficulty processing sensory input that causes pain and confusion in people with ASDs.

AIT takes place over 20 30-minute sessions. Before these sessions begin, the child's hearing is evaluated to determine which frequencies cause "auditory peaks," which denote sounds that the child is overly sensitive to. Then, during the 30-minute sessions, the child listens to sounds filtered through a machine that randomly chooses both high and low frequencies.

It filters out or reduces the volume of the sounds that cause auditory peaks. Upon completion of the first five hours of therapy, the child is re-tested to determine if the auditory peaks are still occurring and if new peaks have appeared. The therapy is then modified to accommodate any changes. Once all the sessions have been completed, the child is tested a third time. This test should show that the auditory peaks have disappeared.

Dr. Berard does state that children may experience behavioral changes during the days over which the therapy is occurring. Changes include agitation, hyperactivity, and mood swings. There is no definitive explanation for these changes, but therapists have noted that it could be the therapy itself or it could be dietary changes since parents sometimes ply their children with junk food to get them to sit for the therapy.

Advocates of Auditory Integration Therapy state that children experience the following benefits:

- A lessening of over-sensitive hearing
- Better control of vocal volume
- Better interaction and expressiveness
- Increased eye contact
- Better understanding of language and its use

- More age appropriate behavior
- Better performance in school
- Better social skills
- Increased comfort level
- Less easily distracted
- Better self-esteem

Numerous studies surrounding this therapy have been conducted. In 1997, Link studied three boys with autism who underwent Auditory Integration Therapy. No changes to over-sensitive hearing were found and very few benefits to behavior and cognitive skills were noticed.

In a 1995 study by Rimland and Edelson, 18 children (ages 4 – 21) were given a multiple criteria assessment over three months. The children who participated in the experiment showed a decrease in behavioral problems as opposed to the children in the control group who did not. These behaviors were not, however, related to sound hypersensitivity or in the areas of comprehension and language.

23.4 Dolman/Delacato method

Dolman and Delacato believe that children should learn to crawl or creep before learning to walk.

Three times a year, the Delacato Centre holds week-long courses in January, May and September. Parents make an appointment to learn how to conduct the therapy at home.

In a study by Rimland and Edelson, 445 parents of autistic children who participated in the therapy reported seeing improvement in their children.

The Dolman/Delacato method is also known as patterning. Advocates of this method view autism as being the result of a brain injury. The idea with this therapy is that in children with autism (and other disabilities) the brain can be taught to accept new experiences through patterns of movement. New pathways in the brain are forged by making the child crawl or move as children do at earlier developmental stages.

Before therapy begins, the child is assessed to determine which requirements must be met in his or her therapy sessions. Then, the child participates in therapy sessions lasting for an average of two hours per day, during which he or she performs exercises based on physiotherapy, occupational therapy, and education. The parents may carry out this therapy at home.

Advocates state they've seen results ranging from extremely successful to noticeably successful.

Success in the Dolman/Delacato method rests on the shoulders of the parents. The more work the parents do with the child, the more success will be noticed. Parents who work extensively with the child will also see results more rapidly. It is claimed that within eight months from the beginning of the therapy, some children from ages 2-10 years old are re-classified as 'high functioning.'

For children with more serious forms of ASD, benefits such as better eye contact, improved attention span, improved behavior, and better language skills are seen.

23.5 Snoezelen

This popular treatment involves the use of different multisensory stimulants that help calm down an autistic child. This includes the use of different colored lights, sounds and scents in a controlled environment to provoke a positive response from the child with autism.

Snoezelen, or controlled multisensory stimulation, is used for people with (severe) mental disabilities, and involves exposing them to a soothing and stimulating environment, the "snoezelen room." Such rooms are specially designed to deliver stimuli to various senses, using lighting effects, color, sounds, music, scents, etc. The combination of different materials on a wall may be explored using tactile senses, and the floor may be adjusted to stimulate the sense of balance.

Originally developed in the Netherlands in the 1970s, snoezelen rooms have been established in institutions all over the world. In Germany, for example, there are more than 1200 snoezelen rooms.

Snoezelen might be beneficial to people with developmental disabilities, dementia, and brain injury. However, research on these matters is scarce, with variable study designs.

The term "snoezelen" (pronounced like "SNOOzelen") is a neologism formed from the Dutch "snuffelen" (to sniff, to snuffle) and "doezelen" (to doze, to snooze).

Summary
Proving that a treatment is effective is very expensive and time consuming. Thus, there are a number of treatments which are supported by anecdotal evidence but no rigorous scientific research. These are considered "alternative autism treatments." Some alternative treatments could prove useful to you, and others might be fraudulent, so consider them carefully. Five alternative therapies are described here: Facilitated Communication, Holding Therapy, Auditory Integration Therapy, Dolman/Delacato Method, and Snoezelen. Many treatments for autism are complementary to one another, so you may find that one or more alternative therapies can help your child.

23.6 Other Alternative Treatments For Autism

As more research is done on autism, doctors and researchers are finding alternative ways to treat it. Medication can have nasty side effects. Parents are looking for different, natural ways to treat their autistic children.

There have been some alternative methods in treating autism that are more common than others. Some work alone while others are used in combination. There is no telling which method will work best for your child. Speak with your doctor to learn about alternative treatments for autistic children.

- **Music Therapy**: Autistic children have been found to respond to music in a number of ways. Sometimes the music makes them happy and they want to move around, helping with their motor skills. Other times children sing along to the words of the song, helping with speech therapy. This has been seen in children who do not even talk. Music therapy is a natural way to help autistic children.

- **Sensory Integration**: Everyone, autistic or not, has a certain smell that reminds them of something happy. Or the touch of a certain cloth will invoke specific feelings. This holds true for some autistic children as well. Researchers have been using sensory skills to get autistic children to react. The autistic children rely more on their hearing, touch, taste and smell to understand and communicate. This is also used to calm autistic children down by using specific odors or textures. (See 21.4 & 21.5)

- **Nutritional:** An autistic child's diet can affect their reactions. Doctors have used many different diets. Some of the popular diets are gluten-free, which is no wheat products, or removing dairy from the diet. Certain ingredients in foods make autistics act out or have bad reactions. Learn what they are and eliminate them from your child's diet.

- **Omega 3**: Omega 3 is a fatty acid that has been found to have health benefits, which include better sleep patterns, better social skills, and better general health. These are all positive effects for a child with autism. While you can buy Omega 3 at many nutritional stores, discuss with your doctor the benefits of trying Omega 3 in your autistic child's diet. Omega 3 and other essential fatty acids are needed in a child's normal growth pattern. However, no major studies have been done on the benefits of fish oil for autistic children.

- **Play Therapy:** Play therapy works well because it doesn't feel like work. Autistic children are in a more relaxed atmosphere and have a chance to react naturally. When a therapist begins playing with the autistic child, this will give the therapist and the child a chance to bond. The child will learn to trust the therapist through playing, which will make the sessions easier. By creating bonds through playing, autistic children can learn to play well other children their own age.

Good treatment plans may use some of these alternatives along with medication, or you can try them out before resorting to medication. Every child is different, so some of the alternatives therapies could work well for one autistic patient while not work for another.

Don't get discouraged if it doesn't work for your child. Just look for ways to keep your child happy while giving your child the best care.

23.7 Holistic Medicine

The following are some of the general holistic or alternative medicine systems that can be helpful to people with ASDs.

- Homeopathy
  This is a natural and holistic form of medicine that is based on nature. Homoeopathic remedies are recommended for people with ASD because the use of the correct homoeopathic medication can help the patient improve his or her physical, mental, and emotional state.

- Acupuncture
  Developed and derived from China, acupuncture is recommended for people with ASDs because of its potential effect on the patient's nervous system and on the GI tract. If acupuncture is done and applied properly, it can heal various nerve damages and can even improve the patient's gastrointestinal functions.

- Chiropractic treatment
  Because of the adjustments made to the patient's spine and other body structures, chiropractic treatment is said to help autistic children to develop positive behaviors by adjusting some of the patient's senses.

- Naturopathy
  This holistic medicine is based on the principle of using products that come from nature. Naturopathy uses nutritional and natural medicine to treat patients.

- Orthomolecular medicine
  This approach uses mega dose vitamins in therapy. But since vitamin overdoses have evident side effects, make sure that you discuss its possible advantages and disadvantages with a licensed physician or registered nutritionist.

- Osteopathy
  Just like in chiropractic adjustment, osteopathy adjusts the patient's muscular-skeletal system to improve the function of the brain.

Craniosacral therapy, an osteopathy-related treatment, is usually recommended for children with neurological problems such as ASD.

- Ayurveda and other traditional medicine
  Going back to basics, traditional and natural products have become a trend in the medical field nowadays. Among these traditional medications, herbal remedies are being used by more people with illnesses and even those who have family members with ASD. Ayurveda from India and various traditional Chinese medicines are well-known in this category.

These holistic medications suggest that appropriate and balanced diet, healthy lifestyle, and various therapeutic meditations can help people with ASD cope with their condition. So far, the only proven benefit of these to autistic people is that they cleanse the patient's digestive tract.

Chapter 24 Dietary interventions

In an effort to do everything possible to help their children, many parents continually seek new treatments. Some treatments are developed by reputable therapists or by parents of a child with ASD. Although an unproven treatment may help one child, it may not prove beneficial to another. To be accepted as a proven treatment, it should undergo clinical trials, preferably randomized, double-blind trials that would allow for a comparison between treatment and no treatment. Some of the interventions that have been reported to be helpful to some children, but whose clinical efficacy or safety have not been proven, are mentioned below.

Dietary interventions are based on the belief that 1) food allergies cause symptoms of autism, and 2) an insufficiency of a specific vitamin or mineral may cause some autistic symptoms. If parents decide to try a special diet for a given period of time, they should make sure that the child's nutritional status is measured carefully.

A diet that some parents have found to be helpful to their autistic child is a gluten-free, casein-free diet. Gluten is a casein-like substance that is found in the seeds of various cereal plants – wheat, oat, rye, and barley. Casein is the principal protein in milk. Since gluten and milk are found in many of the foods we eat, following a gluten-free, casein-free diet is difficult.

A supplement that some parents find to be beneficial for an autistic child is Vitamin B6, taken with magnesium (which makes the vitamin effective). The result of research studies is not conclusive; some children respond positively, some negatively, some not at all or very little.[lxxxvii]

In the search for a treatment of autism, there has been discussion lately about the use of secretin, a substance approved by the Food and Drug Administration (FDA) for a single dose normally given to aid in diagnosis of a gastrointestinal problem. Anecdotal reports have shown improvement in autism symptoms, including sleep patterns, eye contact, language skills, and alertness. Several clinical trials conducted in the last few years have found no significant improvements in symptoms between patients who received secretin and those who received a placebo.[lxxxviii]

Karyn Seroussi, the mother of a formerly autistic boy, researched how dietary changes can affect autism, and used dietary exclusion to improve her son's condition. Such treatments are part of the controversies in autism. She is known for her parent support advocacy efforts, and is the author of a book entitled Unraveling the Mystery of Autism & PDD: A Mother's Story of Research and Recovery.

Seroussi's work primarily addresses the debate between parents and professionals about what causes autism, and advocates the belief that in most cases it is a medically treatable disorder, through dietary and behavioral interventions, which needs to be diagnosed early and investigated appropriately.

Author Karyn Seroussi says her son now has no traces of autism, due in large part to a strict GFCF [gluten-free, casein-free] diet. Some parents report improved eye contact, less constipation or diarrhea, and better behavior. However, other parents do not notice a difference in their children.

Besides gluten and casein, some parents report that removing corn or soy led to equal or greater improvements in their children. Because soy protein is similar to gluten and casein, some diet proponents recommend removing it if the child seems sensitive.

Dietary and Other Interventions
In the past several years a great deal of emphasis has been placed on using a diet to control a number of conditions, including autism. There has been much talk about whether food sensitivities and allergies are the underlying cause for the severity of some symptoms of autism or, indeed, the symptoms themselves.

Although some people claim results of diet changes to be as dramatic as complete recovery from autism, most people agree that a change of diet isn't a cure for autism because, in fact, there is no cure. However, proponents of dietary management of autism agree that many symptoms will decrease in severity and some may even disappear.

The most widely used diet for autism management is the Gluten Free/Casein Free (or GFCF) diet.

In addition to the theory of dietary management of autism, some believe that autism can be managed through the use of supplements to replace nutrients that are lacking.

24.1 The GFCF diet

Interest in a Gluten Free/Casein Free diet for people with autism began in the early 1980s, when researchers noticed that autism symptoms resembled the behaviors animals displayed under the influence of opioids like morphine. As a result, a researcher by the name of Jaak Panksepp suggested that individuals with autism have higher levels of opioids that naturally occur in the brain than people without autism. Beta-endorphin is the most well-known of these opioids. It is also known as endogenous morphine and there is a known association between its effects and the symptoms of autism.

Shortly after Panksepp introduced the idea of increased opioids, Christopher Gillberg, another researcher looking into the theory, showed proof of increased levels of "endorphin like substances" found in the cerebro-spinal fluid of some autistic individuals. Those individuals who had self-destructive behaviors and seemed to feel pain less acutely than non-autistics were more likely to have elevated levels.

The amount of these substances is too high to have originated in the central nervous system, so the conclusion is that they could only have come from certain foods not being completely broken down by the digestive system. While the majority of these substances are released through the urine, some will go to the brain and disrupt normal activities.

Casein, which is found in both human and cow's milk, has been proven to break down in the stomach into casomorphine, a substance that clearly has opioid properties. Gluten, found in certain grains, breaks down into gluteomorphins. People with autism are thought to have an intolerance for or an allergy to foods containing these substances. As a result, the GFCF diet was created.

Some parents, doctors, and researchers have reported that children placed on a GFCF diet show at least some improvement in speech and/or behavior while others report striking improvements. Another reported effect of the diet is a reduction in bouts of diarrhea or loose stools, a problem common among autistic children.

Another theory supporting a switch to a GFCF diet is the notion that children with ASDs suffer from a condition commonly called "leaky gut." Leaky gut is thought to be the result of small holes in the intestinal tract that could be caused by too much yeast growth. Yeast is also found in many of the products that contain gluten. This overgrowth of yeast may cause symptoms such as:
- Confusion
- Problems with stools
- Fatigue
- Hyperactivity

Starting a GFCF diet
Initially, one must understand that a gluten-free diet is not a cure for autism. It primarily lessens the symptoms of autism in the child. Further, one must stick to this diet for several months rather than a few weeks. While the child's gluten-free diet does its job well, it takes a long time to remove the gluten that is already consumed. In certain cases however, people do find immediate results.

Before making changes to your child's diet, consult your child's physician and work with someone qualified to make sound nutritional recommendations. It's very important that your child continue to receive all the necessary vitamins and minerals to remain healthy while improving symptoms through dietary management. In general, children with autism need the same nutritional input as children without autism, so it's a good idea to follow the Recommended Daily Allowance (RDA) guidelines.

You may find it useful to remove one food at a time from your child's diet, then observe his or her behavior for a short period of time before removing another food. This will enable you to determine specifically which foods cause problems for your child. During the period of observation, keep a diary of the food you've removed and detail changes in your child's behavior. You may also find it helpful to ask people who don't know that you've made changes to your child's diet whether or not they notice any differences in the child's behavior.

Many people who advocate the GFCF diet recommend removing milk products first because the body is able to remove casein faster than gluten. It takes about a month for the body to flush itself of casein. After a month has passed, you can begin removing foods that contain gluten from the diet. Gluten can take up to six months to disappear from the body. For that reason, it's a good idea to give the diet itself a six-month trial period before deciding if it is helping your child.

Signs of a food allergy or intolerance:
- Red cheeks
- Red ears
- Dry skin
- Headaches
- Hyperactivity
- Tantrums
- Problems with bowel movements
- Amounts of substances akin to opioid peptides in their urine

Foods to avoid
Gluten is a protein found in many types of grains and food starches, and is hidden in foods you wouldn't expect to find it in. To remove gluten from your child's diet, avoid the following foods:
- Wheat
- Oats
- Barley
- Rye
- Spelt
- Semolina
- Couscous
- Malt
- Some vinegars
- Soy sauce
- Certain flavorings
- Artificial colors
- Hydrolyzed vegetable proteins
- Licorice
- Most processed foods
- Self-basting turkey
- Some cold cuts
- Prepared stocks and soups

- Modified food starch
- Caramel coloring
- Breads
- Bakery items
- Cereals
- Cookies
- Crackers
- Pizza
- Any foods with questionable ingredients, such as "natural flavorings," "flavor extracts," or "spice extracts"
- Pharmaceutical products that use gluten as a binder

Casein is found in dairy products. To remove casein from your child's diet, you'll need to avoid:
- Milk
- Cheese
- Butter
- Yogurt
- Ice cream
- Whey
- Some margarines
- Some soy cheeses
- Some hot dogs
- Foods containing caseinate
- Foods containing lactose

Obviously there are a lot of foods that you'll need to remove from your child's diet and it won't be easy to do. Many of the foods on the list are foods that children love. However, advocates of the diet insist it's worth the effort. It's important that all people who will be responsible for the care of your child are aware of the dietary changes and are on board with your decision to follow the diet, or at least in agreement enough to not sabotage your attempts by sneaking beloved (but forbidden) foods to your child. Take the time to explain what you're doing, that you've taken the appropriate steps to make certain your child's nutritional needs are still being met, and why you feel it necessary to make changes.

Foods to include
Many supermarkets carry gluten-free substitutes for the foods your child loves. For example, you should be able to find bread, crackers, cookies, pretzels, waffles, and pastas made from gluten-free flours like rice or potato flour. You may even be able to find gluten-free flour on the shelf so you can bake your own foods. Your community may also have a health food store that carries GFCF foods, or you can use the Internet to find websites that will assist you in finding foods that fit into the diet. To make certain you maintain a good, balanced diet for your child, be sure to include plenty of:

- Eggs
- Meats
- Vegetables
- Fruits
- Nuts

Other GFCF foods include:
- Rice
- Quinoa
- Amaranth
- Potatoes
- Buckwheat flour
- Soy
- Corn
- Beans
- Tapioca
- Poultry
- Fish
- Shellfish
- Teff
- Sorghum

Dietary supplements and autism

Because of their unusual attachments to routines or items, people with ASD often restrict their own diets by eating only certain types of food. And, to make matters worse, many autistics suffer from gastrointestinal problems. As a result, many are lacking essential vitamins and minerals.

Although there's still more research to be done concerning the subject of nutrition for autistic people, a great deal of research has already been published.

Published results include:
- The Southwest Autism Research Center studied 400 people with autism over 30 years ago. Of those people, 48% had chronic diarrhea or constipation, conditions that prevent the body from properly absorbing nutrients.

- In August 2000, Dr. Emar Vogelaar studied 20 children with autism and found that over 50% of them were deficient in vitamins A, B1, B3, B5, biotin, selenium, zinc, and magnesium. They were also deficient in amino acids and essential fatty acids.

- Dr. William Walsh studied 500 children with autism and found that over 99% of them had a higher Serum Copper:Plasma Zinc ratio than was normal. This showed that autistics should avoid taking supplements that contain copper and should take more zinc to improve the immune system.

- Dr. Landgreme discovered that 22% of autistic children had a low output of urinary calcium, which suggests they need more calcium.

- Dr. Waring conducted research showing that autistic children have twice as much sulfate in their excretions as do non-autistics, but have just 20% of the normal levels of sulfate in their blood. A lack of sulfate may cause compromised development of the brain, a susceptibility to heavy metal poisoning, and inflammation of the intestines.

- Research also showed an existing B12 deficiency in autistic children with increased urinary methylmalonic acid, which can cause a variety of health issues, including general fatigue.

Many parents of autistic children have reported that their children's symptoms improved, as has their general health, when certain vitamins and minerals were introduced. Only rarely are there reports of negative effects as the result of supplement introduction.

Supplements that have shown benefits in children with autism are:
- Vitamin B-6 and Magnesium: B6, which must be taken with magnesium to be effective, helps the body make neurotransmitters necessary for proper functioning of the brain.

- Cod Liver Oil: Improves eye contact and behavior. Cod liver oil is an excellent source of vitamin A and Omega-3 fatty acids.

- Vitamin C: Reduces the severity of ASD symptoms.

- Multivitamin/mineral complex: Improvements in sleep patterns, gastrointestinal problems, language, eye contact, and behavior.

Starting a supplement regimen
Prior to beginning a supplement regimen for your child, it's advisable to have a complete blood test for vitamin and mineral levels. However, since the blood test must measure all vitamins and minerals, it can be quite costly.

Therefore, many parents decide to introduce supplements slowly, trying a new one for a period of time and noting the effects. This method of introducing supplements can be safe and effective, but it will take a significantly longer time to achieve the desired results than using a blood test.

Many people combine the use of supplements with the GFCF diet. A healthy diet is a key step in making the use of supplements effective. Also, since many autistic children have leaky gut, they are unable to adequately absorb supplements. Following the GFCF diet improves leaky gut and enables the body to appropriately absorb the vitamins and minerals.

Parents should choose supplements that do not contain copper since many autistic children are naturally high in copper and too much copper can be toxic.

It's extremely important to stick to recommended allowances of vitamins and minerals. Too much of certain types can actually harm your child. If you are uncertain how much to give your child, consult your physician or a qualified nutritionist.

Tips for a Successful Supplement Regimen
Starting a supplement regimen can be costly, especially if you're using the trial and error method. Also, getting children to take supplements that sometimes have an unappealing flavor or odor can be difficult.

Here are some tips to help reduce costs associated with starting a supplement regimen and to help your child adjust more easily to the changes:
- When introducing new supplements, introduce them one at a time and observe changes for about three weeks. Keep a diary noting changes in behavior as well as any physical changes. Use these notes to determine if the supplement is working for your child.

- If your child refuses to take the supplements, try:
  - Placing the supplement in his drink
  - Adding tiny drops of cod liver oil to favorite foods
  - Sprinkling ground supplements on foods
  - Use a syringe to squirt the supplement into the child's mouth
  - Give doses in multiple sittings instead of all at once

- When introducing new supplements, buy them in small sample-size quantities. If they don't work, you won't have as much waste.

- Find out the proper use of supplements. For example, ask if they should be taken with food, on an empty stomach, in the morning, or at night.

- Take a break from all supplements two to three times each year. Supplements can build up in the body and overload the system. Taking a break allows the body to naturally reduce unnecessary levels.

- Never give random supplements to your child. Approach introduction systematically and with a lot of thought.

Summary
Based on the belief that symptoms of autism may be caused by food allergies and/or vitamin or mineral deficiencies, dietary interventions have been developed. Many have not been tested clinically, but that doesn't mean they don't work. Often, such treatments might help one child but not another. Some

parents have found a gluten-free, casein-free diet to be helpful. Others have reported similar or greater improvement from the removal of corn or soy. Whatever diet you try, you should monitor the results carefully. B6 with magnesium has been reported to be beneficial by some parents, but research results are inconclusive. Anecdotal reports have shown that secretin has reduced the severity of autism symptoms, but clinical trials have shown no significant improvements as a result of secretin when compared to a placebo. There is a great deal of published research on vitamin and mineral deficiencies in autistic people. You should approach the topic systematically rather than randomly, and document your results.

Chapter 25 Medications used in treatment

Drug therapy

Strongly opposed by many parents of autistic children, this treatment for childhood autism is seen as a highly controversial subject. While use of anti-seizure medication is effective for children who suffer from seizures, parents point out that most of the drugs used in this treatment aren't really appropriate for use on autistic children. Many autistic people themselves actively oppose the prescription of drugs to control the behavior of autistic children.

Distinguishing between helpful, analgesic, and damaging treatments is not clear-cut. The repayment of drug usage in autism is doubtful. Crusade groups such as Autistic People Against Neuroleptic Abuse have recommended that even though disposition, apprehension and obsessive disorders do take place in a number of people with autism, autistic people are not commonly psychotic, apprehensive, miserable or bipolar and they disapprove of the over-prescription of drugs to take care of these morose psychological circumstances.

As you have seen, there are a number of treatments for childhood autism available today. These treatments are products of studies by professionals and are aimed to help autistic children live a normal life.

There are, however, a number of groups which say that autism does not really need a cure since it is a part of the personality of the child. The same groups have been criticized for promoting this view of doing nothing.

This view, though, has its points considering the fact that autistics are prone to stress, anxiety and self-doubt. People feel that trying to change a child with autism is likely to further isolate the child. Treating them normally, however, would be the correct way to get them to act normally.

All these types of treatments for childhood autism have their virtues. However, you need to pick one that you think will be the best for your child. To do this properly, you need to get as much information as you can and base your decision on this.

Medications Used in Treatment

When starting a treatment plan for an autistic person, doctors will usually look at different medicines that can help out. Because an autistic person can display different symptoms, the medication plan is going to be different for every person. There is no medicine that is going to cure autism, but medication is used to lessen the symptoms to help people live full, functional lives.

Parents may not want to start their children on medication right away when there is a diagnosis of autism. This is understandable because some people don't want to have their children go through a lifestyle of taking pills daily.

There are other options to consider. Alternative treatments include changing a child's diet or offering them natural treatments.

Here is a look at the types of medication a person with autism might have to take:

- *Antipsychotic*: These types of medications are used for behavioral problems. This can include a variety of problems such as aggression, tantrums or insomnia. This medication should not be the first option for the child. Behavioral therapy should be sought out and tried before resorting to these types of pills.

- *Anticonvulsant*: This is to help control seizures if an autistic person suffers from them.

- *Anti-anxiety and anti-depression*: Autistic children can have a hard time controlling their feelings. Sometimes they laugh and cry without being prompted. These medications are used to control those feelings and random outbursts. However, these medications have some serious side effects. If your child does take these, watch for odd behavioral changes, ones that weren't present before the medication began.

- *Sedative:* If your autistic child suffers from insomnia or other sleeping disorders, a doctor may prescribe a sedative to help the child sleep better. There are natural alternatives that you may want to seek out before trying sedatives.

- *Stimulant*: Some children who suffer from autism are hyperactive and these medications are used to help children focus better. This is often used when a child becomes school-aged to help them to pay attention and help with their education. This medication is useful for those children who can't seem to stay focused on any certain areas.

Medicine should be a last resort for parents when treating their children. You don't want the children to become dependent on the medication. Another problem with medicines is that it may control the issue, but have side effects that cause new problems. You also want to discuss long-term side effects with your doctor.

If you notice the medication is not helping, talk to your doctor. Your doctor may prescribe an alternative medication or try a different course of action. It's important to keep the lines of communication open with your child's doctor because this will help in getting the best treatment plan for your child.

Biomedical Treatments for Autism
People have commonly thought of diseases and abnormalities in the bodies as the queer workings of fate. But now we know that certain changes in the hormonal levels of the body or specific viral infections and bacteria cause diseases and other abnormalities, and we understand the mechanisms that

work in many conditions. This way, we have learned to hypothesize and create solutions to intervene with the diseases and disorders.

Sadly though, among the many for which mankind hasn't discovered cures yet are the syndromes, disorders and diseases that affect the brain and its functions. This probably springs from the reality that we still cannot understand "the organ that understands." It, in a sense, is still a veiled mystery to us.

Once we have learned the backgrounds of these brain diseases, we can surely find existing cures to combat them. But so long as we lack understanding, we can never get from square 1 to square 2.

When using biomedical treatments, we should not give way to margins of error. Remember that we are dealing with neurons, the central nervous system, and the sensitive brain. Any grave damage is likely to be permanent.

Autism is permanent. Once it develops in a three-year-old child, he will have to carry it all his life. Symptoms may subside with proper conditioning and training, but still they are inside the person and they can manifest at any moment.

Biomedical treatments for autism must be done with great caution. We are dealing with complex body mechanisms and responses plus serious conditions that can significantly affect a person's entire life.

Chemical intervention in a normally functioning brain is difficult and dangerous enough, and much more so when dealing with an abnormal brain that has different transmissions. Therefore, the effects of treatments in people with autism are far more unpredictable than in the normal population, and unpredictable enough so as not to provide comparison from one autistic person to another.

It is unavoidable therefore that medical prescriptionists will somehow experiment on what will best work for a case and what must not be used. There are general medications that have the same effects for each case, but because of the unpredictable nature of autism, doctors will have to discover which create effects, whether good or bad, to the patient in question.

There are several controversies and questions that have risen with the use of drug interventions with autism. Generally, experts believe that drugs may help control the display of symptoms but they are said to have sub-minimal or minimal effect on the condition itself.

Biochemical treatments of autism don't rely solely on drugs and medications though. There is said to be a significant relationship between biochemical processes and the body's physical processes. This is the main reason why physical therapists contribute significantly to any treatment of autism that aims to intercept with biochemical processes.

However, as with drugs, therapies are not the universal cure to autism, nor do they have constant effect in any particular patient due to varying responses.

We can now produce therapies that work better, because we are already determining the biological factors of autism. Nonetheless, we still cannot be confident that individuals displaying autistic features will always react in ways we perceive to be true.

Medications are often used to successfully treat behavioral problems, such as aggression, self-injurious behavior, and severe tantrums that keep the person with ASD from functioning more effectively at home or at school. The medications used are those that have been developed to treat similar symptoms in other disorders. Many of these medications are prescribed "off-label." This means that the FDA has not officially approved them for use in children, but the doctor prescribes the medications if he or she feels they are appropriate for your child. Further research needs to be done to ensure not only the effectiveness but also the safety of psychotropic agents used in the treatment of children and adolescents.

A child with ASD may not respond in the same way to medications as typically developing children. It is important that parents work with a doctor who has active experience with children with autism. A child should be monitored closely while taking medication. The doctor will prescribe the lowest possible effective dose. Ask the doctor about any side effects the medication may have and keep a record of how your child responds to it. It will be helpful to read the "patient insert" that comes with your child's medication. Some people keep the patient inserts in a small notebook to be used as a reference. This is most useful when several medications are prescribed.

Anxiety and depression
Selective serotonin reuptake inhibitors (SSRIs) are the medications most often prescribed for symptoms of anxiety, depression, and/or obsessive-compulsive disorder (OCD). Only one of the SSRIs, fluoxetine (Prozac®), has been approved by the FDA for both OCD and depression in children age 7 and older.

Three that have been approved for OCD are fluvoxamine (Luvox®), age 8 and older; sertraline (Zoloft®), age 6 and older; and clomipramine (Anafranil®), age 10 and older.[lxxxix] Treatment with these medications can be associated with decreased frequency of repetitive, ritualistic behavior and improvements in eye contact and social contacts. The FDA is studying and analyzing data to better understand how to use the SSRIs safely, effectively, and at the lowest dose possible.

Behavioral problems
Antipsychotic medications have been used to treat serious behavioral problems. These medications work by reducing the activity in the brain of the neurotransmitter dopamine. Among the older medications are typical antipsychotics, such as haloperidol (Haldol®), thioridazine, fluphenazine, and chlorpromazine. In more than one study, haloperidol was found to be more

effective than a placebo in treating serious behavioral problems.[xc] However, haloperidol, while helpful for reducing symptoms of aggression, can also have adverse side effects, such as sedation, muscle stiffness, and abnormal movements.

Placebo-controlled studies of the newer "atypical" antipsychotics are being conducted on children with autism. The first study, conducted by the NIMH-supported Research Units on Pediatric Psychopharmacology (RUPP) Autism Network, was on risperidone (Risperdal®).[xci] Results of the 8-week study were reported in 2002 and showed that risperidone was effective and well tolerated for the treatment of severe behavioral problems in children with autism. The most common side effects were increased appetite, weight gain, and sedation. Further long-term studies are needed to determine any long-term side effects. Other atypical antipsychotics that have been studied recently with encouraging results are olanzapine (Zyprexa®) and ziprasidone (Geodon®). Ziprasidone has not been associated with significant weight gain.

Seizures
Seizures occur in one in four people with ASD, most often in those who have low IQ or who are mute. They are treated with one or more anticonvulsants. These include such medications as carbamazepine (Tegretol®), lamotrigine (Lamictal®), topiramate (Topamax®), and valproic acid (Depakote®). The level of the medication in the blood should be monitored carefully and adjusted so that the least amount possible is used to be effective. Although medication usually reduces the number of seizures, it cannot always eliminate them.

Inattention and hyperactivity
Stimulant medications such as methylphenidate (Ritalin®), used safely and effectively in people with attention deficit hyperactivity disorder, have also been prescribed for children with autism. These medications may decrease impulsivity and hyperactivity in some children, especially higher functioning children.

Several other medications have been used to treat ASD symptoms; among them are other antidepressants, naltrexone, lithium, and some of the benzodiazepines such as diazepam (Valium®) and lorazepam (Ativan®). The safety and efficacy of these medications in children with autism has not been proven. Since people may respond differently to different medications, your child's unique history and behavior will help your doctor decide which medication might be most beneficial.

Summary
There is no known cure for autism – it is a life-long condition – but there are some treatments available to make life easier for the child and parents. Goals of treatment include reduction of problem behaviors that interfere with learning, and fostering growth in areas that include communication, cognition, and self-help skills. The treatments focus on improving the overall functioning of the child with autism.

Behavioral therapy and training are often used to promote favorable behaviors and to prevent and discourage undesirable behaviors[xcii]. For example, discrete trial training is one-on-one teaching where small parts of behaviors and skills are taught to the child in short, repeated sessions[xciii].

Drug treatments are available to treat some of the symptoms of autism, such as over activity, repetitive movements, aggression, and self-injury. Tranquilizers, at low doses, are thought to be able to reduce problem behaviors. Other drugs, such as risperidone, selective serotonin reuptake inhibitors, antidepressants, and anxiolytics, have also been used to treat the negative symptoms of autism.

HOME, EDUCATION, LEISURE, WORK, INDEPENDENCE, & PLANNING A FUTURE

Chapter 26 @Home

Another distinction that we will elaborate on from Chapter 26 onwards is the impact of autism through stages of one's development. There are many ways to look at the impact the disease has on the child or adult diagnosed with autism. A helpful way to look at this is to make distinctions in the major hemispheres in which a person has to function.

In this part of the book we will start with distinctions in:

- Autism and family
- Autism and school
- Autism and work
- Autism and leisure
- Living with autism

Every family member has another position, another relation with the autistic family member. This means the reciprocal adaptation for everyone is different. A younger brother might adapt less than a granny. The demands on a mother can be more than those on a father.

Autism presents challenges for the entire family of an individual with autism.

Parents

Parents of children with autism face all the normal pressures of parenthood such as keeping a child safe, coping with normal misbehavior, and ensuring their children lead a happy, healthy life. But they also face significant difficulties as a direct result of autism, which poses its own set of parenting questions, like:

- How do I keep my child safe when he wanders out of the house, doesn't understand the dangers of everyday items like appliances, and for instance presents self-destructive behavior?
- How can I be certain my child's special educational needs are met?
- How do I make sure the needs of my other children are met?
- How do I avoid undue stress on my marriage because of the added pressures of autism?
- How do I handle the mental and physical changes that come with adolescence in a child who doesn't understand these changes or the social issues that come with them?
- What will happen to my child when I'm not there to take care of him anymore?

For parents, having a child with autism can be both stressful and frustrating, especially when you see other parents with normal children. However, no matter how hard you want your child to be as normal as possible, all you can do is lessen the effects of the disorder and make your child live a happy life. Autism sustains a great amount of misery and pain to both you and your child. But this does not mean you have to sit down and watch hopelessly as your child grows up differently. As mentioned, you can do something about it to minimize its effects.

One thing you should know is that autism is undetectable before birth and the first expressions can appear a year or two after giving birth. This is why you as parents should recognize the early signs of autism as early as possible, because it can hit any child in different ways.

Early signs of autism are language delay, repetitive use of words or phrases in a normal setting, resistance to change and insistence on a single activity cycle, fondness of spinning objects, obvious fear of things, poor concentration, lack of sensory pleasure, detachment from the real world, and lack of interest in toys.

If you notice some of these signs, approach a doctor who can provide clear answers on the condition of your child. Then, if your child has been diagnosed with autism, provide your child with an early intervention program. The early preventive treatment is the best thing you can do to alter the effects of autism on your child. People who can recommend early intervention programs include pediatric psychologists, occupational therapists, developmental pediatricians, speech or language pathologists, and early childhood educators or special education teachers.

It must be reiterated that an early intervention program must be done as soon as your child is diagnosed with autism. Both therapeutic and educational services are significantly important to reduce the effects of autism. These programs will also help to prevent your child from developing problems associated with autism like repetitive behaviors.

Depending on the program and the case of your child, you can choose to enroll your child in either a special school that support students with autism, a regular school with normal students, or a private school that provides low student-to-teacher ratios in classrooms, giving each child with autism closer therapeutic and educational attention.

As a parent, you should be informed on how to deal with autism. This will enable you to help your child as he grows up. It is especially important for you to keep the following rules of thumb on how to interact with your child:

- Let your child develop a sense of security and peace in your presence.
- Develop routines in and out of the house. Rules on the expected attitude inside and outside the house must be made clear.
- Don't be restrictive but be strict. Make sure you restrict patterns that would worsen your child's condition. No means NO.
- Provide affection in as many ways as possible.

Son or daughter

If your father or mother is autistic, this can lead to cumbersome situations. In general, more house rules are needed because the parent with autism tries to keep control by means of rules.

For children the most important issue is, however, that the parent with autism cannot always sense well what goes on in the child's mind and thus the parent is not always able to give the child the support he needs. This can obstruct developing an emotional bond between the two. The child will receive only a few compliments given by the parent with autism, will probably receive much criticism, and must consider the parent's handicap all the time. This can lead to an imbalance in which the child more or less takes over the parent's role. Moreover the non-autistic partner, most frequently the mother, will have extra tasks, as a result of which the child can also lay a lesser claim on this parent.

Having a parent with autism leads to a particular educating. Children must learn to accept that their parent is not the same as other parents. Raising a child lays a heavy claim on the autistic parent's flexibility. Unexpected events are more or less common during the education and upbringing of children. Spontaneous sleepover parties, changes in plans, and not accepting parental authority seem to be a prominent part of educating children. These situations are very difficult for an autistic parent.[xciv]

Brother or sister

Siblings, too, face difficulties not present for their peers without autistic brothers or sisters. They find themselves faced with a sibling who may take little interest in them, demands a great deal of attention from parents, and exhibits embarrassing behaviors.

All these concerns are legitimate. With the proper education, a common goal, and strategies in place to enable the family to appropriately cope, living with autism can be a very manageable situation.

Being a brother or sister of someone with autism means having to take into account your autistic brother or sister. This expands itself as time goes by to eventually taking responsibility for this brother or sister who can't stand his or her own ground socially. Because of this you learn to be social, but at the same time you get less chance to be a carefree child. This responsibility usually does not decrease when one grows older. Requests from the parents to look after the autistic brother or sister are sometimes made directly and sometimes implicitly.

Most striking for someone with an autistic brother or sister is that much attention goes out to the latter; as a result they themselves get less attention, so they might end up feeling less important.

A second notable element is that the autistic brother or sister cannot play well with other children. The "playing age" lies much lower than the calendar age. Because children outside the family often bully or tease the autistic child, parents expect their brother or sister to compensate by tagging along with the autistic brother or sister. As a brother or sister you might not always feel like doing so.

For the child with autism, having a brother or sister means following a full-time social development course by watching and listening to how their brothers and sisters perform. This is very favorable for further development. Parents must, however, make sure that the brother or sister is not hindered in their own development and that they themselves receive proper attention.

A third element can be the difficulty in taking friends and boyfriends or girlfriends home, because they are also expected to consider the autistic brother or sister along with the other children.[xcv]

A family of their own
People with autism can also found a family. This asks an extra effort from the partners, but it can lead to a deeper relationship. When there are children, however, autism often leads to problems, because a much larger effort is asked from the partners, and also because children tend to disturb the quiet autistic patterns.

Sharing domestic tasks is not easy for most men, but for someone with autism it is an even larger problem. Taking care of children is no simple thing. Women with a male partner have to adapt their expectations anyway because one might be less inclined or able to combine tasks, but with an autistic partner this even more strongly applies.

The upheaval which having a family brings is contrary to the slowing down/time out which someone with autism necessarily needs. As a result, the parent with autism will weigh heavily on the other family members, and the non-autistic parent will compromise to keep the peace.

A family means constant movement. It also seems hectic because there's always a mess that needs to be cleaned up. There's always someone demanding attention and things that need to be done immediately without the possibility of retreating for a moment or two.

The most difficult fact is that the person with autism hardly has enough time for himself, and even if there is enough time, there are these continuous disturbances. This can lead to escalations with physical and verbal violence.

Relationships
A relation between people is always a work of art. The high percentage of divorces illustrates this clearly. Relationships in which one of the partners is autistic have a double problem, namely the effort to mold the relationship into something good, and difficulty in understanding what a partner with autism brings to it. Forming a relationship means a transition from quickly understanding each other in the courting phase, through a phase where you discover you might not know and understand each other as well as you thought as in the amorous period, to the process of nevertheless learning to understand

each other. A relation means consideration for each other, sensing what keeps the other busy, and trying to adapt your behavior.

In general with an autistic partner the ability to sense and flexibility toward behavioral change is lower than in people without autism. Broadly speaking the intention to adapt is larger: autistic people are mostly characterized by trying to do their best. However their willingness is much larger than their possibility. Because the autistic partner is concerned with seemingly unimportant things, the partner without autism has often difficulty believing this is inability rather than uncooperativeness.

Moreover, the partner without autism has limited possibilities for enjoying things together, such as going out to parties, because the partner with autism wants to avoid groups of people. The partner without autism must take over tasks and show more adaptive behavior than he or she may have anticipated at the beginning of the relationship, and this will be more than seems to be the case in other relationships. The positive aspects of the relationship, like honesty and loyalty, are large, but are at risk of being left out of the picture.

Often partners of people with autism are the first who cry out for help, because they feel overloaded or exhausted. They only have an eye for the negative aspects in their responsibility and sometimes say that they have the feeling of having an extra child, instead of a partner.

Frequently the autistic partner is the man. The female partner is often extremely sensitive, empathic, and very verbally gifted. In fact, you will notice a pattern that you often see between men and women, but more extremely. By the time help is finally offered, the patterns in the relation have reached extremes. It frequently involves a very eloquent woman and a man whose spirit is broken.

The fight between the partners goes out of control because the partner with autism tries to understand what is said and sometimes takes it literally, or forgets, or isn't able to focus on the emotional aspect. The man's speech will frequently be overshadowed by the woman's words.

The endless discussion to get clarity can drive the partner without autism nuts. She simply wants the other to be able to sense what's going on and while she may be stronger in argumentation than the partner with autism, she might lose the argument while at the same time she feels she is right. The autistic partner however is not particularly interested in winning the argument, but is desperately trying to understand and as a result comes up with arguments which turns the conversation into a kind of debate instead of attempting to get clarity.

It can help to simply stop to the discussion and return to the good intentions of both which are usually there.

The partner without autism expects the other to share feelings and ideas. But for men with autism this certainly means asking too much. The woman expects the man to see that she does not feel 100% lately. For someone with autism this is quite difficult to notice and express.

Even for someone without autism it is often difficult to discover how the other feels and exactly what the other needs. This is more or less always the case in a man/woman relationship and even then it is not always clear for the non-autistic partner.

Being considerate of each other and sensing each other's needs is of the utmost importance in any relationship. The part of the problem in a heterosexual relationship that is caused by man/woman differences is larger than the aspect added by the autism.

Summary
Having an autistic family member is a challenge, and the nature of the challenge varies depending on the relationship. If you're the parent of an autistic child, your challenge is to raise a happy and functional child without neglecting any siblings. If you have an autistic parent, to some extent you will find yourself raising yourself, as well as leaning more heavily on the other parent. If you have an autistic brother or sister, your parents may expect or even ask you to help raise your brother or sister. Autistic people who have families of their own will find the hectic pace and inability to plan for every contingency to be stressful. If you are a non-autistic person in a traditional male/female relationship with an autistic person, your partner's lack of empathy may be trying.

26.1 How to cope as a parent of an autistic child

Parenting an autistic child indeed calls for a lot of courage, patience and optimism. While it is sometimes rewarding when the schedules follow on unperturbed, sometimes you wish to rush away from the stress and vent all your frustrations. One thing we must understand is that your frustrations, stress and depression can severely harm your child. To be a successful parent you must be a happy and contended individual because you further pass on this happiness to your child. Given below are a few ways to help you through your journey with your autistic child.

Support Groups
The local support groups are a collection of parents going through a similar scenario. It gives you a chance to talk and discuss your problems with people who can relate to them. They might help you with suggestions and some unexpected solutions for the daily routines and other activities for the child. Also, they provide an opportunity to meet various people and listen to their experiences and learn from them. It allows you a break from the therapists and doctors as well.

Writing Journals

Penning your feelings, thoughts and expressions is often a great mechanism to emotional relaxation. One can keep this journal private enough. This stress buster allows you to be friends with yourself and chalks out some individual moments for you. It might also help you chart your child's behavior on a day-to-day basis.

Getting Away

We all crave a break sometimes, where we just want to be alone or with our spouse.

There are several activities that cannot be done with the kids whether autistic or not. Look for a qualified babysitter for your child and go out on a night date with your spouse. Carry on with the activities you always wanted to do but were never able to make time for – for instance, catch your favorite film, play some interesting sports and games, or merely take a long drive to your choicest food joint. In case you cannot make plans outside home, enjoy a relaxed hot bath after the child is asleep. Pamper yourself sometimes and follow your heart.

This will relax your tensions and help you become a better parent, which will help your child.

Ask for Help

All of us want to give the best to our children all by ourselves. In our efforts to be a super mom, we often tend to forget that our frustration and anger always affects the child. We must understand that there is no harm in seeking help. Until and unless we communicate our problems, no one can help as people cannot be mind readers.

Summary

Parenting an autistic child surely requires help. In case you are trying a treatment which is not effective enough, talk to someone and seek guidance. Convincing an autistic child to do certain tasks gets very tough. In such times having someone for the simple tasks makes the situation easier to tackle. Seeking help from your spouse and talking out your problems with him/her makes a lot of difference.

26.2 Let your child be a kid

Parenting an autistic child, we often forget that your child's life needs something more than the doctors and therapists. We become so protective and concerned about every little movement in their lives that we allow them no time to be kids. It is indeed important and helpful to allow them a little time in the day to let them do what they like.

Here are a few things that will surely pamper the kid within your child.

1. Let your autistic child choose his activity or game at a certain time each day. It may be playing with his favorite toy or game or pursuing a hobby

like drawing or painting. This provides a break from doctors and therapies for the child.

2. Plan activities outside the home for your autistic child. For instance, a dinner at the food joint he relishes the most, or a picnic at a near by park. Such activities can be planned once a week. At times the child prefers spending time with his grandparents as well.

3. If you keep your child too protected and do not let him mingle with the other kids, he might develop a sort of phobia. Let him run, jump and yell like the other children. Kids love to get dirty and they have real fun doing it. It won't harm him to get dirty. A bath can wash away the mud but he will have his share of fun.

4. Being autistic doesn't mean that your child cannot lead a normal life. You must teach him to have courage and achieve whatever he aspires to do. His condition should not become a hurdle in his path.

5. At this tender age, kids often hold on to all possible excuses to get special treatment. Don't let autism become a reason or excuse for your child. Punish him for his mistakes and make him face the consequences. This will help him become a strong individual in the long run.

6. Give simple tasks to the child that are part of his or her daily chores like making the bed or packing a school bag. Make sure the child is able to do them and reward him for the same. This will enhance his confidence and give him a sense of accomplishment.

7. Inspire your child to do his best in all aspects of life and show him that you have expectations from him. If your child is not made to use his full potential he shall never come to know his real strength.

Summary
Playing in mud, getting dirty, slipping down and yet smiling, fiddling with a favorite toy, yelling around cheerfully – that defines fun for kids. Do not be a guard over your child, be a guide and let him be free sometimes. Even though he has special needs, he will be much happier when he can freely choose (some of) his activities.

26.3 Autistic children need schedules

Children at all ages, whether 3 or 13, often complain of boredom. Making them do what you want but they don't is indeed cracking a hard nut. Especially when dealing with special needs like those of an autistic child, a schedule is a great help. To be an efficient parent, we must manage several activities every day, such as the child's school, therapy, doctor's appointments, homework and studies, daily chores, etc. The driving force behind all of these is your child's health and growth.

Scheduling creates a pre-defined structure for the child in which he knows what to expect next, what he will do tomorrow, and where he will be at a given point in time. Often autistic children have certain anxiety issues. Whenever they are left free to think widely without any guidance, they might shift to such depressing thoughts. A well-designed schedule leaves less or no extra time unguided and hence the anxiety level drops greatly. This avoids any breakdowns in the necessary daily chores and the medical procedures.

Making them do something essential but undesirable to them like completing homework becomes easier with a schedule. You make them shift to a task like 'study' or 'homework' after completing the prior task and aim to accomplish the same in order to move to a welcome 'activity' like 'drawing' or 'outdoor games.'

With numerous check-ups, therapies and medical needs, managing your child's timetable can sometimes be quite cumbersome. For instance, appointments with a therapist and a doctor might overlap. A schedule helps you keep a track of each appointment without fail.

Once you have made a schedule for your child, draft it in the form of an attractive chart in his personal space or room. Let him follow the steps one after another on his own, of course with your able guidance. This will enhance his self-confidence and his decision-making skills.

At times the autistic child has a problem reading the words. In that case, use a 'visual schedule,' in which every task or activity is allotted a symbol – a garden for outdoor games, a stack of books for studies, and a stethoscope for a doctor's appointment, and a handshake for his therapy hours.

In case of any change in the schedule, explain this to your child in detail in time. As the child will be planning things according to the schedule only, even a slight change could upset him. So involve him in the change and the decision, as this will allow him to feel more independent and confident.

In our day-to-day lives, there can be many hassles in sticking to a set timetable, but try to do so as much as possible. For instance, if your child is used to waking up at 7 in the morning, continue the same on the weekends as well. Similarly, try not to change his bedtimes too much, as proper sleep will keep your child healthier.

A sample schedule is shown below:

7 AM	Wake up, brush your teeth, bathe, put on your uniform, pack your bag
8 AM	Breakfast
8:15 AM	Board the school bus
2 PM	Come home, wash your hands, change your clothes
2:30 PM	Lunch
3 PM	Nap Time
4 PM	Have milk, study time

5:30 PM	Leisure
6 PM	Outdoor games
7 PM	Watch cartoons
8 PM	Bathing
8:30 PM	Dinner
9 PM	Bedtime

Summary

As a parent, you are sure to see improvement in your child with the defined schedules. Ensuring that something is always planned for him will make his and your life far easier and more smoothly managed.

Chapter 27 @School

Getting an education requires a great deal of independent planning, the extent of which depends on the sort of study. Working independently involves planning one's study. The EF, the executive functions, play an important role in these tasks.

Men with autism find it difficult to maintain this responsibility and to remain aware of "the big picture," so they often depend heavily on their instructors. They require a lot of support and try to deal with their uncertainty by discussing all details.

This is often difficult for instructors. Men with autism require far more hours than other students and seem to obsess over minutiae. But these aren't minor details for the autistic man, who will sometimes lose sleep over a question that others would see as unimportant.

Men with autism find it difficult to learn from books because it requires distinguishing between main themes and side issues, and translation from theory into practice.

Also, autistic students have difficulty with social interactions with teachers and other pupils. They can become isolated and have problems with rejection. Breaking through this isolation requires heavy involvement from the training staff.

27.1 Factors to consider when teaching a child with autism

Teaching a child with autism is a challenge for most people, especially for parents who have not yet accepted the condition of their child or who have not been informed of what needs to be done to ensure a good education for their special child.

Autism is a mental disability that attacks the ability of the child to move, communicate, think, and feel normally. Knowing this will enable parents and others involved in teaching the child to use the right guidelines to properly educate an autistic child.

Here are the factors to consider when teaching a child with autism:

Instructional formats or curriculum
There is no single and general effect of autism. Different children with the same disorder happen to have different conditions. Each one requires a special instructional format or curriculum to be applied. Thus, the way of teaching is not based on autism itself but on how it affects the child. However, there are

general instructional formats or curricula that can be given to every autistic child. The difference is only in the teaching approach.

Communication concerns

The way instructions are given to children with autism should not be the same as with non-autistic students. Since autistic children have difficulties understanding things verbally and cannot communicate well verbally, instructions should be given in a different way. The classroom should be equipped with things that enable children to learn even without verbal instructions. Visual aids make it easier to communicate with special children. Instructions and rules outside the curriculum that they need to learn and understand should be given in the way they understand best. The main point is to communicate properly and effectively.

Age

Autistic children with the same physical age may have a different mental age. Knowing the mental age of the child will provide an easier learning process for both the child and the teacher or parents.

For young autistic children, parents must apply an early intervention program that will enable the child to be guided correctly in terms of discipline, motor skills, and communication. This must be done as soon as you discover that your child is autistic.

Meanwhile, instructions for elementary students may include manners of integrating with other people or making friends. In other words, autistic children should be trained to be sociable in this period of learning.

Autistic children in their high school years must learn how to integrate not only with other people but also with the whole community. Learning how to work, live, participate and recreate with other people is very important in this stage.

Behavioral factors

Autistic children need guidance on how to behave by themselves and with other people. This is because they are especially passive or have developed destructive or excessive behaviors. In the past, the approach to change this behavior was often by punishment. Today, the approach is by positive behavior support (PBS). This approach treats the children with dignity and respect that will not only improve their self-esteem but also improve their behavior dramatically without using punishment. Special children need affection and care. This approach caters to these needs.

27.2 The importance of teaching writing to a child with autism

A child with autism is often described as being confined in his or her own world. This is because the child has limited ability to interact with other people.

A specific character of the autistic spectrum is the inability to properly grasp the concept of language.

Teaching writing to a child with autism can prove very valuable to both the teacher and the student. On the student's side there are a variety of advantages that he or she can gain from the ability to write.

In teaching a child with autism to write, you give him or her the precious ability of interaction. Autistic children often fail to communicate with other people because face-to-face verbal interaction is just too intimidating for them. Writing, however, allows them to express their feelings on a much more impersonal level.

Did you know that computers are now being used to enhance the communication skills of autistic children? Teaching writing to a child with autism will equip him or her with the knowledge necessary to improve his or her communication skills. This is because teaching writing to a child with autism helps him or her to initiate the interaction.

Teaching writing to a child with autism does not only help him or her in developing communication skills. It also helps them to develop hand-eye coordination and grace in movement. Many people react with disbelief when informed of this fact. However, when you study the history of specific cultures you will see the meaning behind this.

Miyamoto Musashi, also known in Japan as the sword saint, developed his swordsmanship through calligraphy. In fact, when you study Chinese martial arts history, you will find that many warriors took up calligraphy in order to improve their skill. And what do you think calligraphy is? It is learning how to write beautifully.

Let's now switch to the teacher's perspective. What advantages can teaching writing to a child with autism possibly give to the teacher?

Well, there is always self-fulfillment. Abraham Maslow categorizes the need for self-actualization as the highest need that a man can fulfill. This means that the quest for self-fulfillment is the noblest quest known to man. In teaching writing to a child with autism, people find self-fulfillment because they learn how to take pride in the achievements of the student.

They realize just how much impact teaching writing to a child with autism has. They learn the value of their help and just how much progress they have made with the child. They also learn how to appreciate their own abilities.

Because of the development of technology, many people forget the value of being able to write. They seem to feel that they do not really need the skill since they can send any message using the keyboard. The skill of writing is especially diminishing today because people can send messages using video or audio.

Teaching writing to a child with autism lets them rediscover the value of being able to write.

There are many advantages to be gained from teaching writing to a child with autism.

27.3 Teaching strategies for child with autism

There is one truth, and you might not believe it yet, but sooner or later you probably will. Children with autism are far more normal than you maybe would have first imagined. They have the same sensations, feelings and emotions that we all have. Only their reactions to stimuli are different. This results in their inability to create socially normal interactions. They, in a sense, fail to express their reactions in ways we think are normal.

A child with autism will communicate his behavior and reactions through emotions. If he wants something, for example, he will draw attention by screaming or banging his head against the wall.

Now, when you are teaching a child with autism, you must remember that he needs different methods before he understands what you are trying to tell him. In this section, we will provide various teaching strategies for autistic children.

A child with autism is basically a visual thinker. They may understand things when used in verbal form but they can better cope with visual aids. Their thoughts work like videotapes that comprehend sequences of pictures. So the best way to maximize this is to use various teaching methods that employ visual techniques in general.

Therefore, verbal instructions don't register well on them. The most that they can remember is a three-stepped verbal instruction, but still this would be quite a challenge on their memory. You may write your instructions on a piece of paper and have it understood before you leave them with your instruction. This is important to apply with all things that they have difficulty creating a mental picture of, such as phone numbers and sequences.

Work on their strengths. In rare cases, children with autism have developed extra skills that are not usually present in normal children. These skills include mentally solving complex math problems, working with a computer, or extremely good drawing or painting skills. If you notice this in your child or pupil, there is no reason for you to ignore this. You have to focus more on what they excel at than on what they are incapable of doing.

A child with autism has the tendency to focus more on a single thing, like a ball or the tire of a car. If you identify things to which they are fixated, it is best to use these in encouraging them to study. When doing math problems, use ball figures as examples. Or when telling them stories that are associated with tires, like cars, give extra focus to the things that interest them most.

Since they work more visually, it would be good to devise means of education with more tangible forms of examples. For instance, for counting you can use visual objects like blocks in different colors and shapes.

Though these teaching strategies are simplified for children with autism, there is still a large chance that they will not learn easily. Don't get frustrated; both of you will get through it. Just be patient in repeating lessons and counsel their parents to follow up at home. Teaching must not stop at school.

27.4 Your child's educational plan

The common thread in autism is the presence of a developmental disability, more specifically, a disorder of communication which manifests itself differently in each person. But whatever the level of impairment, the educational program for an individual with autism should be based on the unique needs of the student. If this is the first attempt by the parents and school system to develop an appropriate curriculum, conducting a comprehensive needs assessment is a good place to start. This evaluation will become the blueprint for your child's educational plan.

When the diagnosis Autism Spectrum Disorder is made, it is of utmost importance to contact the child's day care center, playground or school. After all, a child/young one with an ASD needs more guidance and support from his environment to be able to function optimally. The day care center, the playground and the school are important aspects of the life of a child/young one.

In addition to exchanging information about the diagnosis, it is important that the following questions are discussed:

Has the diagnosis been recognized?
Is there a difference in the conduct of the child/young one there and at home?

Experience teaches that some children with an ASD show problematic conduct at home. Parents believe that these problems are due to strain/excessive demands at school.

The problem is that the child adapts himself to school and seems to be doing well there. Maybe the child burdens himself to the utmost to adapt and behave as desired. At home in familiar surroundings, the child is released and this may result in difficult conduct. During a conversation between parents and teacher, different visions about the child's functioning become apparent.

The other way around can also be found, where the child shows problems at school but all goes well at home.

Regular and permanent consultation between parents and school about the signals a child gives at home and at school are very important. Does the child/young one shape up optimally? Does the schedule for the day/teaching satisfy the requirements of the pupil? Some points of reflection are:

Does the child have one or various teachers?
What is the size of the groups or classes? Are there combined classes? Is there more emphasis on group teaching or individual teaching? Is the teaching structural or aimed more at independence? Is there a great deal of cooperation in groups or not? Is the child/young one in need of extra support and working within the schedule for the day at school? Is there, within the daily schedule or school, sufficient knowledge of ASD?

Is it necessary to investigate the cognitive and/or didactic skills of the child/young person further?
Depending on the replies to these questions it will become clear whether the child/young person is content and develops sufficiently during daily activities or at school, whether additional coaching is required, or whether another type of program/teaching should be chosen.

When the child/young one develops well within the present schedule for the day or school, it is important to closely follow the progress and to remain in consultation so that you are warned in time if things stop going well.

Educational planning for students with autism often addresses a wide range of skill development, including academics, communication and language skills, social skills, self-help skills, behavioral issues, and leisure skills. It's important to consult with professionals trained specifically in autism to help your child benefit from his/her school program. But bear in mind that even the most well intended advice might generate inappropriate curriculum models and impair the child's ability to develop to his/her full potential. That's why it's important to get a wide range of opinions and to keep a close eye on your child's progress or lack thereof. Most professionals agree that individuals with autism respond well to highly structured, specialized education programs designed to meet the individual's needs.

Based on the major characteristics associated with autism, there are areas that are important to look at when creating a plan: social skills development, communication, behavior, and sensory integration. Programs sometimes include several treatment components coordinated to assist a person with autism. For example, one individual's program may consist of speech therapy, social skill development and the use of medication, all within a structured behavior program. Another child's may include social skill development, sensory integration and dietary changes. No one program or diet is perfect for every person with autism. It's important to try several approaches and find the ones that work best on an individual basis.

Important cornerstones in program and education for children and young ones are clarity, structure and predictability. Structure can be introduced in time, space and activity. Introducing structure does not mean that the child/young one himself is to be structured but that the surroundings are fitted to the child.

The structure should be inviting, and offer safety and positive confirmation. The structure may never be an end but it is a means to support the child/young one. The structure can be offered with help of photos, drawings and pictograms or written texts, depending on the possibilities and needs of the child.

With all of that said, parents and professionals need to work together. Teachers should have some understanding of the child's behavior and communication skills at home, and parents should let teachers know about their expectations as well as what techniques work at home. Open communication between school staff and parents can lead to better evaluation of a student's progress. Community goals like purchasing meals and grocery shopping should be reinforced through work at school, just as parents' goals for their child outside of school, such as the development of leisure activities, should be reinforced. Cooperation between parents and professionals can lead to increased success for the individual with autism.

Academic goals need to be tailored to the individual's intellectual ability and functioning level. Some children may need help in understanding social situations and developing appropriate responses. Others may exhibit aggressive or self-injurious behavior, and need assistance managing their behaviors. No one program will meet the needs of all individuals with the disability, so it is important to find the program or programs that best fit your child's needs. Exactly like with treatment approaches, educational programs should be tailored to your child's individual needs, be flexible and be re-evaluated on a regular basis.

27.5 Available resources for special children

There is no more painful experience for parent or sibling than knowing that his or her most precious child or beloved sibling is diagnosed with a lifetime condition such as autism.

Considered as the most common form of developmental disorder in the group of autism spectrum disorders (ASDs), autism is known to affect people across the globe regardless of race, gender and overall status in life.

Characterized by impaired social interaction problems with others, autism is known to affect not only the patient's social skills but also his or her means of communicating, whether verbal or nonverbal. It is evident in his unusual, routine or repetitive and limited lines of interests and set of activities.

Studies show that autism can be detected as early as the infancy stage. Infants who cannot respond to their parents or other people, those who tend to be absorbed by a certain thing for long periods of time, those who do not respond when their names are called, and those who shun eye contact with others have early tendencies of autism.

In toddlers, autism can be detected if the child starts to withdraw from people, stops communicating with a specific group, and develops indifference to other people. Autism in the preschool stage can also be determined if the child shows difficulty in understanding and interpreting others' thoughts and feelings, cannot take in social cues from a person like a facial expression or tone of voice, and has a hard time showing empathy because they lack it.

Another distinct sign of autism in children is repetitive activities or movements like sudden twirling or rocking and recurrent self-abusive behaviors like heavy banging of their heads and biting themselves. Delayed speech is also another noticeable symptom of autism as well as less sensitivity to pain but over-sensitivity to various sensory stimulations such as mild touch or soft sound.

These are just some of the behaviors that indicate autism. While some of them may seem normal, parents should be very observant of their child's behavior because the range in impact of these symptoms or behavior can be extreme and disabling in the long term.

Available resources for special children

Teaching a "special" child can be exhausting and draining, especially if the parents do not know the proper way to do it. But parents with autistic children are often unaware of the many resources available for them and for the education of their children. With these various support systems and institutions, parents and other family members can learn to adjust and eventually thrive.

One of the most reliable public resources for educating an ASD child is the school. In fact, a school with a system designed for the ASD child can be an enormous resource and help. Teachers with a deep understanding of the disorder and experience in training and teaching autistic children can help you guide their learning. By building on the child's interests, they encourage the child to show his or her talents in various fields such as art, music, mathematics, or memory.

Today, there are many special schools for autistic children that employ trained and qualified staff. But, if your budget cannot afford this specific type of schooling, you can choose from various public schools that offer special curricula for autistic children. Several public schools even have exceptional education departments with programs that are designed to meet the needs of ASD children.

Besides schooling, another means of educating ASD children is by incorporating various alternative treatments such as special diets or a facilitated communication strategy for the child. Although these approaches have not been proven scientifically, they can be effective for your child. You can also ask around, especially parents who have autistic children, on how they teach them. Some of the treatments may work for your child, but make sure that you consult a professional first.

Lastly, you can opt for the service of occupational therapists (OTs) in teaching an ASD child because they are trained to teach special children to improve various motor delays such as writing, dressing, cutting, and coloring.

27.6 The ABCs of teaching social skills

Experts say that one of the best things parents can do before they start teaching their child with ASD is to talk to other parents who are in the same situation. They can get advice on effective methods and treatments for teaching ASD children with basic social skills. But, before trying any method or alternative treatment, parents should discuss it with their physician first.

The following are some tips for parents before they start teaching their children the basic social skills they need to learn:

- Muster lots of patience. Since the symptoms of autism are characterized by repetitive activities and poor social skills, parents should be patient with their children, especially in behavior management.

- Educate yourself. Read all you can about the disorder and how to teach your child basic social skills. It will also help if you familiarize yourself with disability rights so you know what your child's rights are when it comes to government assistance, education, and possible benefits.

- Familiarize yourself with Non-Profit Organizations (NGOs) that focus on autism so you can get help in teaching your child when it comes to social skills.

- Don't stop giving your child treatments. Autism affects your child's language development; that is why you need to continue giving him or her speech therapy while you're teaching him or her other social skills.

- Don't force the special child to do a task. Studies show that autistic people strongly oppose any changes in their monotonous set of activities or routine. So it is not advisable for parents to repeatedly drill a task into a child because it can cause trauma.

The teaching attitude
Teaching an ASD child can be a major stressor in the lives of parents, especially when they are still confused and frustrated. The best thing to do is to be the best parent any child could have: patient, understanding, loving, caring, and persistent. Social skills such as saying "hello," taking turns, sharing, waiting, listening, potty training, and staying on topic or practicing reciprocal conversation can help your child to live as normal a life as possible.

The following are just some of the steps for teaching your autistic child basic social skills.

1. Target one skill at a certain time. By doing this, you can promote understanding and achieve success in the goal of teaching him or her a specific social skill. It will also be beneficial for you both to break down a set of social skills and work on each skill individually.

2. Practice positive reinforcement. Reward the child for learning the targeted skill. Other external reinforcements may be required to motivate your child. All you need to do is to explain the importance of the skill in an easy-to-understand manner.

3. Teach each social skill in a 1:1 setting. Autistic children can easily be distracted by certain things around them so it would be advisable to teach them in a place where there are no possible distractions in order to get an initial response.

4. Work on individual skills in different settings. After the child has mastered a specific social skill, parents or educators should begin teaching another skill in a different setting. This will allow the child to differentiate one skill from another. To maintain a specific skill that has been mastered, use verbal praise.

5. Always be consistent. In teaching social skills to special children, consistency is the main key for success.

6. Take time to evaluate the child regularly. By doing this, you can get enough information about their personality, weaknesses and strengths. Once you have this information, you will know how to teach a specific social skill to a child.

7. Assess the child's readiness. Before teaching any social skill to an autistic child, make sure that you have already assessed his or her readiness. This is very important because his or her interest in learning the social skill will be the main key to succeeding in the teaching process.

27.7 Teaching students with autism

In the United States, the Individuals with Disabilities Education Act was passed in 1990. It "mandates suitable educational plans for children with developmental disabilities or delays," including autism[xcvi]. It states that the government must grant a free and equal education to all students, regardless of their disability or learning delay.

A widely discussed subject that is centered on education is the inclusion of students with disabilities in the classroom. Students with autism are being included in regular classrooms with students who do not have disabilities. The non-disabled students will model appropriate behaviors for the student with autism. Studies have shown that inclusion is beneficial to both the student with autism and their non-disabled peers[xcvii].

When teaching a child with autism, Egel suggests focusing on two areas: "the use of functional activities and an effort to make programs appropriate for the student's developmental level and chronological age." Smith, Polloway, Patton, and Dowdy[xcviii] also point out that educational programs should teach the child life skills and help them to deal with daily needs.

When teaching children with autism, a structured learning environment is important. It is helpful to be consistent and to develop predictable routines[xcix]. Additional strategies for the teacher to use when teaching a student with autism are listed in the book by Smith, Polloway, Patton, and Dowdy. They include:

- Speak slowly and state positively what to do (ex. let's walk)
- Provide visual instruction and information as well as verbal
- Encourage communication by responding to words rather than to behavior
- Provide written words and pictures to aid communication
- Use cooperative learning to promote social interaction

Peer buddies and peer tutoring can be used in the classroom to help teach the child with autism. In the peer buddy approach, the child with autism is paired with a student of normal development. The children are encouraged to talk and play to promote social interaction. Peer tutoring again involves one typical student and one child with autism, but the child with autism is being tutored. This approach can be varied by having the child with autism tutor a younger, normally developed student.[c] These approaches are most appropriate when the child has high functioning autism.

Integrated play groups are also useful to help teach the student appropriate behavior. The teacher can provide a structured environment that optimizes the interaction between the child with autism and the other students[ci]. Fennick and Royle point out that when a child with autism is allowed to play with children without disabilities, they will use appropriate play and social behaviors. They found that the results were even more dramatic when the child with autism was allowed to participate in their favorite play[cii] activity[ciii].

27.8 Giving your child with Asperger's syndrome an education

Working with children affected by Asperger's syndrome is truly a challenge to most teachers, young or experienced. This is especially due to the fact that they are different individuals with needs that should be especially studied and provided for.

Superficially, they may appear to be like normal children. However, a quick look at how they behave will tell you otherwise. They may also present exceptional talents such as keen memories or paying attention to details, which may not be found in children with a 'normal' brain. Some may even be mistaken for geniuses who can store large amounts of data in their brain without making mistakes recalling these facts.

However, many of them are weak in comprehension and have poor cognition. But as a teacher to your pupil or child, it is only fitting that you discover his fortes and try working on them. No child is ever deprived of all capacities. Somehow, there are skills that you might find worth the risk of training.

Like most of the developmental disorders, Asperger's syndrome affects the communication facilities of a person affected by it. Therefore, the major areas concerned are those that are closely related with language, speech, and social interaction. These also include both verbal and non-verbal communication.

Because of these lacks, children with Asperger's syndrome fail to recognize social cues and facial expressions, and in general they lack empathy. They may express obsession with details of their own interests but may fail to give the other party a chance to talk and discuss his interests in depth.

The aggravation of this syndrome may range from mild to severe. Thus, the categories in between are truly hard to recognize and we still don't have enough understanding of the true nature and root of the disease.

Because Asperger's syndrome is said to be high-functioning autism, people rarely recognize its presence until the signs have become extremely obvious. This means that the syndrome normally begins to materialize at grade school, when the child is exposed to the world beyond home.

Immaturity, failure to communicate well, and misbehavior are among the most prominent signs of this syndrome in school. However students do quite well when it comes to academic affairs. They normally outshine other children in specific fields. But when they are faced with issues relating to communication and social interaction, they seem to have problems.

Special education is not always applicable to children with Asperger's syndrome since many of them have average and above average intelligence and in most cases are capable of behaving normally.

Another thing that you should watch out for is that each child with Asperger's syndrome requires a different method of special education. Like most disorders and diseases directly related to problems in the brain, these children must have an especially structured form of learning that is well adapted to their conditions and capacities.

To better maximize the child's potential and your time in teaching, it is advised that parent do follow-ups at home. This will help best since the child will have a continuous environment for learning. Parents must take an active role in seeking the thresholds for their children when it comes to learning.

Summary

Education requires planning one's study time, reading books, determining which are the main issues and which are only side issues, and interacting with instructors and classmates. These are all skills where the autistic student is severely challenged. Thus, the instructors must be heavily involved in helping the autistic student to overcome these challenges, and the parents should pay particularly close attention to the child's education. As with all matters related to your autistic child, an educational program must cater to your child's individual needs and be closely monitored, because every autistic child is different, just as every non-autistic child is different.

Chapter 28 @Leisure

Someone with autism will mostly want to spend his time on his own. Nowadays the computer is becoming an important leisure activity. Problems with the surroundings arise when time is spent with others. If participation in larger groups takes place in a structured setting, for instance a chess club, where it is very clear what is to be expected, this kind of activity will normally not meet much resistance. If one offers an autistic person the freedom to choose which leisure activity he wants, it probably will not be a group activity.

The characteristic of leisure time is that it has no obligations and it should not impose pressure on someone.

In groups, however, obligations often arise as well as peer pressure. For people with autism, this is a reason not to choose group activities. In this sense, the preferred leisure activity will imply fewer problems with the surroundings, because autistic people will often make solitary choices.

However, resistance to change and new things can hinder the autistic person from going out and trying new activities. Someone may wish to try a new activity during a holiday but be afraid to take the first step. In this case stimulating and supporting surroundings can help.

Leisure activities
Leisure means time to be filled up. People with an ASD generally have many difficulties in imagining what can be done with time to spare: how to oversee and organize it, how much time an activity might take, and with whom this time should be spent.

Many people with an ASD have therefore trouble dealing with their free time and for them leisure is difficult to get through. They prefer to have something programmed or to continue working. For this reason, people with an ASD are grateful for support offered by someone who teaches them to pass free time, to organize it, and to help them oversee the time/activity. Sometimes it is necessary to help children play; e.g. what are the possibilities of specific games. It is often difficult to find suitable recreation for people with an ASD.

Taking part in group activities is limited because it requires social skills, exactly the weak points of people with an ASD.

A number of parents of children/youngsters with an ASD choose not to inform the supervisors of the handicap. Others do inform supervisors and they do this with or without consulting the child/young one. Experience teaches us that informing and advising supervisors leads to more positive experiences because more understanding, support, explanation and protection can be offered.

One cannot always predict whether an activity will suit someone with an ASD. Much depends on specific interests and possibilities of the person with an ASD. In general, individually directed and/or structured activities are more effective. Activities such as judo or other defensive sports, athletics, chess, computer clubs, and scouting often prove to be suitable.

Autism and the Christmas Holidays
Many parents of children with autism or other neuropsychological disorders mention that the Christmas holidays are a particularly difficult time for them. Of course, any holiday can be difficult for any child because of the temporary changes in routine, but Christmas is usually the most difficult holiday for parents of children with autism or other neuropsychological disorders.

There are no surefire techniques to use with your child that will insure a "Martha Stewart Christmas." Families who have children with autism or other neuropsychological disorders have used the eight tips below to make their Christmas better.

Children with autism are visual learners, so take pictures of what is going to happen at Christmas – the tree, the gifts, the relatives – and start showing these pictures to the child with autism several weeks before Christmas. Tell a little story to the child while he/she is looking at the picture about how to behave, what's going to happen, and what the child can do if it is too much. If possible, include your child in the pictures. A picture of the child going to his room to escape the noise and confusion when he/she gets overloaded seems to help, too.

1. Try to keep your child in his or her usual routine as much as possible.

2. Sensory over-stimulation – the lights, the sounds, the smells, the relatives touching your child – are the main culprits during the holidays. Eliminating or minimizing these culprits is your best bet.

3. Some families who have children with autism or other neuropsychological disorders wait until Christmas Eve to put up their tree and decorate.

4. Some families let their children do all the decorating. The child may line up or stack decorations rather than decorate in the traditional way, but so what?

5. Rather than trying to do the Christmas shopping with your child in a crowded, noisy mall, many families shop by catalog or online and let the child point to or circle the toys he/she wants. Websites such as www.stars4kidz.com offer a variety of toys for children with autism or other neuropsychological disorders. Just type "autism toys" into your search engine.

6. Tactile toys are often a better choice for children with autism or other neuropsychological disorders. Toys that make sounds or involve too

much stimulation or are too complex may cause an adverse reaction in the child. As mentioned above there are websites that sell toys designed for children with autism or other neuropsychological disorders. Try ordering some of these toys and then let your child select the ones to play with as they are unwrapped.

7. Talk to relatives before they come over about the best way to behave with your child.

8. Generally, children with autism or other neuropsychological disorders do better in the morning than in the late afternoon or evening when they are tired. It may be better to schedule Christmas events at these times.

The parents of children with autism or other neuropsychological disorders need to relax themselves. Often the child picks up on the parents' stress and that is enough to ruin Christmas.

Last but not least, realize that you are probably not going to have perfect food, perfect decorations, and perfect gifts. Christmas with children with autism or other neuropsychological disorders may not be traditional, but it can still have real meaning.[civ]

Holidays

Holidays mean a lot of excitement, celebration, festivities, and spending time with the family. It might sound very exciting for us, but can be very tedious and overwhelming for an autistic child.

Does that mean that parenting a child suffering with autism means no holidays at all? Certainly not!

With a few precautions and tips you can spent a wonderful vacation with your family and your autistic child.

Here are a few points to remember:
1. Keep the time span shorter. A reduced time limit means no over-tiring schedules for the child. A lot of emotions and excitement can be a major problem trigger for the autistic child. A shorter time span will help him balance himself as it won't be as overwhelming for the child.

2. Let him pick the activities of his choice. If the child is not willing, do not force him to join any activities. For instance, when the whole family is having dinner at the table, your child might not want to join them, preferring to eat in a calm place. Let him do so, as this will comfort him the most.

3. Stick to your daily schedule as much as possible. If your child is used to sleeping at 8 in the night, do not keep him awake forcibly for longer hours. If it is unavoidable, try giving him an afternoon nap. Even your family would not like to meet an irritated kid. Also, handling a sleepy child will also be a tough job for you as a parent.

4. Distribute the activities over a few days. It is not necessary to visit all the relatives in a single day. Be aware that an autistic child cannot handle a lot of new acquaintances together. Give him time and breaks so that he enjoys the meeting and family atmosphere rather than getting stressed. Even the family would love to meet your child when he is in the right mood and frame of mind.

5. Do not drag your child in to long hours of shopping. Christmas rush in the malls and markets often annoy adults as well, so why would you expect your child to handle it easily? A child with autism will naturally feel uneasy. So, look out for a good qualified care taker and let your child be at home while you are shopping. Otherwise, leave the child with your spouse, or other responsible family member. Even as a parent, it would be tough for you to handle your child in such scenarios.

6. Do not open all the presents at one go. Kids are naturally attracted to presents and gifts. Their excitement is worth seeing as they open the wrapper and unfurl the surprise. These emotions could be too overwhelming for the child and could act as triggers in autism. Opening a few presents at a time will help your child bear the excitement and enjoy the festivity of Christmas in a better way. Let him relish a few pieces and after a few days open the rest.

7. Do not disturb your child's diet for the sake of fun. If your child is following a special diet plan, be firm and ensure that none of the family members share restricted food with the child. Some people might be of the opinion that your diet plans are not beneficial or are not worthy enough. You must stick to your decision and follow your beliefs for the benefit of your child.

8. Be with you autistic child and let him feel the vacations. Holidays at the core are all about having fun with the family. Do not alienate your child from the group. Include him in the fun and enjoyment along with the rest of the people and let him feel the vacation mood. Be optimistic and thank God for everything in life and make it a point to pass on this optimism to your child.

9. Reward your child for his good behavior during the outings. Children love to face challenges and win prizes. Reward your child for being good and behaving well while being with the family. This wll give him a sense of achievement and drive him to behave better and avoid all sorts of mischievous behavior.

10. Be patient when your child gets stressed out or shows anxiety.

Being a parent of an autistic child may require a great deal of planning and patience. Yet, during holidays, try to forget the problems of daily schedules and have a wonderful time with your kid. Your stress and agitation will surely add to his anxiety and stress. Count on all the good things in life and relax your mind and heart.

Summary
Leisure time is, by definition, time when you aren't compelled to do anything. To an autistic person, who needs structure and routine, it can be painful. Given a choice, the autistic will choose solo activities, or else a group activity with a great deal of structure, such as a chess club. Social skills are the weakness of autistic people.

Holidays are also stressful times for the autistic because they represent a deliberate, chaotic disruption of normal routines. But that doesn't mean that you can't make the holidays meaningful and enjoyable for your autistic child.

Chapter 29 @Work

Depending on the degree of autism, the work situation can demand much of autistic people. They are generally very conscientious and want to do their work well, but it is very difficult for them to know when something is good enough. They can become very uncertain, the result being that they regularly ask if something is well. This can irritate their colleagues and their employer.

Another aspect of work is interaction with colleagues and customers. The degree of development of social skills and the possibility to assess social interaction plays a large role.

At work the structure is only partly clear. It is expected that people understand what must be done and take initiative in doing it.

People with autism frequently overlook things because they cannot be busy with two things at the same time and are easily confused by a quantity of tasks.

Furthermore, it also generally takes them longer to do tasks according to a certain routine. They must continue to concentrate on what must be done for quite a while before the task becomes a habit. The consequence is that they are less flexible, because they must concentrate and because they must make a lot of effort to change their routine. This also makes it cumbersome to do new things at the same time. It is advisable for them to learn only one new task at a time.

In addition to these weaknesses, there are also strengths that need to be mentioned: the effort it takes people with autism to distinguish main issues from side issues ensures that they have a sharp eye for detail.

This talent makes them exceptionally suited for jobs that demand a great deal of precision. Being an employer of someone with autism means that you must be willing to be flexible in organizing the work, in the tasks that must be carried out, and in the way tasks are presented.

If that succeeds, the person with autism proves to be someone who is precise, conscientious, and reliable, someone who keeps his promises, someone who has an eye for detail and is well informed on the rules that apply in the company.

Finding a paying job does not suit everyone with autism. Autism is an impairment which can lead to restrictions in several fields of functioning. At work you need skills in different areas such as social contacts, information processing, and planning.

Frequently, adaptations in the workplace are necessary. These adaptations mostly concern rest, structure, reducing the stress of high expectations, and reducing unexpected tasks. Inertia in information processing and working more slowly than other people is a problem people with autism will face.

The quality of the work done can be very good; the quantity however can vary from less to problematic. Someone with autism in general works very precisely and has an eye for details. For some activities this can be necessary. On the job, giving the person with autism activities to exploit his special qualities can do the trick.

The solution to the 'work problem' can be finding a suitable job. People with autism often look for jobs in which they can help other people. In this kind of work the appeal for adequate social interaction is eminent.

If a nurse enters a hospital room, she must assess within a few seconds which patient needs her attention first. To do this, she must use the patient information, the course of the sickness, her general knowledge, recent events, and the picture of the patient now lying in his bed. She must form this mental picture of all the patients in a very short time. People with autism need time to be able make such an assessment.

Another aspect of caring professions is that there is much need for cooperation. You must know what your colleague does or what you can expect of him. For people with autism this is an extra difficulty.

Continuous moving about between various tasks can lead to problems. Performing administrative work and taking telephone calls at the same time can prove to be a problem. People with autism need more time to return to their original task and thus they make more mistakes if they are interrupted. Adaptations in the nature of the activities can be a solution. It can also be helpful to incorporate less difficult activities in periods when the telephone must be answered.

To work for someone with autism means a mixture of very positive and cumbersome characteristics and a larger claim on accompaniment by the surroundings.

Summary
The workplace traditionally requires social skills and multi-tasking, making work very challenging for the autistic. They require more time to learn new skills, they must concentrate on what they are doing, they require more time to turn these new skills into habits, and they can be inflexible. But they excel in jobs which require precision and attention to detail. They are honest, reliable and hard working. If an autistic employee knows what to do, he or she will do high quality work. Quantity might be variable, however. They are also attracted to work in which they can help other people. If you can find a suitable job for an autistic person which plays to his or her strengths rather than being impeded by his or her weaknesses, or if you as an employer have the flexibility to create such a work environment for an autistic employee, the results will be satisfying to everyone involved.

Chapter 30 Independence

For many people with Asperger's syndrome, living on their own is the usual situation. The fact that independent living is not suitable for everyone only becomes obvious after the step is taken and things do not work out the way they are supposed to.

Living on your own means waking up in time for work or study, paying your own bills, keeping your house clean, staying healthy by eating good meals, keeping up good personal hygiene, and keeping in contact with your neighbors. The attention and energy spent on these tasks must be in balance with other life tasks such as work, training, relations, and friendships. In people with autism this balance can be upset.

Living on your own, with all the tasks that go with this responsibility, can take someone with autism so much energy that there there's no energy left for other matters.

Constantly being forced to remember the things that have to be done can also drain the person. These people have to put in more effort to make even the simplest of tasks succeed. A practical helpful solution can be a drawing board or school board to write all the do's and don't upon. Even then, getting things done can be quite difficult because this person might not be able to judge correctly when things are done sufficiently.

People with autism often have peace of mind after everything is done, even the finest details. An autistic person is uncertain when judging whether or not something is done adequately, which makes this peace of mind difficult to find. However, the repetition of behavior brings rest and decreases the feelings of anxiety.

Another problem with living on your own is the difficulty in bringing structure and keeping control of all the necessary things that need to be done to keep the household going.

The household can be neglected and the administration not kept up, as a result of which bills are not paid. Frequently, professional support is necessary, but it is important that this reflects the wishes and possibilities of the one with autism.

Within the framework of experimenting with independence, someone with autism can restrain its surroundings a lot. Sometimes it is not simple to understand the reason for the 'keeping back' behavior of autistic people.

If you live independently, you have to handle and maintain ordinary contacts in your neighborhood. For the person with autism this is not always easy. Do you have to let in someone who asks for a cup of sugar? Who do you have to say hello to and what does it mean if your neighbor ignores you in the early morning? Does he dislike you or is he simply only half awake?

People with autism who have no regular daily routine are often tempted to change their day and night rhythm. Sometimes they enjoy being awake at night because it is much quieter then. The passage of the day into the night can be a difficult moment, as a result of which they will postpone more and more and start living at night. At night, however, they must take into account the sounds that they themselves produce. Sometimes this is difficult for people with autism, because they are not conscious of the noise they make.

Living arrangements for the adult with an Autism Spectrum Disorder

Independent living
Some adults with an ASD are able to live entirely on their own. Others can live semi-independently in their own home or apartment provided they get assistance with solving major problems, such as personal finances or dealing with the government agencies that provide services to people with disabilities. Family, a professional agency, or another type of provider can provide this assistance.

Living at home
Government funds are sometimes available for families who choose to have their adult child with ASD live at home. These programs include Supplemental Security Income (SSI), Social Security Disability Insurance (SSDI), Medicaid waivers, and others. Information about these programs is available from the Social Security Administration (SSA). An appointment with a local SSA office is a good first step to take in understanding the programs for which the young adult is eligible.

Foster homes and skill development homes
Some families open their homes to provide long-term care to unrelated adults with disabilities. When the home teaches self-care and housekeeping skills and arranges leisure activities, it is called a "skill development" home.

Supervised group living
People with disabilities frequently live in group homes or apartments staffed by professionals who help the individuals with basic needs. These often include meal preparation, housekeeping, and personal care needs. Higher functioning people may be able to live in a home or apartment where staff only visits a few times a week. These people generally prepare their own meals, go to work, and conduct other daily activities on their own.

Institutions
Although the trend in recent decades has been to avoid placing people with disabilities into long-term care institutions, this alternative is still available for people with ASD who need intensive, constant supervision. Unlike many

institutions years ago, today's facilities view residents as individuals with human needs and offer opportunities for recreation and simple but meaningful work.

Summary

Living alone and independently is a balancing act for anyone. Work and study, finances, hygiene, health, and neighbors require attention and energy. So do other life tasks such as training, relationships, and friends. The person with ASD must concentrate harder on each of these tasks, and thus may not have the energy to do them all. Things can be neglected, and the problems only become obvious after the person has tried living alone and discovered that it didn't work.

If living independently doesn't work, other options are semi-independent living, living at home, foster homes, skill development homes, supervised group living, and institutions. Some combination of these methods, or moving from one to another as is most suitable at a given time in a person's life, is also an option.

Chapter 31 Planning a future

As your child becomes an adult, through treatment and individualized education, his or her symptoms may lessen. However, autism is likely to affect the individual throughout his or her life. They will probably always have difficulty relating to others and communicating effectively. The good news is that many adults with autism are able to live meaningful, productive, and independent lives. And, for those who are severely affected and unable to live on their own, some early planning and public resources can help to assure the best possible life for your adult child.

Planning for your autistic child's future

It's important to start thinking at an early stage about how your child's life will play out. This is especially true if the child will need lifelong care. Having a plan for the future will alleviate stress for you, family members, and even the autistic child.

Unfortunately, research in the United States shows that less than 20% of families with disabled children have planned for the future. Making a plan can be difficult and even overwhelming, but because it is such a crucial step in your child's life, finding the help you need to develop the plan should be a priority. Professional services are available to assist with future planning, but they can be costly. If you find the cost to be too high, you can create a good plan on your own.

A comprehensive plan should be formulated and put in writing so that all concerned are clear about your wishes and those of the child (if he or she is capable of participating in planning activities). Professional financial planners recommend that the plan cover four key areas:

1. Lifestyle
2. Legal
3. Financial
4. Government Benefits

If you're creating the plan with minimal or no professional assistance, breaking the plan down into these four areas may make the task more manageable for you. Tackle each piece of the plan separately and work through it until it's done.

1. The Lifestyle section of the plan should include information about:

- Where your child will live
- Personal care needs
- Whether or not your child will have ongoing educational needs and the provisions for those needs

- Career or job goals and planning
- Social life
- Religious activities
- Health care
- Behavioral needs
- Legal guardianship
- Funeral arrangements

When considering your child's personal care, think about special needs for bathing, dressing, and toileting as well as activities he or she enjoys, dietary needs and medication. Make certain you specifically explain all of these things in writing. If your child has special "quirks" such as methods of communicating thoughts and feelings or routines that help him or her get through the day, it may be helpful to actually videotape these activities since they may be difficult to explain in writing.

2. The Legal portion of the plan must address the family's wishes for any assets that are to be distributed. An executor must be appointed. It may also be a good idea to set up a trust. This section of the plan is likely to require the assistance of a lawyer. However, if you've done your research and have carefully thought through what you want to include in the plan and steps you would like to take, you can minimize the time involvement of a lawyer, and therefore your costs.

3. Financial planning may be the most difficult and daunting part of future planning. The first step is to establish a monthly plan based on the needs the child has today and to project that plan into the future. You will then need to make a determination of how much money must be deposited into a trust to ensure the child will have enough money for the rest of his or her life. Remember that autistic children have normal life expectancy.

Finally, the family will need to find a way to fund the trust. Consider any stocks, mutual funds, IRAs, real estate, or other assets you currently have. In addition, it's never too late to begin saving for your child's future.

4. The final portion of the plan, Government Benefits, will depend on where you live. Look into laws, services, and benefits available to your child. If your child is entitled to benefits, don't be afraid to claim them. Your child will need all the help he or she can get.

Finding the right living arrangements
There are several options for living arrangements for adults with autism. Potential arrangements include:

- Living independently: If your child is able to live on his or her own, the decision about where to live is a pretty simple one. If your child needs just a little help with major tasks like financial planning, consider hiring someone to assist with these responsibilities.

- Remaining at home: If you choose to have your child continue living with you, there may be financial assistance available to you from the government.

- Skill development homes or foster care: Some people accept people with disabilities into their homes and provide long-term care. When those people help the autistic person to continue learning skills, such as personal and housekeeping skills, and assist the person with engaging in social activities, the home is considered a "skill development" home.

- Supervised group living: Group homes where professionals handle day-to-day tasks like cleaning, meals, and personal care are available for adults with disabilities. And, if your child is capable of handling most aspects of everyday life on his or her home, there are group homes available in which professionals only check on the person a couple of times during the week.

- Institutions: While the term "institution" has a negative connotation and many people today choose to avoid this option, it should be noted that good, long-term care institutions are available where residents are treated as individuals with important needs.

Making the leap from school to a career or job

Probably the best advice that can be given regarding helping your child to make the leap from school to a career or job is to take it slowly. In fact, this is the advice that Temple Grandin, Ph.D., an extremely successful adult with autism, gives. Dr. Grandin offers the following tips to help people with autism find the right employment for them:

1. Slow transition: Allow the child to begin working while still at school. This could be part-time work or a few hours of volunteering each week.

2. Find employers who are supportive: Locate people who are prepared to work with your child and who can accept and incorporate his or her unique abilities and interests into the workplace.

3. Look for a mentor: A mentor might be someone who works in the career field your child is interested in. The mentor should be someone who can help your child learn important social skills as well as career-specific ones.

4. Take the time to help employers and other employees learn about autism: Employers and employees need to be given the opportunity to learn more about autism and your child's special needs in terms of the labor force. They should also be assisted in understanding how autistic people interact socially and what your child's specific limitations are. Helping others to understand autism and your child will avoid situations that could get your child fired.

5. Consider freelance work: Freelance work provides your child the opportunity to have meaningful employment while avoiding difficult social situations.

6. Create a skills portfolio: In a normal employment situation, the interview process is largely about personality, the ability to effectively communicate, and being able to work with others. Because of the unique social aspects of autism, it's important that your child learns to sell his or her skills instead. If possible, avoid the personnel department altogether and try to get directly to those in charge of the area he or she would work in – they are more likely to respect your child's skills.

Finding a fitting job

Many adults with autism find employment in areas that were once their obsessions. For example, Temple Grandin's occupation as a designer of livestock handling equipment grew out of one of her childhood fixations.

However, careers and jobs must build on the unique abilities and strengths of the person with autism while minimizing weaknesses.

Dr. Grandin states that most people with autism have poor short-term memory. For that reason, employment in the following fields should be avoided:

- Cashiering
- Restaurant cook
- Waiting tables
- Dealing cards in a casino
- Dispatching
- Taking dictation
- Receptionist
- Telephone operator

The job your child does take should take into consideration the way he or she processes information. People who are "visual thinkers" should look for jobs that don't require them to process information quickly and that make good use of their long term memories and visual thinking skills. Jobs that meet this description include:

- Computer programmer
- Commercial artist
- Photographer
- Equipment designer
- Animal trainer
- Veterinary technician
- Mechanic
- Computer or small appliance repairman
- Web page designer

- Video game designer

Those who fit into the category of "non-visual thinkers" are usually good with numbers, facts, and music. Good jobs for these individuals include:

- Accountant
- Librarian
- Engineer
- Journalist
- Copy editor
- Taxi driver
- Statistician
- Physicist
- Mathematician

Those who are non-verbal or have limited verbal skills may find employment in the following areas:

- Library reshelfer
- Factory worker
- Janitor
- Shelf stocker
- Warehouse worker
- Gardener
- Data entry personnel
- Fast food

Financial and insurance implications

Caring for a person with autism can be very costly. Treatment may be ongoing throughout the person's life. The United States spend $90 billion annually on autism related issues and 90% of this amount is spent on adult services. That said, it should come as no surprise that autism can be a great financial burden on families and adults with autism. Families who don't receive government benefits typically spend about $12,000 yearly to ensure their autistic child receives the appropriate treatment.

While many people have insurance coverage, a great number of insurance companies don't cover autism treatments or cover them to a lesser extent than treatments for other conditions. In fact, research shows that in the year 2000 43% of the families with autistic children were denied coverage for the disorder. That is because autism is classified as a "mental disorder" and mental disorders are generally not covered to the extent of medical disorders.

Insurance companies claim that covering autism and other Pervasive Developmental Disorders would be too costly. However, studies show that the cost to insurance companies would actually be fairly insignificant while taking a huge burden off the families themselves.

The best defense against unwarranted expenses is to educate oneself in applicable laws and government services. Apply for those services and benefits for which your child is qualified and perform a follow-up to make certain your request is processed. Speak to other parents in the same situation and find out which resources have worked for them.

It is especially important to look into the question whether or not your adult child with autism will be eligible for insurance benefits through his or her employer. If so, determine whether the coverage will pay for any autism treatments he or she is receiving. Because of privacy laws, your child may need to complete paperwork to allow you to discuss coverage issues with the insurance company. Make certain this paperwork is on file for anyone who will be assisting your child with medical claims. This, too, should be a provision for which you make arrangements in your child's plan for the future.

If your child will not be eligible for health insurance through his or her employer, determine which governmental aids may be available. Your child may qualify for free health coverage or treatment. Sign your child up for each and every one of these benefits to ensure his or her needs are completely met.

Strategies for everyday living
Financial and employment issues aside, just carrying out normal daily activities like getting out of bed and getting ready for work can present unique challenges for adult autistics. Below are some ideas for handling some common everyday problems adults with autism face. It should be noted that these strategies might not work for every person with autism since each individual has a different set of symptoms. Or, the strategies may need to be modified to meet individual needs.

- Make very detailed checklists. Include each step that must be completed. For example, a morning checklist might include things like "brush teeth," "eat breakfast," "shave," and "shower." They should also include items the person needs to take with them for the day, like keys or a lunch.

- Use a PDA to remain organized and provide reminders for tasks that must be completed.

- Get rid of any clutter in the home. This will help you stay organized and help eliminate confusion.

- When considering tasks that need to be done, decide whether you really need to do them. And, if you do need to do them, don't worry about perfection.

- Follow a daily routine. It will eventually become habit.

- Break big jobs like housecleaning down into small jobs, like cleaning a portion of a room. This makes tasks more manageable and you'll be able to complete them in short periods of time.

- Ask for help when you need it.

- Use specific areas for specific tasks. For example, if you work out of your home, set aside a desk or other area that you use only for work. This will allow the space to serve as your reminder that when you are there, you are supposed to be working.

- Use pillboxes to help you take the proper dosages of your medication. Adults with autism often forget if they took their medication or not, which can lead to overdosing. The pillbox should be divided into morning, afternoon, and evening sections and should have a section for each day of the week. Make taking medication part of your checklists.

People with autism may have difficulty remembering which clothing items they wore recently. This may lead to wearing certain things more often than is acceptable in the non-autistic world. Try always hanging clean clothes up on the right side of the closet and taking clothes to wear from the left side of the closet. This will keep your wardrobe rotating.

Summary
Early intervention for your ASD child is necessary to meet his or her immediate needs, as we've discussed before, but it's also important to think about your autistic child's future at an early stage. Where will your child live when he or she is an adult? How will you manage the transition from school to career or job? What about financial considerations, insurance, social life, and religious activities? By deciding the answers to these questions early, based on your child's needs and abilities, and his or her input if he or she is able, and putting them in writing, you will have clear goals that you and your child can work toward as he or she grows into adulthood. This will lead to greater fulfillment for everyone and ensure a good quality of life for your autistic child. You can create this plan by yourself or you can get assistance.

A COURSE OF LIFE

Chapter 32 Autism and course of life

Another way to look at the impact of autism on an individual is to look at its impact through someone's course of life.

We will distinguish:
1. Babies and Toddlers
2. Childhood
3. Puberty/Adolescence
4. Maturity
5. Middle Age
6. The Elderly

In the previous chapters we outlined a picture of the nature of autism, the impact it has and the possible aids. It makes a large difference, of course, whether we are discussing with someone with autism, with Asperger's syndrome, or someone with autistic characteristics such as PDD-NOS.

32.1 Babies and toddlers

Being a baby involves rapid development in basic fields of feeling, seeing, eating, talking and walking. From a social point of view, attachment is a central feature. This means that the baby will try to attach to people in its surroundings; that means trying to bond with these people. It uses everything it has to bond: babbling, smiling, grabbing, and crying.[cv] Many autistic children resist or ignore contact with their parents as a baby. They often cry, they hold their arms limp along their body when they are picked up, they hardly if ever smile, and sometimes they push the other away.

The toddler too is actively involved in keeping his caretakers near to ensure help is there when it is needed.

Kids with autism are not able to do much bonding. This makes it more difficult not only for themselves but also for their surroundings. The caretaker, usually the mother, will try to make contact with the child. A parent may feel rejected when the baby doesn't make contact or even does not seem to be interested in making contact. The young child with autism seeks even less consolation or help and seems deeply involved within himself. Some parents will feel rejected. Others, however, will feel very close to their child because it will not break the symbiotic relationship with the caring parent.

So it is not a first example of the stubbornness phase, which is part of healthy development and is an illustration of the first separation from the parents, while the child keeps depending on the parent or caretaker at the same time.

The parent will keep supplying the help that is needed. As said before, some parents will feel rejected and others won't. The child will keep using the parent as if the parent was an instrumental part of itself. For instance it will grab its parent's arm and point to an object it would like to have. It doesn't reach the point of being able to function autonomously on its own. This is another illustration of the fact that the child has difficulty in bonding in a safe manner, because this child is not able to let loose. It hardly makes eye contact, and the gaze is often seen as empty, gazing past another person or fixating on the tip of somebody's nose. This gaze is perceived as 'penetrating.'

Bonding is a complicated social activity and requires development of social insights. It means actively working on the 'theory-of-mind,' which implies the development of a theory over one's own thoughts and feelings and those of others.

In this phase, children are not at all occupied with bonding. Sometimes they are still busy with subjects that ripen quicker with the average child. For instance the body still has to learn how to digest food, the immune system needs to be activated, their senses still need to develop further, their motor senses need more development too, language needs to be formed, and the child needs to be toilet trained.

Children with autism need a lot of energy to manage this development because this maturation passes at a slower pace. This can mean problems with being held, being cuddled, etc.

During childhood, development of cognitive skills and playing with other children is very important. Children with autism, however, are still busy bonding with people in their direct surroundings and still have problems understanding how the world turns. They are busy exploring and getting used to people in their direct vicinity and they are certainly not active in playing with each other in a social manner.

Kanner uses Frederick as an example. Frederick first pays attention to people around him and people coming to visit. When Frederick first gets to know his family he should already have been busy with finding friends at school, playing with other children in the sandbox in the playground.

Learning starts with copying actively. In its own way the child copies internally and externally what he sees and says 'yes' to the world around him. An autistic has problems copying and often stays trapped in what is known and familiar, showing safe repetitive behavior. The child seems to say 'no' to the world.

There is a tendency to stick with known territory (need for sameness) and repetition of the same behavior. Changes in surroundings are not accepted, because this makes the surroundings unrecognizable. The child is very frightened of the unknown and unexpected. This can lead to panic attacks and tantrums. Other children are often avoided because they show unpredicted behavior. This is caused by the autistic's inability to empathize with other children's interests, feelings and games. Sometimes the autistic child chooses a much younger child to play with. This child will have to follow the orders that the autistic child makes up according his own ideas and thoughts. Sometimes the child will adore and be totally fixated on an older favorite friend.

Children with autism are usually late in development and understanding reciprocity. As a result they 'use' other children for a longer period as a tool in their game without proper realization that the other child has needs of its own. They do not play games that coincide with their calendar age but often according to their 'development' age, which often is much younger.

The expectation that children with autism can easily get along with their peers is often too high. As a result the daily stress the autistic child feels rises. And thus daily rituals and obsessions increase.

Children with autism lose themselves often in certain subjects or manners. Trains and dinosaurs are very popular with autistic children. They give them the rest they need. Every child will have his own favorite subject. Many children will keep asking questions about their favorite topic endlessly. Sometimes certain stereotypical mannerisms will be endlessly repeated, like turning switches on and off, turning objects such as buttons, etc.

32.2 Childhood

Impairment in Language Use
Many autistic children do not reach the level of active language use. When there is no significant development in language skills before the age of six, the prognosis is dim and the child will stay autistic. Passive use of language (understanding spoken language) might be well developed, even though this might not seem obvious.

Speech develops more slowly and is filled with unripe elements and a different syntax. These children often do not talk about themselves as I but in the second or third person (pronominal reversal). They also tend to imitate adults with the same intonation or by changing each sentence in a question (echolalia).

Some children copy the adult's language perfectly without understanding exactly what the real meaning is (delayed echolalia). They often use a language with their own words and word combinations from existing words: neologism. Their voice melody is even, metallic, or insecure questioning. Other people's sayings are taken literally (literalness). Humor, jokes, etc. can thus become very threatening to an autistic child.

Impairment in handling information
Oversensitivity to sensory sensations makes these children often react with panic or anxiety when confronted with sudden or hefty sensations such as harsh noises or changes in light and darkness.

The skin can also be seen as a large sensory organ, and their skin isn't considered as a division between themselves and their surroundings. They are very receptive to changes in mood in their vicinity. They can, however, shut out outside impressions by pretending to be deaf or simply pretending not being able to see you. Sometimes they will lock themselves in a cupboard. Sometimes they can become panicky or start a screaming fit due to a small scratch on their hand, while a severe injury on for example their foot will hardly evoke a reaction.

The way they handle food might also be different. They might reject all kinds of food or might for instance only enjoy porridge; their senses are often used in a sensopatic (feel and act) manner: moving fingers quickly back and forth near their ears, moving their open hand up and down in front of their eyes, losing themselves in the changing light fall.

Some may kick on hearing noises. Background sounds are often heard in a crystal clear manner. There is a weak integration of sensory input. Keeping a bird's eye view and being able to distinguish important from unimportant things is lacking or costs a lot of effort. They often like to smell things or people and often put objects in their mouth. Remarkably, a lot of these children are fond of music or even musically talented.

Impairment in motoric and motorial development
Motoric development of a child with autism is usually delayed. Often this development shows leaps and bounds in different dimensions: long periods of status quo, then a sudden acceleration, sometimes after an illness. The rough and fine motor system is often unripe or lagging behind. You can often see stereotyped or ritual behavior like rhythmically walking back and forth. Excitement can lead to fluttering hands and tiptoe walking.

Older children often move their upper body forwards and backwards. Sudden panic or anger can lead to shouting fits accompanied with hitting, kicking or spitting on others. Sometimes auto mutilation occurs, where the inwardly directed anger can be focused on specific senses, sometimes on other parts of the body, for instance head banging. Over-activity can alternate with periods of stillness. Facial expressions are often plain and express stupefaction. When they are small, these children often make a perfect, beautiful impression: these are princes or elf children.

Impairment in cognitive development
Nowadays it is assumed that about half of the children suffering autism function on a mentally handicapped level. Some of these children have partial, very talented powers such as a phenomenal memory for figures or certain events. Their imagination and thoughts are very visually oriented.

Working with non-speaking autistics through 'supportive communication' has taught us that they are capable of intelligent thoughts but at the same time they have difficulty using language as a medium to express these thoughts. It is clear that 'normal' intelligent tests are not fit to work with the autistic child's different level of consciousness.

Phases in treatment

It is important to distinguish phases in development.[cvi] Roughly speaking one can distinguish three phases:

1. The first phase creates the foundation for optimal functioning. A clear and understandable day structure is offered and healthy habits are developed. A central place is taken by the need for structure and boundaries, needed for functioning on a normal day-to-day basis. When the child has autism, the main focus will be on treatment in this first phase, as steps from the second and third phase are not always reachable. Children with ADS often reach the second or third phase after intensive coaching. Serious events, however, or a transition to a next development phase (like entering puberty) can lead to a (temporary) relapse.

2. The second phase follows the first phase when the child has found enough self-confidence and strength. In this phase the child has to come to terms with his or her differentness and learn to cope with it and learn to integrate it into their lives. They have to accept and understand safe coping mechanisms for anger and fear and at the same time take distance from them, because they are no longer necessary and they can be replaced by more effective coping and defense strategies that have to be learned.

   Besides continued support and coaching to handle daily life, several therapies can be used to get rid of old pains and to learn how to make new choices, for instance creative therapy or music therapy. In other cases visual communication can help to develop young underdeveloped areas. Everything that helps strengthen the will of life, which helps the development of courage and happiness, is of the utmost importance.

   In the coaching of parents the emphasis will lie on recognizing certain problems the child might have.

3. The third phase consists of consolidating and integrating what is learned outside the therapeutic context, in real life, at school or at work. It is always dangerous to assume that these children/adolescents are already there, while the newly learned capacities are still fragile. A setback when the first challenges occur is always a possibility.

It is very important for the child to collect successful experiences in 'normal' life in whatever setting this may be, and to experience problems that can be handled. The child will learn that life goes on and that it isn't necessary and that it does not help to hide or to fall back on old defense strategies. The third phase comes to an end when the newly learned skills become an automatic part of one's behavior and personality. Self-confidence will grow. There will be less or no need for stressful behavior.

Activities you can do with your autistic child

Special attention and extra patience are some of the most important virtues you must have to raise a healthy child, even if he has autism. And since an autistic child has certain deficiencies in terms of learning, you should give extra attention to the specific points he has to improve on. In view of this, you can adapt the following activities to develop skills that are lacking in your child:

1. Physical activities

Walking and simple aerobics
Most children with autism find it difficult to take the first step or make each part of the body move together as one. This is because autism affects the visual, auditory, and tactile stimuli, impairing children who have normal motor skills. In several cases, autistic children possess a low level of physical fitness since they cannot move normally and prefer to stay in their comfort zone. Providing physical activities for your child will let him develop physical fitness and minimize the effects of lack of body coordination as he grows up. Of course, physical activities will provide healthy benefits to your child as well. The regular movements of the body will increase the level of correct response, improving the behavior of your child.

Body movements
Simple clapping of hands and movement of the feet are enough to start your child improving his motor skills. This is especially important if your child is between 10 months and 2 years old, because his arms and limbs should move normally to avoid any deficiencies as he grows.

Swimming
Swimming is considered a total body workout and is very beneficial to a child with autism. It enhances the physical capability of the body to improve movement and develop the best motor skills among all types of physical activities.

2. Mental activities

Puzzle games
Puzzle games improve the imagination of your child, especially in the stage of early development. These games will also improve their intellectual capacity to explore and to learn. Aside from this, puzzle games are fun and exciting for a child with autism.

Computer games
There are several games that are made especially for children with autism. These games can be found online and can be played for free. They are both enjoyable and educational for your child.

3. Emotional activities

Story telling
Although some autistic children have attention deficiency, taking time to read them stories can result in several benefits. This is because the child feels that he is cared about. Aside from this, the connection you make with your child through these activities is worth the time you spend telling them stories.

Walk in the park moments
If you let your child stay inside the house most of the time in his early stages of development, he may not be able to see how the outside world functions. It might induce fear about facing other people, which will add to his difficulties as he grows up. When he eventually faces the world on his own, he needs to know how the world functions. A walk in the park can introduce him to the world step by step.

Puberty/Adolescence
During puberty and adolescence, contact with one's peers is very important. Adolescents like to experiment with finding out how the world works. Being part of a group and functioning within a group is equally important.

For youngsters with autism, this is a different matter. Their experience with peers at elementary school has left much to be desired. Often they have been bullied by classmates and are wary of staying in touch with others of the same age. When they reach puberty they have just arrived at dealing with others in a manner that was okay at elementary school but does not suffice in their new environment. The games (which were useful in learning social skills) they played (as if they were real) are no longer played during puberty. People expect the youngster's social skills to already be more or less developed for use in this stage of life to find friends and seek a partner.

Youngsters with autism, however, are very busy developing cognitive skills in this period of life. Elementary school has often provided insight in strong cognitive skills and talent on one hand and learning disabilities on the other hand. Their skills give them an anchor point and raise their interest. That is why the development of cognitive skills can lead to some peace of mind.

The transition to young adulthood is marked by the realization that one is different from others the same age and the difficulty they have fitting in.

32.3 When your child grows up

Growing up
Experts say that parents who have autistic children should prepare them for the challenges that will face them as they grow up. For effective and successful explanation of the things mentioned, parents need to explore various tools, resources, options, and ideas to make the process of preparing the child easier. The following discusses the advantages and disadvantages of teaching and preparing autistic children for the outside world.

1. School and schooling. There are cases of autism and ASDs that are highly functional and enable the person to acquire education, even a college education for that matter.

PRO: This can help your child to acquire more knowledge and a chance to live a normal life. School and schooling can also help him or her to pursue a career after college.

CON: Your child might be teased and bullied by other normal kids. When this happens, your child's behavior will be greatly affected because the traumatic experience in school will be on his or her mind. Make sure that the school environment has a developed curriculum for ASD children. Otherwise, it is not advisable for him or her to go there.

2. Teach the child needed social skills.

PRO: This is a very good way of preparing your child for other groups within the society. Social skills such as greeting, listening, waiting, and maintaining a conversation can help the child meet and make new friends.

CON: Teaching and enforcing these social skills without assessing his or her readiness may pressure the child and oppose whatever you're teaching. Make sure that the child is willing to open up to the social community before you enforce various social skills.

3. On sex and sexuality.

PRO: It is very important to educate your autistic child about sex and sexuality to avoid possible sexual abuse. Make them understand the difference between a good and bad touch, the proper behavior inside a bathroom, and who can ask her or him to undress.

CON: Unless you want to confuse your child, you should talk straight when teaching about sex and sexuality, especially in explaining body parts. Don't be too vague or complicated in explaining things about it unless you want your child to explore it on her or his own.

4. Physical changes during puberty. Explaining the physical changes from childhood to adulthood will avoid fear and confusion in your child.

PRO: By doing this, your autistic child will slowly understand that the different changes in their body are normal and not something to be afraid of.

CON: They might explore it on their own especially in public. Proper guidance should be given at all times.

5. Hygiene. It is important to keep them clean to prevent possible allergies or diseases.

PRO: Teaching them day-to-day hygiene will make them understand the importance of being clean and neat. You can do this by demonstrating the basics of hygiene and safety.

CON: They might use various hygiene products the wrong way, which could lead to allergy or accident such as being poisoned.

32.4 Young adulthood

This is a period in life that is stressful, due to several changes occurring at the same time. For a young adult without autism this is a heavy task to fulfill. For a young adult with autism, this might be a period when it becomes obvious that they are not able to function on their own or can do so only with difficulty.

Starting a higher education often coincides with living on your own. Thus the inability to live on one's own might only then become clear.

Living in student dorms or your own room outside the family surroundings means running your own household, running errands, cooking, and doing administration in addition to studying.

Many students find this too difficult to cope with. Studying while taking care of all these new tasks will drain one's energy, so little to no effort will be put in developing new relationships. A new environment also implies meeting new friends and forming relationships. This is an area in which autistics do not excel.

Sometimes differences in development between young adults with autism become manifest in this period. When a young adult lives at home, parents or family members do many things without even giving them a thought. Everything happens in well-known surroundings with the structure, rules, etc. he or she is used to. When this young adult leaves home to live alone, this structure vanishes and he must build and get used to a new structure. This appears to be quite difficult for many young adults and even more complicated for sufferers of autism.

In class teachers expect a lot more independent studying than most autistics can handle. They have difficulty planning their study and doing their assignments.

During this phase the sense of being different and having difficulty fitting in with others has a heavy impact. While their peers are busy spreading their wings and becoming wholly independent, young autistic adults find themselves lonely and sometimes even depressed. Their cognitive skills no longer provide a safe haven as they discover that bonding with others just doesn't work the way they would like it to. They notice their peers, old classmates, and others from their neighborhood develop relationships and form careers. They notice that their own talents are not developed to the fullest extent and that they fall behind in lifework.

Dealing with the Autistic Adolescent

Adolescence is a challenging phase of life even for non-autistic children. And it's a challenge for both the parents and the child. Adolescents begin to feel the need to pull away from parents and develop their individuality. They may place more stock in what their peers think than in the thoughts of their parents. They challenge rules, snicker at their parents' "old fashioned" way of doing things, and generally want nothing to do with any suggestions made by their parents. On top of all of that, there are physical changes to contend with. It is during adolescence that children begin to mature sexually, so there are hormonal issues to contend with.

Children with autism have compounded difficulties with adolescence. While they may want to break away from their parents and become more independent, they may lack the necessary skills to do so. They may also lack the ability to communicate their newly found frustrations and feelings. And, sexual maturity can lead to inappropriate behaviors, including the unintentional breaking of social taboos.

Dr. R. Kaan Ozbayrak, MD, contends that there are three factors that determine how an autistic child will react to peers in his or her adolescent years. Those factors are:

- Level of Interest: Many autistics are simply not interested in people around them. If your child is interested in his or her peers, social interactions will be determined by the remaining two factors.

- Level of Avoidance: In children who are interested in others, the amount of social anxiety they experience will determine how they interact with their peers. It may be difficult to tell the difference between lack of interest and anxiety. The good news is, once you've determined the problem is anxiety, it's simpler to treat than lack of interest.

- Level of Insight: If your child is interested in others and doesn't avoid them, his or her understanding of autism will be the key factor in how he or she interacts with peers. Children who aren't aware of the disorder and how it affects them may have more difficulty with social interaction.

An interesting result of ASD that many parents have noticed is that children with autism are often more comfortable dealing with younger children or with adults than they are with their peers. This may be because younger children are less likely to judge them and are more accepting of autistic behaviors, so they feel safe to the autistic child. And, adults feel safer, too, because they are more likely to be tolerant of aberrant behaviors, and therefore less critical.

Managing loss of normalcy
No matter what their developmental level, most children with autism eventually see that they aren't like others their age. This generally happens during the adolescent years. Like parents and grandparents, the child may also experience grieving over the loss of "normalcy." It's important for parents to understand the grieving process, and to help the child understand as well.

Those who are grieving generally experience:

- Anger
- Denial
- Depression
- Acceptance
- Adaptation

These feelings may not happen in the order listed, and the child may move back and forth between them, accepting the disorder one day and feeling angry the next. While you may be tempted to ignore the process at times in the hope that it will simply go away, that's probably not the best step. Try to deal with the process as calmly as possible and encourage your child to talk about his or her feelings. Your positive modeling can help your child through this very difficult time.

Children with autism may become depressed during adolescence because of all the added pressures. If your child shows signs of depression, talk to a physician or psychiatrist immediately. Depression is a serious condition.

Signs of clinical depression include:

- Long periods of sadness
- Quick to anger so that family members are on edge
- Inability to fall asleep or stay asleep
- Fatigue
- Loss of appetite
- Low self-esteem
- Remarks about hating life and hating others, and wishing he or she were dead
- Loss of interest in previously enjoyed activities
- Withdrawal from the family
- Wrongly blaming himself/herself for things that go wrong

On a positive note, some autistic children deal with their loss by embracing their disorder and finding their identity there. They join support groups for children and adolescents or find other ways to get in touch with them, help educate others about autism, set up websites about autism, and generally help generate support for the disorder. If this is the tack your child takes, encourage him or her by finding ways to help. Or, you could get involved right alongside your child and make it a family effort. However, keep in mind that this is a time when your child will want to strike out on his/her own, so your presence may not be wanted. If that's the case, take a step back and allow your child to spread his/her wings.

Using interests to boost self-esteem

Children with autism tend to become interested in one subject and will learn everything about it that they can. Unfortunately, that might also mean that they will bore others with incessant talking about the subject. Your child's interests might just be a means of boosting low self-esteem during adolescence.

Instead of avoiding the subject, discover ways to use the interest to help your child become engaged in new ways of learning or interacting with others. Try to find approaches that will challenge the child. Make creativity part of the approach. Your interest in the subject and your child's ability to teach you about it will provide feelings of pride and help the child through an otherwise difficult time.

Autism and Developing Sexuality

Although your child may not progress socially at the same time as his or her peers, his body will keep up with normal physical development. Therefore, your child will begin to experience sexual maturity at the same time as those around him/her. These changes cause very real worries for parents. These worries include:

- Fear that the child's behaviors will be misinterpreted
- Fear that the child will be subject to abuse due to their lack of social understanding
- Fear of an unplanned pregnancy
- Fear that the child will never have the chance to enjoy a normal sexual relationship
- Fear of sexually transmitted diseases

Then there's the inappropriate behaviors autistic children may exhibit due to budding sexuality, such as touching themselves in public, taking off clothes, public masturbation, inappropriately touching or staring at others, and talking about inappropriate subjects in public.

The best way to deal with your child's budding sexuality is to make up your mind to talk about it. Don't just address the subject in passing or when it comes up; make time to sit down and discuss it. Ask your child what he/she knows about sex and honestly answer questions in an age-appropriate fashion. Talk about normal behavior and behaviors that shouldn't occur in public. Be open to listening to whatever your child has to say. It's important that your child feel that he/she can come to you to discuss feelings, frustrations, and questions.

If talking to your child doesn't work, ask your physician or other professionals with experience in this area for assistance. Your school may even be able to point you in the direction of resources.

32.5 ASD and adolescence

Facing the challenges of ASD during adolescence

Today, many autistic adults are able to successfully deal with their situation and are actually successful in their respective fields. These successful individuals were able to make it despite their challenging condition because of the proper transition from childhood to adolescence and to adulthood.

Experts say that the transition of autistic children from childhood to adolescence is very important because this will determine if they are capable of pursuing different fields later on.

Being a parent of an autistic adolescent is indeed an exhausting and tiring job, but this is not the time to show weakness. In fact, this is a very crucial time because you have to teach your autistic child how to deal with imminent challenges ahead.

1. Social skills. Various social skills such as proper interaction and dealing with others should be emphasized to autistic adults so they can learn to fit into the social community.

2. Sex and sexuality. Educating your autistic adolescent about sex and sexuality is very important because it can veer them away from possible sexual abuse. You make them understand who is authorized to touch them or ask them to undress, the difference between a good or bad touch, how to behave in a bathroom, independence inside the locker room, and the importance of reporting recent events. Parents can also educate their children about sex and sexuality by being proactive, speaking technically and concretely about body parts, being consistent in reminding their children about sexual safety, reinforcing appropriate behavior at all times, and by redirecting inappropriate behaviors especially masturbating in public.

3. Physical changes during puberty. Be sure to explain the different changes in their body and make them understand that these changes are normal.

4. Hygiene. You can teach them day-to-day hygiene by demonstrating the basics of hygiene and safety.

5. Getting a college education. You should help them understand the process of getting a college education, such as gaining an admission to a desired college, moving away from home, managing emergent social situations and conditions, time management, transportation, budgeting, completing specific course work, securing services needed, and life after college.

This may sound like a daunting task, but if you have taught him properly throughout his life this training will be a natural extension of what he has learned. Remember, patience is the key here.

32.6 Transitioning to adulthood

Around the age of 14, parents should begin thinking about how their autistic child will make the leap from school to adulthood. Ultimately, the goal for the child should be to lead as normal and independent a life as possible. As with your child's elementary and secondary education, good planning is key. Develop a plan geared toward making your child's adult life successful and fulfilling in terms of career, social activity, and community involvement. Your child's transition plan should incorporate:

- Individual interests, needs, skills, and preferences
- Strategies for a successful life after schooling ends
- Long range goals and activities designed to reach them
- Services that will help reach goals

Again, the plan should be written down, but it shouldn't be just words on a paper – it must involve action. Once you've identified areas of interest for your child that could blossom into a career, take action to find opportunities that will provide experience and training to help achieve career goals. For example, if your child is particularly interested in animals, look for opportunities to volunteer at animal shelters, zoos, farms, or veterinary offices. You might also find it helpful to seek out opportunities outside of the child's particular set of interests to provide your child with new options.

In reality, the steps required to help your autistic child become a successful adult aren't much different than steps for a non-autistic child, just more intensive and time consuming.

When your child is around the age of 14, begin exploring possible careers, talking to school counselors about your child's capabilities, participating in job assessment activities, and talking to people or reading books about careers of interest.

In high school, take another look at the transition plan to make sure it is still geared toward your child's current interests and remains realistic. Your child should begin taking courses that will enable him/her to enter a university or vocational school to pursue a program in his area of interest. Allow your child to participate in activities that allow him/her to "try out" a career field, such as summer jobs, volunteer work, or part-time work. If your child plans to attend college or a vocational program, begin researching potential schools, and tests that are necessary for enrollment. Identify schools that will be able to accommodate your child's special needs.

After high school, you will need to identify services and benefits your child may be entitled to. Contact local agencies for help in applying for programs or assistance for your child.

32.7 Maturity

During maturity, differences between people with and people without autism are very easily found. Of course this also depends on the severity of the autism. It also depends on whether or not autism has been diagnosed. When autism isn't very predominant, life's duties can be more or less met. However, it takes a lot more energy from the autistic person and the people who are helping.

Maturity is the phase in one's life when families are formed and children are born. So this is also the phase where problems with children having autism become visible and might be a reason to look for autism in the parents. This might be perceived as shocking as well as comforting. The perspective the future holds becomes different, as well as the past. This calls for adjustment.

Children with autism are usually not occupied with founding families but with coping to live by themselves. Letting go of your parents is a complicated process which means that parents as well as their children have to explore the new boundaries that come with leaving the nest. Both have the same worries. They worry that this process might go too fast to keep up, or too slow, and they hope that the child might eventually be able to cope on his or her own.

32.8 Middle age

Middle age is typically the phase of life in which people develop their careers. They have finished their studies and are joining the work force. Their qualities and talents become apparent, their experience increases, and consequently a career develops. With autistic people this is not the way things usually develop. They are often single and in search of a partner. Sometimes they have already given up seeking a partner. The ones with a partner will often notice that tensions within their relationship are increasing.

During this period, because of the still hesitant and unknown diagnostics of adults with autism, perhaps their autism is still undiscovered. It is often a combination of men with autism and women with an empathetic nature. Women's middle age also means that women enter the change of life with all the disadvantages of possible mood swings. Their increasing assertiveness is an advantage. For years, women have adjusted themselves to their husbands and asked their children to adapt to their father. Reaching middle age, women sometimes draw the line. They do not wish to sacrifice themselves any more and want their husbands to change and adapt to their desires.

Especially in the case of a male partner with autism, this process is troublesome. Demanding so much change and adaptation is shocking for the man, and the blame over the past years is very painful. For the woman it is shocking to experience that the adjustment of the past years has not been a sacrifice, but a necessity, and that not all can be changed. It takes a lot of effort from both partners to do the relationship justice and continue it with more knowledge and experience.

The loneliness of people with autism without partners increases during this period. The road to old age can get rough. Expectations are readjusted and there is mourning over lost illusions during this period. During a midlife crisis, people look back, but for someone with autism this crisis usually occurs later.

32.9 The Elderly

When people grow older they tend to look at life based on their self-knowledge and life experience. Because diagnosing an adult with autism (without a mental handicap) has only recently become fashionable, a lot of autistic adults go through life undiagnosed and thus ignorant of the nature of their impairments.

Finding your own identity is the major theme of this life phase. With aging, brain functions become less flexible; this is also the case with autism. This means in effect that their already substandard flexibility even gets worse. They tend to have more problems adjusting behavior and lean heavily on their partner, unless their partner has divorced them or, much more likely, has been found. In their loneliness they can develop into a peculiar character.

Social help during old age is very important. Knowing this aid is available is of utmost importance for people with autism. Where people normally depend on their self-knowledge, people with autism are still busy working on their identity. The diagnosis of autism may even become part of their identity, aggravating their condition after the diagnosis.

Summary
Previous chapters and paragraphs have outlined the nature of autism, its impact, and possible aids. This chapter focuses on how the various ASDs affect a person in each stage of his or her life: babies and toddlers, childhood, puberty/adulthood, maturity, middle age, and old age.

EXTRAS

Chapter 33 Adults with an autism spectrum disorder

Some adults with an ASD, especially the ones with high-functioning autism or with Asperger's syndrome, are able to work successfully in mainstream jobs. Nevertheless, communication and social problems often cause difficulties in many areas of life. They will continue to need encouragement and moral support in their struggle for an independent life.

Many others with ASD are capable of employment in sheltered workshops under the supervision of managers trained in working with people with disabilities. A nurturing environment at home, at school, and later in job training and at work, helps people with an ASD to continue to learn and to develop throughout their lives.

The public schools' responsibility for providing services ends at a certain age that differs by country. The family is then faced with the challenge of finding living arrangements and employment to match the particular needs of their adult child, as well as the programs and facilities that can provide support services to achieve these goals.

Long before your child finishes school, you will want to search for the best programs and facilities for your young adult. If you know other parents of adults with an ASD, ask them about the services available in your community. If your community has little to offer, serve as an advocate for your child and work toward the goal of improved employment services. Research the resources as much as possible for help your child is eligible to receive as an adult.

Recognition of autistic behavior in yourself or your partner

Although, generally speaking people with an ASD do not marry early or enter into a fixed relationship on account of their contactual problems, assistance organizations have of late been more and more confronted by partners who suspect their spouses to suffer from autism or by partners who suspect themselves to be autistic. Partners often ask for a diagnosis and assistance but the person concerned should agree. It is mostly women who suspect their male partner to be autistic; once in a while it is the other way around. Very little is known about autistic adults and especially about adults who have attained a social position. No research has been initiated as yet and there are very few publications on this subject.

Sometimes an autistic partner realizes that he or she has limitations in the social and emotional field. When he or she is prepared to have a diagnosis made, this should be done after discussing possibilities with a social worker. One could ask oneself if and why a diagnosis is necessary. When both partners recognize the autism and learn to live with it, having a diagnosis made may become less necessary. However, when there are problems, e.g. during working hours, a diagnosis can give more clarity and understanding. It will be more difficult when the partner recognizes these problems in the other but the latter denies them.

Perhaps the partner has more problems in recognizing the problems of a child in the family. This partner himself may have experienced a development where more 'aberrant' behavior was considered normal. This may explain cases that went awry in the past. It is sensible to bear in mind that after the diagnosis, the partner stays the same person; he or she will not change as soon as a diagnosis is made.

At this moment diagnostics and aid for adults with an ASD have relatively little to offer, certainly for partners who have socially found a place and who have succeeded in holding their own up to the ages of 40, 50 or 60.

If somebody suspects a type of autism in the partner, he or she can try to strengthen the structure of daily life, e.g. by making clear arrangements and, if desired, making them visual by using a written list where agenda items can be written down and marked out.

Maybe it will be clear that life with such a partner is different. Expectations from the past, living through trying times together, and doing things together will have to be adjusted. It may be important that the person concerned arranges his own activities and contacts. It is not surprising either that, from the circle of acquaintances, reactions of disbelief arise when this is made a subject of discussion. After all, the person has a job and a family, so there is nothing wrong, is there?

Summary
There are adults in mainstream jobs who don't know they have high-functioning autism or Asperger's syndrome. Some of these adults, or more often their partners, are being tested late in life. Diagnostics have little to offer an autistic who's reached adulthood without knowing he or she is autistic, but an autistic and his or her partner can adjust their lives to make things easier. An undiagnosed autistic might also have more problems in recognizing an autistic child in the family. Hospitals and support groups are good sources of information about autism. People with autism, and families of people with autism, will have different needs and lifestyles than those without it, but it doesn't have to be a disability.

Chapter 34 Who looks after the interests of people with an ASD?

Assistance in general

Autism is incurable and therefore a lifelong handicap. The development of a child with ASD depends on his or her intelligence and linguistic development, and the severity of his or her behavioral problems. Supervision, day relief, and education adapted to the circumstances are very important in this respect.

Although the diagnosis, certainly with children, can be made, the question remains what treatment is to be preferred. Exactly like everybody else, people with an ASD have their own characters, and good and bad habits and talents of their own. Not one person with autism is the same. Therefore, supervision, education, and day relief or work will be different for each person. Every autistic has different personal possibilities and needs. Aid and treatment has to be made to measure. For some people with an ASD, less intensive forms of assistance suffice. For others, more intensive aid is required.

In this chapter a number of ways of assistance are mentioned. When reading this chapter, the impression may be formed that the assistance mentioned is available to a great extent. A brief comment on this: specific indication criteria prevail for many types of aid and supply is often restricted and/or under development.

A number of the types of assistance described in this chapter are specifically applicable to people with an ASD but others are certainly not. People with an ASD can use these types of aid, but the knowledge of autism may be present to a lesser degree and surely not specifically focused on them.

Institutions offering aid to children and adolescents with an ASD usually have more extensive resources than those who offer help to (young) adults. For people who come into contact with organizations, it is important to find out whether they have specific knowledge of autism.

Where to go to for information on autism childcare

Autism is a neurodevelopmental disorder which leads to abnormal patterns of behavior, social relationships, and other skills. Although there are genes typically present in all autistic children, many scientists speculate that the problem not only originates from the genetic makeup of a child, but also from triggers that can be found in the environment.

Physically, autism cannot really be detected. There are no abnormalities in the body that indicate autism. However, the impairment of the autistic child actually lies in his or her inability to interact normally with the world outside.

Families who have autistic children often face severe stress. The amount of care that a child with autism requires dictates the lifestyle of the family. The care for an autistic child often takes up a lot of time and family relations suffer because of this.

Respite childcare for autism can be obtained. But many people are bewildered as to where to find such services. Here are some places that you may want to check out in order to look for information on autism childcare:

1. Hospitals – There are actually specialists in autism childcare who can be contacted through hospitals. When you go to a hospital for information on caring for children with autism, you may be able to find out the proper method of caring for the health needs of an autistic child.

2. Hospitals also provide you with connections. You will need help taking care of a child with autism. Hospitals can provide you with information on different specialists who may be able to give you advice and provide you with the materials on autistic childcare you might need.

3. Support groups – There are groups of people who are focused on helping other people learn about proper childcare for autism, so you see, you are not alone in taking care of a child with autism. This means that you will be able to find someone to help you, if you only make the effort to search. These groups will give you inspiration and show you that there is a way to live normally despite autism.

There are different ways to get in touch with these support groups:

- Through your family doctor – More often than not, your doctor will be able to refer you to different support groups that will help you gain the knowledge necessary to take care of a child with autism.

- The phone book / Google – You also need to look in the phone book or a search engine on the Internet for information on how to contact such support groups. They often list their numbers in the phone book or on the Internet for the sole purpose of making themselves more accessible for those who want information on proper autism childcare.

You should not let autism be a hindrance for normal living. People who take care of autistic children often find that they make more progress if they do not treat autism as a disability. No one is saying that you need to ignore autism in order for it to be treated. However, you should not let a child's autism isolate him or her from the rest of the family.

Here is a final thought: whenever you feel stressed out while taking care of a child with autism, don't take it out on the child. Just remember to always count your blessings, because in the end, your blessings will always outweigh your problems.

Chapter 35 Sexual education

Many people with autism remain self-absorbed during adolescence, apparently uninterested in exploring relationships with others. When interest is displayed, the social skills required to make and sustain adult socio-sexual relationships are frequently too immature to allow for success. In addition to poor empathic skills, many people with autism have difficulty with social timing and with social communication, problems that can make it virtually impossible for them to access a social peer group.

Unable to join in and often rejected by the group, adolescents and adults with autism are poorly rewarded for any attempts they make to copy, or respond to, the social behavior around them; understandably, even the more able person with autism may eventually give up the attempt. Their difficulties not only deny them a place among their non-disabled peers, but they are equally unable to find a place among other people with learning disabilities.

Unlike other areas of personal and social need that professional and lay carers can attempt to meet, offering personal help with sexual need is impossible on legal and moral grounds. Providing surrogate sex partners may be unwise. Leaving aside any other considerations, it has to be remembered that many people with autism display poor social discrimination skills and may be unaware of who is available to them as a surrogate and who is not.

If they cannot find their own sex partners and we cannot supply them, what can we do?

Our support is needed in accepting the reality of the expression of sexual needs among people with autism. In addition to understanding their right to express their sexuality through solo masturbation, we have to accept that it is our task to teach them the relevance of time and place. They need, at the very least, sufficient skills to enable them to behave acceptably in open society, without triggering inappropriate or disapproving responses.

It is our responsibility to find training methods that are helpful, realistic and specifically tailored to an understanding of people with autism.

The need to teach sexuality[cvii]
Parents are a child's most important educator. As such, if parents of children with ASD are to foster healthy development in their children, they must understand the issues involved in sexuality for youth with ASDs. Professionals writing about sexuality and developmental disabilities have highlighted why sexuality education is important:

- Many children with developmental disabilities, including those with ASDs, develop physically in the same way as their peers.

- Youth with developmental disabilities need to understand physiological changes that occur during puberty.
- Youth need to understand personal sexual safety issues relevant for their age and developmental level, such as sexual health and doctor's visits.
- Children with developmental disabilities are at greater risk for exploitation than their peers.
- Sexuality education involves an important social/relationship component and is embedded in social experiences (e.g. social skills, friendships, boundaries, emotions).
- Contrary to general beliefs, individuals with developmental disabilities are less likely to engage in inappropriate/dangerous behavior when educated about sexuality and relationships.

Luckily the topic of sex education for people with autism has been receiving considerable interest of late. Several factors have combined to bring this issue into the forefront.

First, as with programs for most handicapped children, programs for people with autism began providing intensive treatment about 10-15 years ago. These programs began with younger children who are now approaching adolescence. Concerns about sex education become greater with all groups of children during this developmental phase.

Second, there are many more programs for children with autism than there were a decade ago, when the rate of institutionalization for adolescents and adults with autism was quite high. This success has brought about more attention to all issues involving older clients.

Finally, the principle of normalization has increased parent and professional interest in sex education for all handicapped children in general and those with autism in particular.

From the Parents' Perspectives[cviii]
Thinking about sexuality education is not easy. Parents of children with ASD may be apprehensive about teaching topics related to sexuality. They may be unsure how to respond to their child's emerging sexual behaviors, particularly if those behaviors are inappropriate (e.g. violating boundaries). It is generally accepted that sexuality needs to be taught within the context of human relationships and that parents are the most important and best sex educators for their children. Professionals working with families of youth with ASD need to better understand parent's concerns, fears, and hopes and how best to support them in educating their children and handling difficult behaviors that might emerge at home, in school, or in the community.

Youth with ASD present unique challenges: sensory issues, difficulties with social understanding, and restricted interests/repetitive behaviors. For examples that are relevant to how we interpret sexual behavior (or behavior incorrectly considered to be sexual), intervene as needed, and select appropriate educational strategies, such as providing visuals for strong visual learners.

How do we think about sexuality?

Many people think of sexuality as sex, when in fact sexuality involves much more than biology and reproduction. The Sexuality Information and Education Council of the United States (SIECUS) defines it this way:

Human sexuality encompasses the sexual knowledge, beliefs, attitudes, values, and behaviors of individuals. Its various dimensions involve the anatomy, physiology, and biochemistry of the sexual response system; identity, orientation, roles, and personality; and thoughts, feelings, and relationships. Sexuality is influenced by ethical, spiritual, cultural, and moral concerns.

The definition of sexuality is particularly important when considering sexuality education for individuals with developmental disabilities. Sexuality is a natural part of who we are as humans, and how sexuality is conceptualized for individuals with ASD depends on a number of factors including their cognitive abilities; language; adaptive, self-care, and social skills; and interest. It is equally important to note that sexuality education differs throughout childhood and adolescence. For example, young children learn about gender, body parts, privacy, and love, while older children learn about friendships, personal safety, and puberty.

Normalization

Ann Craft identifies, in her book Sex Education and Counseling for Mentally Handicapped People (Costello), these main points in the normalization of sexuality for adults with a learning disability:

- The right to receive training in social-sexual behavior that will open doors for social contact with people in the community
- The right to all the knowledge about sexuality that they can comprehend
- The right to enjoy love and to be loved by the opposite sex, including sexual fulfillment
- The right for the opportunity to express sexual impulses in the same form as is socially acceptable for others
- The right to birth control services which are specialized to meet their needs
- The right to marry
- The right to have a voice in whether to have children

People with autism of all levels of severity experience sexual drives, behaviors, or feelings with which, at some point in their lives, they need assistance. The amount of assistance needed may vary greatly among individuals, even those at the same developmental level. For example, one person might simply need instruction on managing himself in public while another needs a thorough sex education course including heterosexual relationships. All individuals, whether with autism or without, require some assistance and the timing and amount should be geared to the level of need.

Parental involvement and participation is a crucial ingredient. In the area of sex education, this is especially important because such perplexing issues require the combined resources of parents and professionals.

It is important for the dialogue between parents and professionals to begin before sexuality becomes a major issue or problem. So much current sex education training is crisis-oriented, which dooms it to failure from the outset. Ideally, professionals should discuss sexuality and handicapped people with the parents by the time the child reaches age 10. Because many parents do not know what to expect, they are very surprised when sexual behaviors appear in their child. If they are prepared for these in advance, they will be less traumatized when they occur and more likely to discuss concerns with professionals as they arise. The sexual behaviors they observe will less likely be construed as deviant, which will make parents more likely to discuss and confront them.

Values and Technique

Any question about sexuality usually consists of at least two parts: which behaviors we *should* teach (values) and which behaviors we *can* teach (technique). Separating values from questions of technique makes it possible for us to deal with both more effectively.

The value issues are the ones that professionals cannot and should not decide alone. They must be addressed through a continuous dialogue with the parents. Examples of value issues are whether or not a person with autism should be allowed to masturbate or whether or not two severely retarded people with autism of the same sex should be allowed to masturbate by rubbing against each other. Although it is not always easy, value questions can usually be resolved if there is a good parent professional relationship involving mutual trust.

Once these value issues are resolved, the problems become a bit more manageable. If everybody is comfortable with an adolescent boy masturbating in the privacy of his own bedroom, the teaching of how to satisfy himself is less of a challenge. Although many professionals will still understandably be uncomfortable about teaching a boy to masturbate, this process is facilitated if they no longer have to worry about its appropriateness.

Sex education is something that can be acquired through a systematic process, just like any other concept or skill. For people with autism, this means that it must be learned in a highly structured, individualized way using concrete strategies whenever possible.

The emphasis on language must be minimal because of the difficulties that people with autism have with communication. Although the implications and possible consequences of sexuality are much different from more neutral contexts for many of us, creating extreme emotional reactions at times, we must understand that these emotions, at least initially, are not experienced in the same way by our clients. Therefore, teaching sex education must involve many of the same techniques as teaching sorting, matching, letter identification, and the many other skills we teach which have much less of an emotional overtone.

Although sex education must be taught as one teaches other skills, there are also some differences in terms of the priorities we attach to sexual behavior and our tolerance for deviance in this area. Although people with autism do not, at least initially, see sex as very different from most concepts, the rest of society obviously does. We must therefore be very careful to emphasize sexual behaviors as an important priority and to be less tolerant of deviations in this area than we might be with more harmless self-stimulatory or other unusual behaviors.

It is probably obvious to most parents and professionals that society is quite frightened about the sexuality of individuals with handicaps. Although this might seem silly to us, recent surveys suggest that these fears plus concerns that group homes for handicapped people will lower property values are the major reasons why communities oppose these programs. Those working with handicapped people must keep this in mind when setting appropriate priorities. Although a person with autism might only be unzipping his fly in public as preparation for the bathroom, the public might very well see this as exposing himself, with very severe recriminations and restrictions resulting.

Levels of functioning
The notion of matching teaching programs to levels of functioning has been a vital part of the effectiveness of development approach programs. Just as two people with autism having differing motivations will not require the same kind of information, a person with no language and a measured IQ below 25 will require very different sex education programs from one who is verbal with a measured IQ around 100. Obviously, a higher functioning person with more language ability will be able to assimilate more information than one with no language and very limited cognitive abilities.

A second reason for matching programs to levels of functioning is that people with autism functioning at different levels will probably have different long-range goals. An individual with autism who is expected to function independently in a normal environment will have different needs than a person expected to live in a group home and work in a sheltered workshop. The former will need more information and a greater ability to function autonomously.

The second aspect of a developmental approach concerns the context in which skills are taught. One of these contexts is that of normal development. In analyzing the sexuality of adolescents with autism, we must not only recognize their differences from non-handicapped peers but also some similarities. The impulsiveness, aggressiveness, confusion, and defiance that often accompany the biological and physical changes occurring in adolescents with autism are often not so different from those same behaviors occurring during normal adolescent development.

The third aspect of a developmental approach is that behaviors cannot be dealt with in isolation but must be considered in the context of other skills. A sex education program must take into account the communication level, social skills, cognitive ability, conceptual ability, and all other aspects of a person's functioning. To be fully effective, each of these aspects must be considered in planning a sex education program.

For example, two adolescents with autism might have the same general IQ and language ability but very different interpersonal experiences. If both express a desire to date members of the opposite sex, then their sex education programs will have to differ accordingly. The person who has never talked to a female, let along a male peer, might have to focus on some simple interpersonal skills such as looking at other people, initiating conversations, and developing appropriate interpersonal strategies. Dating might still be an appropriate long-range goal but this would be much further down the line. On the other hand, a young adult who has already mastered communication skills would be able to focus on applying them in an interpersonal setting. This person's program might be based more on understanding interpersonal needs, what people do on dates, handling sexual issues, and other related concerns. Although both of these adolescents are of approximately the same age and have similar cognitive and communication skills, their social development would dictate different teaching strategies.

Common problems[cix]
Inappropriate Masturbation
This ranges from the socially embarrassing repeated touching of the genital area through the clothing to the more emotive issue of public masturbation. Over-reaction must be avoided as it is likely to make matters worse. Disapproving of the behavior carries the risk of generating anxiety, or of suppressing the behavior, leaving the individual with no release for sexual energy.

The first positive step is to ensure that the individual does not have a health problem. Often the discomfort of a tight foreskin or a vaginal or urinary tract infection results in behavior that people assume to be masturbatory. If a health check finds no physical irritation, then a program of behavior modification should be set up. If the behavior is a severe problem, then the help of a psychologist should be sought in designing the modification program. The aim of the program will not be to stop masturbation, but to approve of it where and when it is done appropriately.

Excessive Masturbation
It is difficult for any individual to pass judgment on the sexual drive of another. Many of us take our own level of need as a norm. Masturbation can be judged to be excessive when the individual is making the genital region sore from

repeated friction, or where the need to masturbate intrudes into his or her ability to take part in training or recreational activities.

Staff groups can be helped in dealing with excessive masturbation if they become involved in training the individual to use an appropriate place for the act. Once this is established, staff can deal with the less emotive problem that he or she is spending too much time in that place.

Setting times when the individual is free to go to a bedroom or toilet to masturbate is a successful strategy. This can be very frequently at first, followed by a slow process of lengthening the periods between bedroom sessions. Wise staff will use favorite activities to lengthen the time between bedroom sessions and to encourage the individual to leave their bedroom after a period.

Inability to Masturbate to Satisfaction
Both male and female may wish to masturbate but be unable to co-ordinate movement to achieve satisfaction, or may be unable to cope with the intensity of feeling prior to ejaculation/orgasm.

Inevitably such problems give rise to frustration that may become acute. They may also be the reason for what appears to be obsessive masturbation, the activity only serving to stimulate further need rather than provide satisfaction. Some individuals may be helped by being provided with privacy and with an understanding that their masturbation is not disapproved of. Others will need practical help.

Both parents and professional staff should beware of providing that help personally. Society is judgmental about any sexual contact between parents/staff and those in their care. When the need for help is realized, it is necessary to discuss that need with medical advisors and to ask for the help of a sex therapist.

Inappropriate Touching of Other People
Over-reaction to this should be avoided. It is not unknown for a person with autism who has a hand flapping mannerism to be accused of touching the breasts of female staff in corridors. This has more to do with the height of hands and the narrowness of corridors than with sex.

In cases of definite and deliberate touching, the motivation of the person with autism should be assessed. It is common for their interest to be based on watching (and hearing!) the resulting upset rather than on sexual interest. A calm response may, over time, reduce and stop the behavior as it becomes less interesting.

Exposing Self
This should not be confused with lack of modesty and lack of understanding of social rules. The man with autism who turns away from the urinal with his penis showing is not sexually exposing himself. He lacks modesty and understanding, and needs training. It is common for males to awake from a

night's sleep with an erection. This is not caused by sexual excitement but by the physical reaction to an overfull bladder. Given the nature of male pajamas and of dressing gowns, the erect penis may easily be displayed during the walk from bedroom to toilet. Again this is a modesty issue rather than a sexual matter and it is important that it is dealt with calmly and sympathetically.

Discrimination training; hygiene; developmental hierarchy

The most basic sexuality skills that all individuals with autism must learn are simple discrimination skills. These include knowing when and where to disrobe, masturbate, touch other people, and related behaviors. For individuals with autism who have little language and are functioning intellectually within the severely to profoundly retarded range, this might be all they are able to achieve in the area of sex education. However, no other skill will be more important for their ability to function in either group homes or sheltered workshop settings.

Discrimination training is often facilitated by environmental changes that make desired behaviors more likely and undesirable behavior more difficult and time-consuming to perform. This can be accomplished by having an adolescent wear a belt to make it more difficult to put his hands in his pants, having an adolescent girl wear shirts without buttons to make it more difficult to remove them, or similar modifications.

The next level of the developmental hierarchy is personal hygiene. For nonverbal clients functioning intellectually in the severely to profoundly retarded range, this training will probably represent the highest developmental level they can achieve. It should include aspects of personal hygiene that will make them more comfortable personally and will also make it more comfortable for others to be around them. Training in this area will include cleaning themselves properly after a bowel movement, appropriate hygiene during their menstrual periods, changing underwear, cleaning themselves appropriately in a bath or shower, using deodorant, and related behaviors.

For more verbal and higher functioning individuals with autism, these same personal hygiene behaviors should be taught. Even though some of this information might seem very basic, for individuals with autism who are not always interpersonally attuned these concepts are often overlooked. Since many of these people are somewhat anxious about discussing sexuality and related issues, some preliminary work on personal hygiene can provide an easier entry into more sexually explicit discussions.

Next on the developmental sequence is information about body parts and their function. Most of the clients who will be at this level will have some language ability and be functioning intellectually within the moderately retarded range or higher. The goal of this phase will be to introduce concepts of body parts and their functions and to be sure that adolescents and adults with autism understand them.

Most sex education books can be adapted for individuals with autism. The most important part is not the materials but to be sure that the client has a full understanding of what the words and concepts mean. Often, individuals with autism can use the right words but have very little understanding of the important concepts. This can be a particular problem in sex education where most of us feel a bit uncomfortable and don't probe for precise meanings. In providing education about body parts and functions to an individual with autism, it is extremely important to be very explicit and concrete, even if this involves using words or terms that one is not normally comfortable with. This embarrassment and discomfort has primarily social overtones which individuals with autism will not understand. Therefore, we must break through some of these barriers if we are to be effective sex educators.

For those who are able to understand the body parts and their functions including reproduction, the final developmental phase is a complete sex education program, including heterosexual relationships. For some individuals with autism, this is a very appropriate and necessary phase. At this level of training, a significant amount of role playing is needed. As in many areas, individuals with autism have difficulty learning when they are only told something. Role playing how to meet other people, how to talk to them, and how to deal with problems that occur is an important part of learning about heterosexual relationships. Role playing helps to make some of the more obscure concepts easier to understand and use.

In counseling adolescents and adults with autism, several other techniques have also proven useful. The early sessions are generally used simply to focus on establishing rapport. This is done to make the clients feel at ease and to reduce the anxiety that many bring to these meetings. Early sessions are focused on topics of interest to the adolescents or young adults which elicit minimal anxiety.

As these sessions progress, the topic is not only sexuality. Issues of concern include personal hygiene, general issues (Why do men have hair on their chests?), how to relate to others, and a variety of other related issues for these clients.

The second aspect of a developmental approach concerns the context in which skills are taught. One of the most important contexts is that of normal development. In analyzing the sexuality of adolescents with autism, we must not only recognize their differences from non-handicapped peers but also their similarities.

There are many developmental changes that non-handicapped adolescents experience which might have relevance to adolescents with autism. During adolescence, non-handicapped children are given more freedom in going from place to place on their own and are also given more responsibility for carrying out tasks independently. Moreover, they are beginning to explore new relationships with the opposite sex and to learn about sexual changes affecting them. Non-handicapped adolescents also begin to form some image of themselves during this time which will later contribute to a career choice.

In considering adolescents with autism, it is probably useful to realize that, in some form, these same general issues will be of concern. The way to deal with them will of course have to be different from what is done with non-handicapped adolescents and will also depend upon developmental levels. However, some general statements and guidelines might be useful.

For example, the issue of additional freedom should probably be addressed. Is a particular being given as much freedom as he can manage in getting from place to place? Are there any situations in which one is accompanying an individual with autism when this is unnecessary? Or could they be helped by some teaching to move more independently?

Freedom, Responsibility, and Independence
Responsibility is another important issue in adolescence. Even though adolescents with autism can't achieve total independence, are there some tasks in which greater independence can be achieved? Some of these might include getting to bed on time, getting one's work done in class, cleaning one's room or doing the laundry. In addition, we might ask about new tasks that could be learned, including preparing simple tasks or a breakfast, buying materials in a store, yard work, or minor household repairs.

During adolescence, there is a search for direction and purpose that most non-handicapped children pursue. Although perhaps less global, similar concerns probably affect individuals with autism as they become aware of their handicaps and the fact that a world exists beyond schooling. Concentrated training toward specific vocational goals might be helpful in providing more direction and structure for these years.

Chapter 36 Research

Experts often say that among diseases and disorders, autism is one of the most poorly understood.

Having read this far, you can begin to understand why that is. The reason for this poor understanding is because the disease itself is complex, and it becomes more complicated when other people who don't have enough understanding and knowledge about it have to deal with a person who is diagnosed with it.

Characterized by difficulty in communication and the inability to develop social skills, autism has a wide range of symptoms and severity. Behaviors that can be associated with autism include impairment in the ability to be friends with people of the same age or other peers, difficulty in the initiation or sustenance of conversations, impaired imaginative skills and social play, stereotyped language use, limited interests, abnormal intensity, preoccupation with or focus on a specific object, and unyielding devotion to monotonous routines.

Advancements and developments in autism

In order to treat autism and other ASDs, doctors and scientists continue to conduct various research and study regarding its development, causes, and more effective treatments. The following are just some of the studies, researches, and new developments regarding autism, its causes, and treatment options and alternatives.

- *Studies on the cause(s) of autism.* Countless studies are being done simultaneously around the world that trace the possible causes of autism. Most of these studies are focusing on various factors such as environmental and genetic areas to determine the possible causes of the disease.

- *Studies of high-functioning autistic toddlers.* These studies focus on measuring the capability and development of autistic toddlers by using computers to give non-verbal tests.

  Research on testing children who have autistic siblings. There are also studies that focus on children raised alongside autistic children in the hope that they can somehow contribute to the betterment of their autistic siblings.

- *Studies on the possible effects of mercury exposure on children with autism.* Ongoing studies focus on the possible effects of mercury exposure in autism. This is done to learn if various environmental factors can cause autism.

- *Studies on the age of children to be diagnosed.* Various studies are also being done to determine which age is the most ideal for an autism diagnosis. This is being done to gather information about the crucial stages and phases when a child's character and personality are formed.

- *Auditory Preference Research.* This research offers revolutionary means of thinking about and treating the disorder by giving the patients auditory stimuli to determine the sound preferences of the autistic child. This reveals that autistic children prefer structures that have speech-resembling sound rather than those sounds created by normal people.

- *Research on the link of Regressive Autism to Autoimmune Enteropathy.* Children with regressive autism have good response to enteric therapy. Various autoimmune mechanisms can be potential avenues for regressive autism treatment in the future.

- *Study on the effect of Risperidone in treating children with autism.* Risperidone evokes a positive response in autistic children, especially in treating various behavioral disturbances, delayed speech and language development, coping with aggression, irritation, and tantrums.

- *Research on Glutamate Neurotransmitter system abnormalities linked to autism.* People who suffer from autism may exhibit particular abnormalities in their AMPA-type glutamate receptors as well as in the glutamate transporters that go to the cerebellum. These abnormalities can result in the possibility of the disorder.

- *Research on the effects of varying plasma fatty acid levels in autistic children.* Varying changes and levels of fatty acid metabolism can lead to some psychiatric diseases.

- *Research involving biological tests* that can detect the brain disorder in high-functioning patients with autism. Special MRI technology can measure differences in the wiring of the brain.

- *Studies of brain tissue samples* obtained after death from autism patients and healthy volunteers. Research has found differences in how genes encode information in autistic and healthy brains. It has also found that most of the autistic brain samples shared common genetic patterns.

Chapter 37 Red flags for autism

As a reminder we have listed the red flags for autism below.

Tip: If you notice some or multiple signs in your child, write them down. Your concerns and observations are of great value for your pediatrician or professionals who are trying to diagnose your child.

Warning Signs of Autism in Early Childhood[cx]
Parents should ask their child's family doctor for referral to a developmental pediatrician for assessment if there are concerns with any of the following:

Communication Red Flags

- ✓ No babbling by 11 months of age
- ✓ No simple gestures by 12 months (e.g. waving bye-bye)
- ✓ No single words by 16 months
- ✓ No two-word phrases by 24 months (noun + verb – e.g. "baby sleeping")
- ✓ No response when name is called, causing concern about hearing
- ✓ Loss of any language or social skills at any age

Behavioral Red Flags

- ✓ Odd or repetitive ways of moving fingers or hands
- ✓ Oversensitive to certain textures, sounds or lights
- ✓ Lacks interest in toys, or plays with them in an unusual way (e.g. lining up, spinning, opening/closing parts rather than using the toy as a whole)
- ✓ Compulsions or rituals (has to perform activities in a special way or certain sequence; is prone to tantrums if rituals are interrupted)
- ✓ Preoccupations with unusual interests, such as light switches, doors, fans, wheels
- ✓ Unusual fears

Social Red Flags

- ✓ Rarely makes eye contact when interacting with people
- ✓ Does not play peek-a-boo
- ✓ Doesn't point to show things he/she is interested in
- ✓ Rarely smiles socially
- ✓ More interested in looking at objects than at people's faces
- ✓ Prefers to play alone
- ✓ Doesn't make attempts to get parent's attention; doesn't follow/look when someone is pointing at something
- ✓ Seems to be "in his/her own world"

- ✓ Doesn't respond to parent's attempts to play, even if relaxed
- ✓ Avoids or ignores other children when they approach

Chapter 38 DSM IV & DSM V

DSM IV

The Diagnostic and Statistical Manual of Mental Disorders (DSM) is published by the American Psychiatric Association and provides a common language and standard criteria for the classification of mental disorders.

It is used in the United States of America and in varying degrees around the world, by clinicians, researchers, psychiatric drug regulation agencies, health insurance companies, pharmaceutical companies, and policy makers. The DSM has attracted controversy and criticism as well as praise.

There have been five revisions since it was first published in 1952, gradually including more mental disorders, although some have been removed and are no longer considered to be mental disorders, most notably homosexuality.

Many mental health professionals use the manual to determine and help communicate a patient's diagnosis after an evaluation; hospitals, clinics, and insurance companies in the US also generally require a 'five axis' DSM diagnosis of all the patients treated. The DSM can be used clinically in this way, and also to categorize patients using diagnostic criteria for research purposes. Studies done on specific disorders often recruit patients whose symptoms match the criteria listed in the DSM for that disorder.

The manual evolved from systems for collecting census and psychiatric hospital statistics, and from a manual developed by the US Army, and was dramatically revised in 1980. The last major revision was the fourth edition ("DSM-IV"), published in 1994, although a "text revision" was produced in 2000.

DSM 5

The next (fifth) edition of the American Psychiatric Association's (APA) Diagnostic and Statistical Manual of Mental Disorders (DSM), commonly called DSM-5 (previously known as DSM-V until the APA decided to abandon the Roman numerals), is currently in consultation, planning and preparation. It is due for publication in May 2013 and will supersede the DSM-IV which was last revised in 2000.

APA has an official development website for posting draft versions of the DSM-5 at http://www.dsm5.org/pages/default.aspx

The proposed changes with regard to autism can be found at http://www.dsm5.org/proposedrevision/pages/proposedrevision.aspx?rid=94

It seems that Rett syndrome, Asperger's syndrome, and PDD-NOS will be removed from DSM V.

The new name for the category, autism spectrum disorder, will probably includes autistic disorder (autism), Asperger's disorder, childhood disintegrative disorder, and pervasive developmental disorder not otherwise specified.

DSM-IV has three general areas of symptoms:
1. Qualitative impairment in social interaction
2. Qualitative impairments in communication
3. Restricted repetitive and stereotyped patterns of behavior, interests, and activities

DSM V proposes two general areas.
1. Persistent deficits in social communication and social interaction across contexts
2. Restricted, repetitive patterns of behavior, interests, or activities

In the DSM V three Severity Levels for ASD will be distinguished for social communication, restricted interests, and repetitive behaviors.

Chapter 39 Conclusion

Autism has been around for thousands of years, well before we had a name for it. Though it was officially discovered more than 60 years ago, there is still much we don't know about the disorder. What we know for certain is that it is a spectrum disorder that affects each individual differently – from mild symptoms to very severe ones. It is not a mental disorder but a physical disorder, and the cause is still unknown.

Although researchers continue to search for answers, the fact that we don't know the cause of the disorder makes finding a cure even more difficult. Several treatments, both standard and alternative, have been presented, and it would seem that the most effective ones work toward behavior modification while using the child's interests and strengths as a means to an end, or at least an improvement.

Standard treatments currently in use include:
- Applied Behavior Analysis
- Floor Time
- Occupational Therapy
- Relationship Development Intervention
- Sensory Integration Therapy
- Speech Therapy
- Sign Language
- Computer Use
- Toys and Stimulation
- Physical Exercise
- Neurofeedback
- Mindfulness

Alternative treatments include:
- Facilitated Communication
- Holding Therapy
- Auditory Integration Therapy
- The Dolman/Delacato Method
- Snoezelen

In addition to these treatments, some people believe autism can be controlled via the use of special gluten free/casein free diets and/or supplements.

Whatever the treatment method used, it's important that it be specialized to meet your child's individual needs because no two children with autism are the same. Children with autism face unique educational, social, and communication challenges. To minimize these challenges, special educational planning and implementation is necessary. As with treatment, education must be individualized to address the child's needs and build skills that are lacking.

As the child becomes an adolescent, a whole new set of challenges will arise. While these challenges are the normal challenges every parent of a teenager faces, they are exacerbated by autism. Autistic teenagers have difficulty communicating with their peers, but at the same time they want to pull away from their parents. This can leave them with no one at all to talk to. They also have the issue of raging hormones, but are unable to understand or appropriately manage sexual behaviors.

Living with autism brings added stress to the entire family. Siblings may sometimes feel as though their own needs aren't being met or aren't as important as the needs of the autistic child. Couples may find their lives revolving around the care of the autistic child and be unable to find time to spend alone, which may cause erosion of the marital bond. And, of course, there are financial stresses and concerns over the future of the autistic child. To make life easier and to manage the stress of autism, it's important that families find ways to reconnect and acknowledge each individual's role and value in the family unit.

People with autism have a normal life expectancy, so naturally plans must be made for their adult life. Many adults with autism are able to lead fulfilling independent lives. They are able to hold jobs and participate in their communities. To help them do so, parents must start making plans early for the transition to the working world. The child must be helped to find appropriate employment that incorporates his or her skills and interests, while keeping challenges associated with autism to a minimum.

In short, a diagnosis of autism shouldn't be seen as a guarantee of a lesser life. New research is being conducted to gather more insight into the disease, its causes, and its treatments that will surely provide even greater hope for autistics than there is today. Parents must remain their children's strongest advocates in education, treatment and society. With the appropriate intervention and assistance, autism can be seen not as a disorder, but as a way of life.

What's next?
Ok, you have come to the end of this book. You may still have some unanswered questions. Do not hesitate to ask these questions of a specialist you trust.

Index

Bibliography

Books/Publications

AAN Guideline Summary for Clinicians. (2006). Screening and Diagnosis Of Autism. www.aan.com.

American Psychiatric Association. (2000). Diagnostic and statistical manual of mental disorders: DSM-IV-TR (fourth edition, text revision). Washington DC: American Psychiatric Association, 2000.

Bashe, Patricia Romanowski and Kirby, Barbara L. (2001). The Oasis Guide to Asperger's syndrome: Advice, Support, Insights, and Inspiration. New York: Crown Publishers.

Blackwell, J., & Niederhauser, C. (2003). Diagnose and Manage Autistic Children. Nurse Practitioner, 28(6), 36-42.

British Columbia Ministry of Education Special Programs Branch. (2000) Teaching Students with Autism: A Resource Guide for Schools. Victoria: British Columbia Ministry of Education Special Programs Branch.

Cohen DJ, Towbin KE, Mayes L, Volkmar F (1994). Developmental psychopathology of multiplex developmental disorder. In: Friedman SL, Haywood HC (eds). Developmental Follow-up: Concepts, Genres, Domains, and Methods. Academic Press: San Diego.

Cowley, G. (2003). Predicting Autism. Newsweek, 142(4), 46-47.

Cowley, G., Underwood, A., Murr, A., Springen, K., & Sennott, S. (2003). Girls, Boys and Autism. Newsweek, 142(10), 42-50.

Cumine, Val, Leach, Julia and Stevenson, Gill. (2000) Autism in the Early Years: A Practical Guide. London: David Fulton.

DiSalvo, C. A., & Donald, P. (2002). Peer-Mediated Interventions to Increase the Social Interaction of Children with Autism: Consideration of Peer Expectations. Focus on Autism & Other Developmental Disabilities, 17(4).

Edelson, Stephen M. (1999) Overview of Autism Center for the Study of Autism, Salem, Oregon.

Evans, Rachel (2006). The Essential Guide to Autism. eBook.

Fennick, E., & Royle, J. (2003). Recreation for Children And Youth with Developmental Disabilities. Focus on Autism & Other Developmental Disabilities, 18(1),20-28.

Frith, Uta. (2005). Autisme: verklaringen van het raadsel. Berchem:Epo.

Frombonne E. Prevalence of childhood disintegrative disorder. Autism, 2002; 6(2): 149-157.

Greenspan, S, I., Wieder, S, & Simons, Robin. (1998). The Child with Special Needs: Encouraging Intellectual and Emotional Growth. Reading, MA: Persus.

Hellemans, Hans, Vermeulen, Peter, Conix, Greet, De Lameillieure, Lies. (2006). Seks@Autisme.Kom. Een programma voor relationele en seksuele vorming voor jongeren en volwassenen met autisme. Uitgeverij EOP. Berchem.

Kupperman, P. (1997). Precocious Reading Skills May Signal Hyperlexia. Brown University Child & Adolescent Behavior Letter, 13(11), 1-3.

Kuder, S. J., & Hasit, C. (2002). Enhancing Literacy for All Students. Columbus, Ohio: Merrill Prentice Hall.

Levinson, B. (Director). (1988). Rainman. United Artists.

Lewis, L. (1998). Special Diets for Special Kids – Understanding and Implementing Special Diets to Aid in the Treatment of Autism and Related Developmental Disorders. Arlington Texas: Future Horizons, Inc.

Longbottom, Linda (2006). So you've been told your child is autistic. Where do you go from here? eBook.

Martin, A. M. (1996). The Babysitters Club: Kristy and the Secret of Susan. Scholastic Inc.

Mijs, Elisabeth J., (2002). Oudercursus Autisme. Autisme en de kindergeneeskunde. Handout. 12 oktober 2002, Eindhoven.

Morrison, James. (2001) DSM-IV Made Easy: The Clinician's Guide to Diagnosis. Guilford Press, New York.

Morrison, James. (2001). American Psychiatric Association Diagnostic and Statistical Manual of Mental Disorders, fourth edition text revision, 2000, DSM-IV Made Easy, Guilford Press, New York.

Myles, Brenda and Simpson, Richard L. (1998). Asperger's syndrome: A Guide for Educators and Parents. Austin: Pro-Ed.

Sayers, Bonnie. (2006). Educational Tips for Families with a Child on the Autism Spectrum. eBook.

Seroussi, K. (2002). Unravelling the Mystery of Autism and Pervasive Developmental Disorder. New York: Broadway Books.

Smith, T. E. C., Polloway, E., Patton, J. R., & Dowdy, C.A. (2004). Teaching Students with Special Needs: In Inclusive Settings. New York: Pearson.

Vermeulen, Patrick & Degrieck, Steven. (2006). Mijn kind heeft autisme. Uitgeverij Lannoo nv, Tielt.

Vermeulen, Peter. (2002). Voor alle duidelijkheid. Leerlingen met autisme in het gewone onderwijs. Vlaamse Dienst Autisme, Gent.

Vermeulen, Peter (red). (2005). Ik ben speciaal |2 Uitgeverij EPO. Berchem.

Volkmar, F. R., & Pauls, D. (2003). Autism. Lancet, 362(9390), 1133-1141.

Volkmar RM and Rutter M. Childhood disintegrative disorder: Results of the DSM-IV autism field trial. Journal of the American Academy of Child and Adolescent Psychiatry, 1995; 34: 1092-1095.

Links

Adams, Ph.D., James. Vitamin, mineral supplements benefit people with autism, Retrieved January 22, 2007, from http://www.eas.asu.edu/~autism/Initial%20Letter%20to%20Parents.doc

Applied Behaviour Analysis (ABA) – Lovaas, Retrieved January 22, 2007, from http://www.autismcanada.org/treatments/aba.htm

Auditory Integration Therapy and the Counseling Center, Retrieved January 22, 2007, from http://www.vision3d.com/adhd/index.shtml

Autism, Retrieved January 22, 2007, from
http://en.wikipedia.org/wiki/Autism

Autism Centre A Therapy for Autism, Retrieved January 22, 2007, from
http://www.theautismcentre.co.uk/therapy-info.html

Autism in Children, Retrieved January 22, 2007, from
http://pediatrics.about.com/library/blautism.htm

Autism Overview: What We Know, Retrieved January 22, 2007, from
http://www.nichd.nih.gov

Autism Stories. Retrieved January 22, 2007
http://aba4autism.com/mothers.html

Autism What About The Diet?, Retrieved January 22, 2007, from
http://www.glutenfree.com

Childhood Disintegrative Disorder, Retrieved January 22, 2007, from
http://info.med.yale.edu/chldstdy/autism/cdd.html

Disabilities – Autism – Occupational Therapy, Retrieved January 22, 2007, from
http://www.webhealthcenter.com/disabilities/autism_occtherapy.asp

Doyle, Barbara T. Autism Spectrum Disorder (ASD): Myths and Facts, Retrieved January 24, 2007, from
http://www.newhorizons.org/spneeds/autism/doyle_myths.htm

Dr. Temple Grandin, Retrieved January 24, 2007, from
http://templegrandin.com/templehome.html

Edelson, Ph.D., Stephen M. Auditory Integration Therapy: Additional Information, Retrieved January 24, 2007, from
http://www.autism.org/ait2.html

Explicit communication. Retrieved January 22, 2007
http://www.autismusundcomputer.de/ucl.en.html

FAQs (frequently asked questions) about MMR Vaccine & Autism, Retrieved January 24, 2007, from
http://www.cdc.gov/nip/vacsafe/concerns/autism/autism-mmr.htm

Floor Time, Retrieved January 24, 2007, from
http://www.aspergersexpress.com/floor_time.htm

Floor Time Basics, Retrieved January 24, 2007, from
http://www.aspergersexpress.com/floor_time_basics.htm

Grandin, Ph.D., Temple. Choosing the Right Job for People with Autism or Asperger's syndrome, Retrieved January 24, 2007, from
http://www.autism.org/temple/jobs.html

Grandin, Ph.D., Temple. Making the Transition from the World of School into the World of Work, Retrieved January 24, 2007, from
http://www.autism.org/temple/transition.html

Hatch-Rasmussen, M.A., Cindy. Sensory Integration, Retrieved January 24, 2007, from http://www.autism.org/si.html

Insuring the Child With Autism Part 1: How good is your coverage? Retrieved January 24, 2007, from
http://autism.about.com/cs/financialissues/a/insureautism.htm

Insuring the Child With Autism Part 2: Are You Covered? Retrieved January 24, 2007, from
http://autism.about.com/cs/financialissues/a/insureautism_2.htm

Mortlock, John, Socio-sexual development of people with autism. Retrieved November 16, 2007 from http://www.nas.org.uk/nas/jsp/polopoly.jsp?a=2187&d=364

Needlman, M.D., F.A.A.P., Robert. Autism Myths and Realities. Retrieved January 24, 2007, from http://www.drspock.com/article/0,1510,4937,00.html

Newschaffer CJ (Johns Hopkins Bloomberg School of Public Health). Autism Among Us: Rising Concerns and the Public Health Response. [Video on the Internet]. Public Health Training Network, 2003 June 20. Available from: http://www.publichealthgrandrounds.unc.edu/autism/webcast.htm

Ozbayrak, M.D., R. Kaan. Meeting the Challenges of Adolescence: A Guide for Parents, Retrieved January 24, 2007, from http://www.aspergers.com/Adolesc.htm

NIH Publication No. 01-4960. Rett syndrome. Rockville, MD: National Institute of Child Health and Human Development, 2001. Available at http://www.nichd.nih.gov/publications/pubskey.cfm?from=autism

Learn and Grow: Understanding RDI with Connections Center, Retrieved January 24, 2007, from http://www.rdiconnect.com/RDI/FAQ_General.asp

Shattock, Paul. The Use of Gluten and Casein Free Diets with People with Autism, Retrieved January 22, 2007, from http://osiris.sunderland.ac.uk/autism/dietinfo.html

Special Diet for Autism and PDD: The Truth About the Gluten-Free, Casein-Free Diet, Retrieved January 22, 2007, from http://www.autismweb.com/diet.htm

Speech Therapy, Retrieved January 24, 2007, from http://www.autismlink.com/info/speech.php

Strock, Margaret (2004). Autism Spectrum Disorders (Pervasive Developmental Disorders). NIH Publication No. NIH-04-5511, National Institute of Mental Health, National Institutes of Health, U.S. Department of Health and Human Services, Bethesda, MD, 40 pp. http://www.nimh.nih.gov/publicat/autism.cfm

Teaching Children with Autism via RDI (Relationship Development Intervention)/Gutstein method, Retrieved January 24, 2007, from http://www.autismlink.com/info/RDI.php

The Importance of an Appropriate Education, Retrieved January 24, 2007, from http://www.autismeducation.net/education.htm

Visual communication. Retrieved January 22, 2007 http://trainland.tripod.com/pecs.htm

What is Autism? – History, Retrieved January 24, 2007, from http://www.naar.org/aboutaut/whatis_hist.htm

Why RDI? – Connections Center, Retrieved January 24, 2007, from http://www.rdiconnect.com/

Other Resources

http://www.autismspeaks.org
Autism Speaks has grown into the nation's largest autism science and advocacy organization, dedicated to funding research into the causes, prevention, treatments, and a cure for autism; increasing awareness of autism spectrum disorders; and advocating for the needs of individuals with autism and their families.

http://www.pathfindersforautism.org/ages
Autism By Age
A look at multiple life aspects — health, social and relationships, education, employment, housing, transportation, financial, advocacy, assistive technology, and support and respite — each addressed by what is needed for every age.

http://www.cdc.gov/ncbddd/autism/index.html
Centers for Disease Control and Prevention

http://www.cdc.gov/ncbddd/actearly/pdf/parents_pdfs/AutismFactSheet.pdf
Autism Fact Sheet

http://www.cdc.gov/ncbddd/actearly/pdf/parents_pdfs/Asperger_Syndrome.pdf
Asperger's Syndrome Fact Sheet

http://www.nimh.nih.gov/health/topics/autism-spectrum-disorders-pervasivedevelopmental-disorders/index.shtml
Natural Institute For Mental Health

http://www.mayoclinic.com/health/autism/DS00348
Through this unique collaboration, you get access to the experience and knowledge of the more than 3,700 physicians, scientists and researchers of the Mayo Clinic.

http://www.AspiesForFreedom.com
Forums, chat rooms and articles about Asperger's & Autism.

http://www.theGrayCenter.org
Non-profit organization dedicated to individuals with Autism Spectrum Disorders and their carers.

http://www.siblingsupport.org
Community Support Group for siblings of people with special health, developmental and emotional needs.

http://templegrandin.com
Temple Grandin

http://www.autism-society.org
Autism Society

http://www.myautismteam.com
MyAutismTeam

DSM-IV & DSM-IV-TR CAUTIONARY STATEMENT

The specific diagnostic criteria for each mental disorder are offered as guidelines, because it has been demonstrated that the use of such criteria enhances agreement among clinicians and investigators. The proper use of these criteria requires specialized clinical training that provides both a body of knowledge and clinical skills.

These diagnostic criteria and the DSM-IV Classification of mental disorders reflect a consensus of current formulations of evolving knowledge in our field. They do not encompass, however, all the conditions for which people may be treated or that may be appropriate topics for research efforts.

The information presented in this book is not meant as a substitute for diagnosis or professional advice. It is merely a presentation of information concerning ASDs and should not be used to self diagnose or treat individuals with ASDs. If you suspect a person of having a Pervasive Developmental Disorder/Autistic Spectrum Disorder, please contact a qualified medical practitioner.

Notes

i http://en.wikipedia.org/wiki/Hans_Asperger,
http://en.wikipedia.org/wiki/Leo_Kanner,
http://en.wikipedia.org/wiki/Lorna_Wing

ii http://www.pbs.org/pov/refrigeratormothers/

iii Rachel Evans, 2006, Essential Guide To Autism, http://www.essential-guide-to-autism.com

iv http://www.timeline-help.com/autism-charts-graphs-timeline.html,
Retrieved 1 November 2011

v http://www.washingtonpost.com/wp-dyn/content/article/2008/06/27/AR2008062703062.html, retrieved 1
November 2011

vi http://www.washingtonpost.com/wp-dyn/content/article/2008/06/27/AR2008062703062.html, Retrieved 1
November 2011

vii Rachel Evans, 2006, Essential Guide To Autism, http://www.essential-guide-to-autism.com, http://www.jaynelytel.com/timeline.html

viii Autism Research Review International (ARRI) (1991, Vol. 5, No. 2)

ix Lisa Jo Rudy,2006,
http://autism.about.com/od/whatisautism/tp/topmyths.htm, Autism
Spectrum Disorders Explained, Rachel Evans, eBook

x http://www.nimh.nih.gov/publicat/autism.cfm

xi USA specific. http://www.nichcy.org or http://www.cdc.gov/ncbddd

xii Lucres MC Jansen, Christine C Gispen-de Wied, Rutger-Jan van der Gaag
and Herman van Engeland, (2003), Differentiation between Autism and
Multiple Complex Developmental Disorder in Response to Psychosocial Stress
published in Neuropsychopharmacology (2003) 28, 582-590.
doi:10.1038/sj.npp.1300046

xiii Howard B. Demb, M.D. & Olga Noskin, B.S. The Use of the Term Multiple
Complex Developmental Disorder in a diagnostic Clinic Serving Young Children
With Developmental Disabilities: A Report of 15 Cases, Ment Health Aspects
Dev Disabil 2001;4(2):49-60

xiv A. Paternotte, R.J. van der Gaag; Balans Belang July 2001, pp. 35-36,34, 3
pages in total

xv Akshoomoff N, Pierce K, Courchesne E. The neurobiological basis of autism
from a developmental perspective. Development and Psychopathology, 2002;
14: 613-634.

xvi http://www.brainbank.org

xvii Korvatska E, Van de Water J, Anders TF, Gershwin ME. Genetic and immunologic considerations in autism. Neurobiology of Disease, 2002; 9: 107-125.

xviii http://www.cbs42.com/content/health/story/Genetic-Basis-for-Autism-Possibly-Discovered/gRmmRq2FkU6fJmr7Sy2krQ.cspx, found 1 November 2011

xix Courchesne E. Carper R, Akshoomoff N. Evidence of brain overgrowth in the first year of life in autism. JAMA, 2003; 290(3): 337-344.

xx http://www.nimh.nih.gov/index.shtml

xxi In an interview (in Balans Belang maart 2001, tijdschrift van Balans, vereniging voor ontwikkelings-, gedrags" en leerproblemen)

xxii http://en.wikipedia.org/wiki/Causes_of_autism#Autism_and_related_disorders

xxiii http://en.wikipedia.org/wiki/Causes_of_autism#Autism_and_related_disorders

xxiv Gardener H, Spiegelman D, Buka SL (2009). "Prenatal risk factors for autism: comprehensive meta-analysis." Br J Psychiatry 195, Geschwind DH (2009). "Advances in autism." Annu Rev Med 60: 367–80.
Patterson PH (2008). "Immune involvement in schizophrenia and autism:etiology, pathology and animal models." Behav Brain Res.
Mendelsohn NJ, Schaefer GB (2008). "Genetic evaluation of autism." SeminPediatr Neurol 15 (1): 27–31.
Meyer U, Yee BK, Feldon J (2007). "The neurodevelopmental impact of prenatal infections at different times of pregnancy: the earlier the worse?" Neuroscientist 13 (3): 241–56.
Dalton P, Deacon R, Blamire A et al. (2003). "Maternal neuronal antibodies associated with autism and a language disorder." Ann Neurol 53 (4): 533–7.
Braunschweig D, Ashwood P, Krakowiak P et al. (2008). "Autism: maternally derived antibodies specific for fetal brain proteins." Neurotoxicology 29 (2):226–31.
Martin LA, Ashwood P, Braunschweig D, Cabanlit M, Van de Water J, Amaral DG (2008). "Stereotypies and hyperactivity in rhesus monkeys exposed to IgG from mothers of children with autism." Brain Behav Immun 22 (6):806–16.

xxv Gardener H, Spiegelman D, Buka SL (2009). "Prenatal risk factors for autism: comprehensive meta-analysis." Br J Psychiatry 195 (1): 7–14.

xxvi Szpir M (2006). "Tracing the origins of autism: a spectrum of new studies." Environ Health Perspect 114 (7): A412–8.

xxvii Fombonne E (2002). "Is exposure to alcohol during pregnancy a risk factor for autism?" J Autism Dev Disord 32 (3): 243.

xxviii Arndt TL, Stodgell CJ, Rodier PM (2005). "The teratology of autism." Int JDev Neurosci 23 (2–3): 189–99.

xxix Roberts EM, English PB, Grether JK, Windham GC, Somberg L, Wolff C(2007). "Maternal residence near agricultural pesticide applications and

autism spectrum disorders among children in the California Central Valley."
Environ Health Perspect 115 (10): 1482–9.

xxx Singh ND, Sharma AK, Dwivedi P, Patil RD, Kumar M (2007). "Citrininand endosulfan induced teratogenic effects in Wistar rats." J Appl Toxicol 27(2): 143–51.

xxxi D'Amelio M, Ricci I, Sacco R et al. (2005). "Paraoxonase gene variants are associated with autism in North America, but not in Italy: possible regional specificity in gene-environment interactions." Mol Psychiatry 10 (11):1006–16.

xxxii Karr CJ, Solomon GM, Brock-Utne AC (2007). "Health effects of commonhome, lawn, and garden pesticides." Pediatr Clin North Am 54 (1): 63–80.

xxxiii Busko M (2008-05-20). "Antiflea pet shampoos with pyrethrin may play arole in autism." Medscape Today. http://www.medscape.com/viewarticle/574799. Retrieved on 2009-06-08.

xxxiv Román GC (2007). "Autism: transient in utero hypothyroxinemia related to maternal flavonoid ingestion during pregnancy and to other environmental antithyroid agents." J Neurol Sci 262 (1–2): 15–26.

xxxv Sullivan KM (2008). "The interaction of agricultural pesticides and marginal iodine nutrition status as a cause of autism spectrum disorders." Environ Health Perspect 116 (4): A155.

xxxvi Kinney DK, Munir KM, Crowley DJ, Miller AM (2008). "Prenatal stress and risk for autism." Neurosci Biobehav Rev 32 (8): 1519–32.

xxxvii Kolevzon A, Gross R, Reichenberg A (2007). "Prenatal and perinatal riskfactors for autism." Arch Pediatr Adolesc Med 161 (4): 326–33.

xxxviii Limperopoulos C, Bassan H, Gauvreau K et al. (2007). "Does cerebellar injury in premature infants contribute to the high prevalence of long-term cognitive, learning, and behavioral disability in survivors?" Pediatrics 120(3): 584–93.

xxxix Murch SH, Anthony A, Casson DH et al. (2004). "Retraction of an interpretation." Lancet 363 (9411): 750.

xl Deer B (2008-11-02). "The MMR-autism crisis – our story so far." http://briandeer.com/mmr/lancet-summary.htm. Retrieved on 2008-12-06.

xli Measles, mumps, and rubella (MMR) vaccine." Centers for Disease Control and Prevention. 2008-12-23. http://www.cdc.gov/vaccinesafety/concerns/mmr_vaccine.htm. Retrieved on 2009-02-14.

xlii Immunization safety review: vaccines and autism." Institute of Medicine, National Academy of Sciences. 2004.http://www.iom.edu/CMS/3793/4705/20155.aspx. Retrieved on2007-06-13.

xliii "MMR the facts." National Health Service.http://www.mmrthefacts.nhs.uk/. Retrieved on 2007-06-13.

xliv http://www.slate.com/id/2211156/

xlv If you are interested in reading more about mercury and autism:

http://www.mercola.com/2000/oct/1/autism_mercury.htm

xlvi Today, with the exception of some Influenza (flu) vaccines, none of the

vaccines used in the U.S. to protect preschool children against 12 infectious diseases contain thimerosal (mercury-containing organic compound) as a preservative.

xlvii Hviid A, Stellfeld M, Wohlfahrt J, Melbye M. Association between thimerosal-containing vaccine and autism. JAMA, 2003; 290(13): 1763-1766.

xlviii http://autism.about.com/od/whatisautism/tp/Additional-Symptoms-of-Autism.htm Retrieved on 2009-08-10.

xlix http://autism.about.com/od/whatisautism/tp/Additional-Symptoms-of-Autism.htm Retrieved on 2009-08-10.

l Reiersen AM, Todd RD (2008). "Co-occurrence of ADHD and autism spectrum disorders: phenomenology and treatment." Expert Rev Neurother8 (4): 657–69.

li http://autism.about.com/od/whatisautism/tp/Additional-Symptoms-of-Autism.htm Retrieved on 2009-08-10.

lii McPartland J, Klin A (2006). "Asperger's syndrome." Adolesc Med Clin 17(3): 771–88., Ehlers S, Gillberg C (1993). "The epidemiology of Asperger's syndrome. A total population study." J Child Psychol Psychiat 34 (8):1327–50., Klin A (2006). "Autism and Asperger's syndrome: an overview." Rev Bras Psiquiatr 28 (suppl 1): S3–S11

liii Zafeiriou DI, Ververi A, Vargiami E (2007). "Childhood autism and associated comorbidities." Brain Dev 29 (5): 257–72

liv Rogers SJ, Ozonoff S (2005). "Annotation: what do we know about sensory dysfunction in autism? A critical review of the empirical evidence." J Child Psychol Psychiatry 46 (12): 1255–68.

lv Williams DL, Goldstein G, Minshew NJ (2006). "Neuropsychologic functioning in children with autism: further evidence for disordered complex information-processing." Child Neuropsychol 12 (4–5): 279–98.

lvi Ming X, Brimacombe M, Wagner GC (2007). "Prevalence of motor impairment in autism spectrum disorders." Brain Dev 29 (9): 565–70.

lvii Filipek PA, Accardo PJ, Baranek GT, Cook Jr. EH, Dawson G, Gordon B, Gravel JS, Johnson CP, Kellen RJ, Levy SE, Minshew NJ, Prizant BM, Rapin I, Rogers SJ, Stone WL, Teplin S, Tuchman RF, Volkmar FR. The screening and diagnosis of autism spectrum disorders. Journal of Autism and Developmental Disorders, 1999; 29(2): 439-484.

lviii Results were published in the Wetenschappelijk Tijdschrift Autisme, number 1, April/May 2002.

lix Engagement, volume 29, number 3, June 2002

lx There are some interesting notes on the prevalence of autism spectrum disorders. You can find them at http://www.nas.org.uk/nas/jsp/polopoly.jsp?d=364&a=2618 by Lorna Wing and David Potter,

lxi http://en.m.wikipedia.org/wiki/Empathizing–systemizing_theory, Found 1 November 2011

lxii Baird G, Charman T, Baron-Cohen S, Cox A, Swettenham J, Wheelwright S, Drew A. A screening instrument for autism at 18 months of age: A 6-yearfollowup study. Journal of the American Academy of Child and Adolescent Psychiatry, 2000; ? 9: 694-702.

lxiii Robbins DI, Fein D, Barton MI, Green JA. The modified checklist for autism in toddlers: an initial study investigating the early detection of autism and pervasive developmental disorders. Journal of Autism and Developmental Disorders, 2001; 31(2): 149-151.

lxiv Stone WL, Coonrod EE, Ousley OY. Brief report: screening tool for autism in two-year-olds (STAT): development and preliminary data. Journal of Autism and Developmental Disorders, 2000; 30(6): 607-612.

lxv Ehlers S, Gillberg C, Wing L. A screening questionnaire for Asperger'syndrome and other high-functioning autism spectrum disorders in schoolage children. Journal of Autism and Developmental Disorders, 1999; 29(2):129-141.

lxvi Garnett MS, Attwood AJ. The Australian scale for Asperger's syndrome. In: Attwood, Tony. Asperger's syndrome: A Guide

lxvii Scott FJ, Baron-Cohen S, Bolton P, Brayne C. The Cast (Childhood Asperger's syndrome Test): preliminary development of a UK screen for mainstream primary-school-age children. Autism, 2002; 2(1): 9-31.

lxviii Some of these tests can be downloaded at this address:http://www.autismresearchcentre.com/tests/default.asp

lxix Tadevosyan-Leyfer O, Dowd M, Mankoski R, Winklosky B, Putnam S, McGrath L, Tager-Flusberg H, Folstein SE. A principal components analysis of the autism diagnostic interview-revised. Journal of the American Academy of Child and Adolescent Psychiatry, 2003; 42(7):

lxx Lord C, Risi S, Lambrecht L, Cook EH, Leventhal BL, DiLavore PC, Pickles A, Rutter M. The autism diagnostic observation schedule-generic: a standard measure of social and communication deficits associated with the spectrum of autism. Journal of Autism and Developmental Disorders, 2000; 30(3): 205-230.

lxxi Van Bourgondien ME, Marcus LM, Schopler E. Comparison of DSM-III-R and childhood autism rating scale diagnoses of autism. Journal of Autism and Developmental Disorders, 1992; 22(4): 493-506.

lxxii Filipek PA, Accardo PJ, Ashwal S, Baranek GT, Cook Jr. EH, Dawson G, Gordon B, Gravel JS, Johnson CP, Kallen RJ, Levy SE, Minshew NJ, Ozonoff S, Prizant BM, Rapin I, Rogers SJ, Stone WL, Teplin SW, Tuchman RF, Volkmar FR. Practice parameter: screening and diagnosis of autism. Neurology, 2000; 55: 468-479.

lxxiii Note: A large part of this chapter will be USA specific when institutions or programs are mentioned. If you live outside the USA you can always ask your doctor or pediatrician for help.

lxxiv Couper JJ, Sampson AJ. Children with autism deserve evidence-based intervention. Medical Journal of Australia, 2003; 178: 424-425.

lxxv American Academy of Pediatrics Committee on Children With Disabilities. The pediatrician's role in the diagnosis and management of autistic spectrum disorder in children. Pediatrics, 2001; 107(5): 1221-1226.

lxxvi Dunlap G, Foxe L. Teaching students with autism. ERIC EC Digest #E582, 1999 October.

lxxvii Department of Health and Human Services. Mental Health: A Report of the Surgeon General. Rockville, MD: Department of Health and Human Services, Substance Abuse and Mental Health Services Administration, Center for Mental Health Services, National Institute of Mental Health, 1999.

lxxviii Lovaas OI. Behavioral treatment and normal educational and intellectual functioning in young autistic children. Journal of Consulting and Clinical Psychology, 1987; 55: 3-9.

lxxix (Porter, 2000; LaVigna & Willis, 1995; Carr, Dunlap et al., 2002; LaVigna & Donnellan, 1986; McLean & Walsh, 1995)

lxxx Autism News, 20 Apr 2005, http://www.medicalnewstoday.com/medicalnews.php?newsid=23153

lxxxi Stephen M. Edelson, Ph.D. Center for the Study of Autism, Salem, Oregon, Signed Speech or Simultaneous Communication, http://www.autism.org/sign.html

lxxxii Stephen M. Edelson, Ph.D. Center for the Study of Autism, Salem, Oregon

lxxxiii Greenspan, S, I., Wieder, S, & Simons, Robin, (1998) The Child with Special Needs: Encouraging Intellectual and Emotional Growth. Reading, MA: Persus.

lxxxiv http://www.myunion.edu/ccmm/documents/Mindfulness_Practice_with_AutismAdrianeK.pdf, retrieved 1 November 2011

lxxxv http://blog.patriciarobinsonmft.com/thriveontheautismspectrum/2010/07/mindfulness-and-dealing-with-stress.html, retrieved 1 November 2011

lxxxvi http://www.wildmind.org/applied/daily-life/what-is-mindfulness, retrieved 1 November 2011

lxxxvii Volkmar FR. Medical Problems, Treatments, and Professionals. In: Powers MD, ed. Children with Autism: A Parent's Guide, Second edition. Bethesda, MD: Woodbine House, 2000; 73-74.

lxxxviii Autism Society of America. Biomedical and Dietary Treatments (Fact Sheet) [cited 2004], 2003. Bethesda, MD: Autism Society of America. Available from: http://www.autism-society.org/site/PageServer?pagename=BiomedicalDietaryTreatments.

lxxxix Volkmar FR. Medical Problems, Treatments, and Professionals. In: Powers MD, ed. Children with Autism: A Parent's Guide, Second Edition. Bethesda, MD: Woodbine House, 2000; 73-74.

xc McDougle CJ, Stigler KA, Posey DJ. Treatment of aggression in children and adolescents with autism and conduct disorder. Journal of Clinical Psychiatry, 2003; 64 (supplement 4): 16-25.

xci Research Units on Pediatric Psychopharmacology Network. Risperidone in children with autism and serious behavioral problems. New England Journal of Medicine, 2002; 347(5): 314-321.

xcii Volkmar et al., 2003, and Blackwell et al., 2003

xciii Blackwell et al., 2003

xciv Delfos, Martine Leven met autisme / Martine Delfos en Marijke Gottmer ; [cartoons: Marcel Jurriens]. – Houten : Bohn Stafleu van Loghum, 2006.

xcv Delfos, Martine Leven met autisme / Martine Delfos en Marijke Gottmer ; [cartoons: Marcel Jurriens]. – Houten : Bohn Stafleu van Loghum, 2006.

xcvi Blackwell et al., 2003

xcvii Smith et al., 2004

xcviii Smith et al., 2004

xcix Volkmar et al., 2003

c DiSalvo et al., 2002

ci DiSalvo et al., 2002

cii Jennifer BattagliaEDU 539 E210/28/03

ciii Fennick et al., 2003

civ Based on http://www.aba4autism.com/mothers.html

cv Bijloo, Marijke (2004) Autisme Spectrumstoornissen uit: Niemeijer, M.H., Gastkemper, M., Kamps, F.H.M. Ontwikkelingstoornissen bij kinderen: medisch-pedagogische begeleiding en behandeling. Assen: Koninklijke van Gorcum

cvi Niemeijer, M.h., Baars, E. (2003) Mensen met autisme beter leren kennen, Louis Bolk Instituut, Driebergen

cvii http://www.autismuk.com/?page_id=1307, Retrieved 1 November 2011

cviii http://www.researchautism.org/resources/newsletters/2007/2007_feb.asp, Retrieved 1 November 2011

cix http://www.nas.org.uk/nas/jsp/polopoly.jsp?a=2187&d=364, Retrieved 2009, http://periodicals.faqs.org/201001/2081727361.html, Retrieved 1 November 2011

cx
http://www.autismontario.com/client/aso/ao.nsf/Durham/Red+Flags+for+Au
tism?OpenDocument